[the 100] best affordable vacations

JANE WOOLDRIDGE
+
LARRY BLEIBERG

NATIONAL GEOGRAPHIC
WASHINGTON, D.C.

Published by the National Geographic Society
1145 17th Street N.W., Washington, D.C. 20036

ISBN: 978-1-4262-0718-1

The National Geographic Society is one of the world's largest nonprofit scientific and educational organizations. Founded in 1888 to "increase and diffuse geographic knowledge," the Society works to inspire people to care about the planet. It reaches more than 375 million people worldwide each month through its official journal, National Geographic, and other magazines; National Geographic Channel; television documentaries; music; radio; films; books; DVDs; maps; exhibitions; live events; school publishing programs; interactive media; and merchandise. National Geographic has funded more than 9,200 scientific research, conservation and exploration projects and supports an education program promoting geographic literacy.

For more information, please call 1-800-NGS LINE (647-5463) or write to the following address:

National Geographic Society
1145 17th Street N.W.
Washington, D.C. 20036-4688 U.S.A.

Visit us online at www.nationalgeographic.com

For information about special discounts for bulk purchases, please contact
National Geographic Books Special Sales: ngspecsales@ngs.org

For rights or permissions inquiries, please contact National Geographic Books
Subsidiary Rights: ngbookrights@ngs.org

Interior design: Sanaa Akkach (Art Director), Linda Makarov (Designer)

Printed in the United States of America
11/QGF-CML/1

contents

introduction

Sometimes, all you want is to bake on the beach under a UV-blocking umbrella. But if a day or two of lounging leaves you wondering, "Now what?" maybe you're craving something more: a vacation that replaces the worry-worn spaces in your soul with possibilities. And one that you can afford at the same time.

This book is divided into four chapters, with vacations that delve into the American mindscape, explore nature, craft new skills, and stretch horizons—both physical and those in our psyches.

What they won't stretch is your budget. Though what qualifies as "affordable" varies, the 100 vacations here are wallet friendly. Some are downright budget savvy; others combine worthy splurges—tours, meals, train rides, and more that offer a bang worthy of the extra expense—with otherwise cost-effective trips. The splurges are highlighted throughout the book.

All of these vacation ideas recognize that soul-satisfying vacations—like the rest of our lives—often involve trade-offs. Plan ahead to visit during a city's off-season "restaurant week," and you might get a meal by a famous-name chef for half the regular price. Opt for a campsite instead of that cozy bed-and-breakfast, and you'll feel better about splurging on a ride aboard a historic narrow-gauge train.

If you're like us, you'll recognize that the most cherished memories rarely revolve around a grand hotel or pricey gourmet meal. Renewal and wonder are priceless.

So put your iPhone in rest mode and leave the laptop behind. Better yet, head to a remote retreat where wireless doesn't work. You'll be amazed at how well the world survives without you—and you without it—at least for a few days.

– Jane Wooldridge and Larry Bleiberg

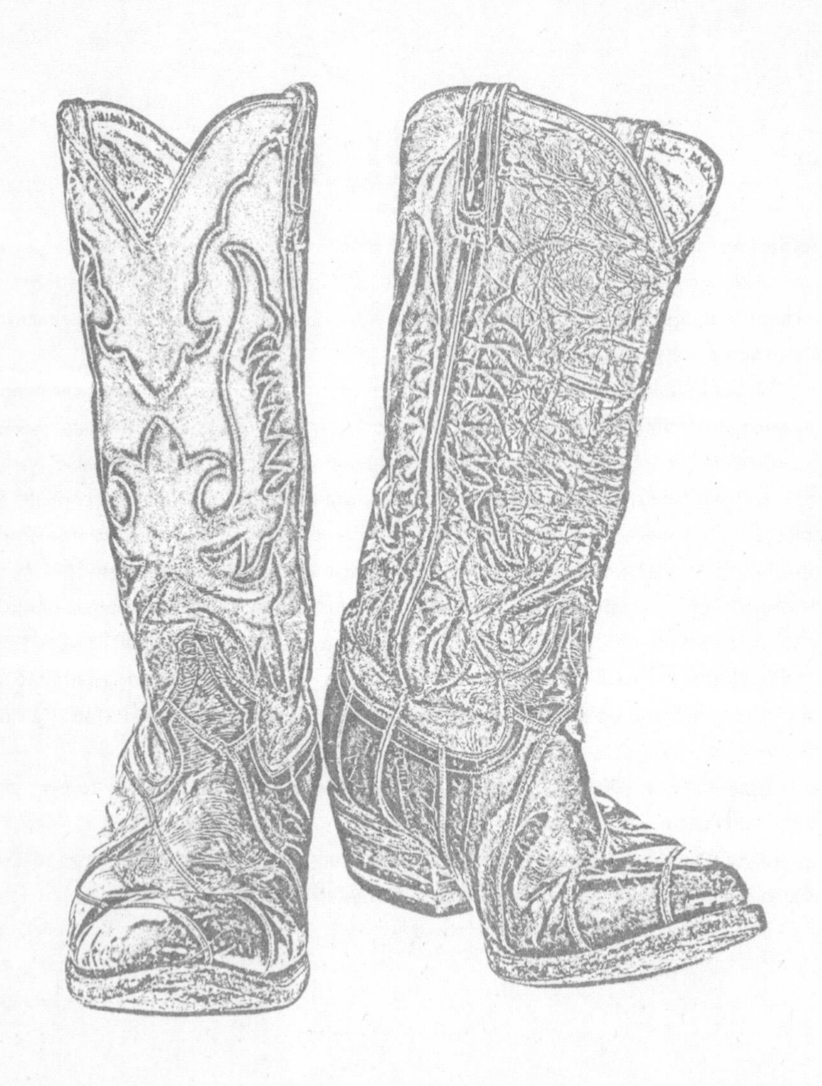

CHAPTER 1

americana

We all have friends who have traveled to the farthest reaches of the globe. They've worn out passports finding their way to the temples of Asia, the majestic castles of Europe, and the incredible diversity of Africa. But ask them about America and they draw a blank. "I'll get to that sometime," the blasé will say. Others, a little shamed, will acknowledge the gap in their travels.

The delightful thing about seeing America is that you're already here. There's no need for visas and intercontinental flights; just point your car to the highway and go. The exotic is right in front of you.

A road trip is the best way to get to know your country—and yourself. And a trip anywhere in the United States will do just fine. For example, a visit to a state fair will tell you as much about human nature as any piece of literature; and Kansas City barbecue and Kentucky bourbon are as much delicacies as Russian caviar and French champagne.

The trips and experiences in this chapter will make you see America with new eyes. You'll see that we have traditions, arts, and history as rich as any country. These vacations let you relive our founding revolution, marvel at the genius of Thomas Jefferson, mourn the tragedies of our Civil War, and see the horrific machinery we were prepared to deploy during the Cold War.

Other trips will introduce you to the heroes of the civil rights movement, make clear that cowboys didn't die out with John Wayne, and showcase sites and museums certain to give you a new appreciation for the nation's capital.

You'll discover corners of our country where nothing seems to have changed for decades—places where you can indulge in folk art, absorb natural scenery, and, most important perhaps, have an unforgettable piece of pie. This is a celebration of all that our nation has to offer, and all that should be celebrated.

relive the american revolution

CONCORD & LEXINGTON, MASSACHUSETTS

Here once the embattled farmers stood,
And fired the shot heard round the world.

—POET RALPH WALDO EMERSON, "CONCORD HYMN" (1836)

1 April 19 is a pivotal day in American history. And although we can't go back in time to watch the Battles of Lexington and Concord, there's another option: Witnessing the springtime reenactment of the battles, when hundreds of dedicated Revolutionary War buffs depict the historic confrontations for thousands of fascinated spectators. There are parades, battlefield encampments, and living history demonstrations open to the public. It's enough to make you don a tricorne hat and whistle *Yankee Doodle*.

"This whole notion about the willingness to stand up and fight for liberty, it comes from here," says Lou Sideris of Minute Man National Historical Park in Concord, Massachusetts. "People really come here and say 'now I know what it means to be an American.'"

The cities of Lexington and Concord work together with Minute Man National Historical Park to re-create these momentous events every Patriots' Day weekend, a Massachusetts state holiday held on the third Monday in April. The major presentations begin on Saturday; by the time the last shot is fired on Monday, visitors will have a new appreciation—and understanding—of the events that launched our nation. Just as the Colonials were volunteer citizen-soldiers, so are the reenactors, who spend thousands of dollars on uniforms and who undergo rigorous training to properly re-create the historic battles.

Here's a quick history primer: The British, tired of rebellious colonists who wouldn't pay their requisite taxes, planned to disarm them. The colonists resented the taxation and wanted freedom from British occupation. The two forces met at dawn on Lexington Green, and shots were fired. The Colonials pulled back; they regrouped a few hours later at North Bridge in Concord. It's uncertain which side then fired first, but in his "Concord Hymn," Ralph Waldo Emerson describes the first shot as the "shot heard round the world." The British soldiers marched 18 miles back to Boston, facing fire all the way. By the end of the day, 73 British and 49 Colonials were killed in action.

The schedule of weekend events can be overwhelming, and—because they are scheduled out of historic sequence—a little confusing. With literally thousands of spectators descending upon the battle sites for reenactments every year, you will need a plan to make the most of your experience. Here are the key events to catch:

- **Commemoration of the North Bridge Fight.** Saturday, 8:30 a.m. The action starts with this battle in Concord. Historically the battle lasted perhaps three minutes, though you can expect it to continue a little longer now. After that, you can visit reenactors encamped in nearby Minute Man National Historical Park, where there will be drill and musket exhibitions, 18th-century artillery demonstrations, and crafts.
- **Bloody Angle Battle Demonstration.** Saturday, around 1 p.m. Unlike at the other Battles of Concord and Lexington reenactment sites, which are relatively compact, the action near the Hartwell Tavern historical area of Minute Man National Historical Park is a running firefight taking place over a half mile, which gives the spectating crowd plenty of room to spread out. In addition, this portion of the park has been restored so spectators see a battle surrounded by trees, not modern-day buildings and traffic. "With the militias moving through the field and jumping over stone walls, it really feels like the original Patriots' Day," Sideris says.
- **Initial confrontation on Lexington Green.** Monday, 5:30 a.m. This reenactment details the initial confrontation on Lexington Green, and despite the early hour, literally thousands of spectators will be on hand, many spending the night. John Ott, the former director of the National Heritage Museum in Lexington, says the sight is unforgettable. "When you see this red mass of troops coming down the road, you hear the drums, and it's amazing. You still get choked up." After the battle, the crowds head to pancake breakfasts at several nearby churches.

Those are just the major presentations. You can also see a Paul Revere reenactor rushing to the Hancock-Clarke House in Lexington warning about the soon-to-arrive British at eleven o'clock Sunday night, or catch parades in Lexington and Concord on Monday.

If you can't make it on Patriots' Day, there are other ways to experience the events. Some locals prefer catching the dress rehearsal of the Lexington Green reenactment, held a week or two before the actual event. The crowd's much thinner and it's scheduled for the afternoon, eliminating the need for a predawn wake-up call. In early March, there's also a reenactment of the Boston Massacre—a 1770 event that led to the Revolution. You'll find the full schedule at www.battleroad.org.

CONFRONTATION AT GETTYSBURG

Less than 90 years after the Battles of Lexington and Concord, another revolution shook America. During the U.S. Civil War, the country nearly tore itself apart. The turning point came near an obscure Pennsylvania town. And after the Battle of Gettysburg, the Confederates' invasion of the North came to an end, as would their rebellion two years later.

During the first week of July, thousands of reenactors and tens of thousands of spectators again invade Gettysburg for a three-day reenactment. Unlike the events near Boston, these battles aren't held on the actual site of the confrontation. Instead, they're staged a few miles away on a farm field; plus admission is charged, about $25 a day with discounts for multiday tickets, www.gettysburgreenactment.com. The events are even more spectacular and heavily attended on the five-year anniversaries of the 1863 battle. Spectators watch the battles from bleachers or many bring lawn chairs. Often visitors come for the morning and head back to their motel to swim returning later to catch an afternoon battle. The biggest crowd arrives on the last day to see Pickett's Charge, which some historians say marked the end of the Rebel cause. The desperate infantry attack resulted in more than 2,600 Confederate casualties. Watching it today, one can see the carnage and sense the desperation the men must have felt that afternoon.

Even if you can't make the reenactment, visitors can see soldiers most weekends during the summer at no cost. The **Gettysburg National Military Park** (717-334-1124, www.nps.gov/gett) hosts visiting "companies," who hold living history demonstrations and are eager to answer questions, which are usually about camp food and battlefield medicine. You'll also find reenactors most weekends camped in front of the **American Civil War Museum** (297 Steinwehr Ave., 717-334-6245, www.gettysburgmuseum.com, $5.50) in the town of Gettysburg. Although the museum charges admission, there's no cost to visit with the soldiers.

Lodging fills up during reenactment weekend, with hotels running from $100–$150 a night. Check with the Gettysburg Convention & Visitors Bureau (8 Lincoln Sq., 866-486-5735, www.gettysburg.travel) for availability, or look in nearby towns, like York, Chambersburg, and Harrisburg, Pennsylvania, and Frederick, Maryland, all within a 45-minute drive. In Gettysburg, most everyone tries **General Pickett's Buffets** (571 Steinwehr Ave., 717-334-7580), where you dine to Civil War–era music and eat your fill of soup, salad, meatloaf or Virginia ham, and dessert for $10–$12.

Lodging can be tricky for this popular event. There are a couple chain motels in Concord. Or look to similar lodging in neighboring towns like Bedford. Both Lexington and Concord have a variety of eateries. In Concord, pick up sandwiches or a picnic at **Concord Cheese Shop** (29 Walden St., 978-369-5778), which dates from 1860. In Lexington, **Via Lago** (1845 Massachusetts Ave., 781-861-6174) offers breakfast and lunch specials like veggie quesadillas ($4.99). [$PLURGE: **For a little splurge, try the famous chicken-pot pie ($13.95) for lunch at Concord's Colonial Inn (48 Monument Sq., 978-369-9200), a historic spot in its own right. It housed some of the Colonials' munitions during the 1775 battles.**]

HOW TO GET IN TOUCH

Concord Chamber of Commerce, 15 Walden St., Ste. 7, Concord, MA 01742, 978-369-3120, www.concordchamberofcommerce.org.

Lexington Chamber of Commerce, 1875 Massachusetts Ave., Lexington, MA 02420, 781-862-2480, www.lexingtonchamber.org.

Minute Man National Historical Park, 174 Liberty St., Concord, MA 01742, 978-369-6993, www.nps.gov/mima.

be corny

MITCHELL, SOUTH DAKOTA

The Indian Corn, or Maiz, proves the most useful Grain in the World.

—JOHN LAWSON, 17TH-CENTURY BRITISH EXPLORER

2 South Dakota knows a thing or two about eye-catching monuments, and though the massive presidential sculpture of Mount Rushmore on the state's western edge is far more famous, the Corn Palace in the small prairie town of Mitchell, 65 miles west of Sioux Falls, is a wonder in its own right.

First created in 1892 as a monumental advertisement for the area's agricultural bounty, the Corn Palace was moved to its current site in 1921. This structure isn't a sedate midwestern show hall—it's a fantasy of Moorish architecture topped with minarets and kiosks. But the real attention grabber? The massive murals that depict American history and achievement, made of 275,000 ears of locally grown corn, plus grains and grasses.

A new theme is chosen each year. Giant tar-paper drawings of the new murals are affixed to the palace in late summer; a crew of about 20 works into the fall to nail the corn in place as the new crop becomes available.

Though sometimes bashed as the "world's largest bird feeder," the Corn Palace and the festival that surrounds it evoke fond memories from many who have seen it.

"I first visited the Corn Palace sometime in the '60s as a youngster with my parents," posted Buck Jones (aka "Sandhills Guru") on a city-data.com forum devoted to the Corn Palace. "I would venture to say that we still visit it yearly . . . Our kids even as adults like to go with us."

Free tours of the 39,000-square-foot Corn Palace are offered throughout the day from Memorial Day to Labor Day. But the palace is at its liveliest each August during its four-day namesake festival, when the grounds are transformed into a midway, rollicking musicians take to the stage, and the toasty smell of roasting corn fills the South Dakota air. Some 40,000 visitors fill the blocks around the palace, eating corndogs and fried Twinkies and barbecue, and catching concerts by name entertainers that, over the decades, have ranged from John Philip Sousa to Willie Nelson and Rick Springfield.

The Corn Palace Festival is part of Mitchell's business week, which includes an agriculture fair called Dakotafest and the Miller Lite Bull Bash riding competition. The Corn Palace Stampede Rodeo takes place in July, a month before the Corn Palace Festival and Bull Bash.

AN ORIGINAL AMERICAN FOOD

Corn is one of our continent's true local foodstuffs, first cultivated by peoples living in what is now central Mexico some 7,000 years ago. Today it's grown throughout the world, but Americans still think of it as an icon of the American landscape.

Celebrate it with a few hours at a corn maze. Dashing through the stalks is great fun, and many mazes have outdoor tables for bring-your-own picnics.

Most open in mid- to late summer (after the corn is tall enough) and stay open into the fall. Naturally, most are in rural settings. Each maze is individually owned, so activities and prices vary, though you can expect to pay around $10 per adult and half that for children under 12.

At the **Sauchuk Farm** (Rte. 58, 781-585-1522), near Plympton, Massachusetts, kids can get their faces painted and ride through the maze on a child-size train. At **Guffey Acres** (1603 N. 400 W, 765-864-0006) in Kokomo, Indiana, small children can romp through a hay-bale maze while bigger kids and adults traverse a convoluted, full-size labyrinth. In Washington State, **Stocker Farms** (8705 Marsh Rd., Snohomish, 360-568-7391) invites locals to design its wacky maze; come Halloween, the corn zone becomes a creepy Field of Screams.

Whether you visit during the festival, the Stampede, or at another time of year, you'll want to check out the Corn Palace memorabilia, local historical exhibits, and a domed mural by WPA artist Oscar Howe. All are on display at the nearby **Carnegie Resource Center** (119 W. 3rd Ave., 605-996-3209, www.mitchellcarnegie.org, closed a.m. & Sun.), founded as a library in the early 1900s with a donation from steel magnate Andrew Carnegie.

If you're interested in pioneer and Native American life, check out the **Dakota Discovery Museum** (1300 McGovern Ave., 605-996-2122, www.dakotadiscovery.com, $5), a kid-friendly interactive center. For American political history buffs and fans of Senator (and onetime presidential candidate) George McGovern, the **George McGovern Legacy Museum** (1200 W. University Ave., 605-995-2935, www.mcgoverncenter.com, closed Sat.–Sun.) at Dakota Wesleyan University recalls his accomplishments.

This is true farm country. Lodging includes campsites, chain motels, hunting lodges (pheasant hunting and bass fishing are big), and working farms like **der Rumbolz Platz B&B** (40732 266th St., 605-227-4385) in nearby Ethan, where a double room costs $70. At **Flavia's Place** (605-995-1562, www.kentoncompany.com), a bed-and-breakfast in Mitchell, rooms start at $60.

HOW TO GET IN TOUCH

Corn Palace, 604 N. Main St., Mitchell, SD 57301, 605-995-8427, www.cornpalace.com.

Mitchell Convention & Visitors Bureau, 601 N. Main St., Mitchell, SD 57301, 866-273-2676, www.visitmitchell.com.

immerse in desert architecture

GRAND CANYON NATIONAL PARK, ARIZONA

People should be looking at the Grand Canyon, but they turn around, and–I've seen it–they literally touch the stonework. They actually physically interact with a piece of architecture.

—FILM DIRECTOR KAREN BARTLETT, *MARY JANE COLTER: HOUSE MADE OF DAWN* (1997)

3 The majesty of the Grand Canyon will overwhelm even the most worldly traveler, but the canyon is not the national park's only attraction. Architect Mary Colter's buildings, constructed a century ago for tourists arriving by railroad, look like rustic landmarks and restored Indian ruins. "Mary Colter's work doesn't stand out from the landscape, it's part of the landscape," says park ranger Maggi Daly. She often encounters visitors on Colter quests, who are seeking out her every work.

Long before women could vote, Mary Elizabeth Jane Colter created these buildings, pioneering what has become known as "parkitecture," the rustic design now common throughout the National Park System. The former St. Paul, Minnesota, teacher was drawn to the region by her love of Native American culture. She designed themed hotels and gift shops for the Fred Harvey Company, which served tourists across the West.

Searching for Colter's eight Grand Canyon park buildings makes for a fascinating vacation. All but one can be seen in a day, as most are clustered along the park's South Rim.

Start with the 70-foot **Desert View Watchtower** at the east park entrance (park admission $25 per car, good for 7 days). The curio shop appears centuries old, but the rough stone exterior hides steel beams and electric wiring. Colter was so exacting that when workers placed a large rock in the wrong place during construction, she ordered the section torn down and rebuilt. While admiring the canyon from inside the structure, look for black glass reflectors by the windows. These reflectoscopes, an invention

GRAND CANYON FACTS

- The oldest rocks are two billion years old.
- The canyon is 1 mile deep.
- It took the Colorado River more than six million years to carve the canyon.
- In 1869 John Wesley Powell became the first European to float through the canyon.
- The park is 277 miles long.

of 17th-century French artist Claude Lorrain, help compress views of the canyon and accentuate its rich colors.

Next stop: Grand Canyon Village, the park's hub, where five Colter-designed buildings stand. The 1905 **Hopi House** is another faux ruin, with low ceilings and traditional design. **Lookout Studio** literally hangs over the canyon rim. And you'll want to stay, of course, at the **Bright Angel Lodge & Cabins** (888-297-2757, www.grandcanyonlodges.com). The wonderful surprise is that rooms start at $79 a night, although you'll have to share a bathroom. The hotel also has a fireplace with a secret: Colter designed it so the rocks match, layer by layer, the geological structure of the canyon. The last two Colter-designed buildings are the men's and women's dormitories for employees; although they are not open to the public, you can easily admire the exteriors, and the park's long-term plan is to convert them to guest housing.

$PLURGE

ABOVE IT ALL

The newest way to see the canyon is not for the faint of heart, nor for the penny-wise. The Grand Canyon Skywalk will have you literally floating over the canyon on a glass-bottomed terrace 4,000 feet above the Colorado River. The view is stunning, and most would agree that the $84 price of admission is worth every penny. The walk is not located at the national park, but a 242-mile drive away on the Hualapai Indian Reservation. *Grand Canyon Skywalk, 888-868-9378, www.grandcanyonskywalk.com.*

Eleven miles west of Grand Canyon Village, reached by the park's free shuttle bus service, which runs throughout the day, **Hermits Rest** is a favorite Colter building. It is fashioned to resemble a hand-built stone hut.

To see the last Colter work, you'll have to hike or take a mule 10 miles down to **Phantom Ranch,** a collection of stone shelters at the canyon bottom. [$PLURGE: **Accommodations at Phantom Ranch range from $42 for a bunk, to $473 for a round-trip mule ride and room and board; reservations are available 13 months in advance. A less expensive splurge is the three-hour mule trip that doesn't reach the canyon bottom. It runs $117.**]

On your tour of the park architecture, be sure to take in the other sights. The park can keep you busy for several days. The easiest way to see the Grand Canyon is to stroll the flat, 12-mile Rim Trail. But you don't have to walk it all–free shuttle buses stop along the route. To hike into the canyon, try the Bright Angel Trail, and if you're feeling ambitious head 4.5 miles down to Indian Garden. But make sure to pace yourself. This is mountain climbing in reverse and the hardest part is climbing back up.

For a true escape, sleep in the canyon itself. While nearly five million visitors come to the park every year, less than one percent camp out (permits required, 928-638-7875, Mon.–Fri. 1 p.m.–5 p.m.). Back on the rim, catch a free ranger talk on the California condor. The species, once on the

SLEEP EASY IN WINSLOW

Long before The Eagles made Winslow, Arizona, famous with their 1972 hit song "Take It Easy," the railroad brought tourists to this desert town. The Fred Harvey Company and architect Mary Colter crafted **La Posada,** styled after a grand hacienda.

The timing was terrible. The hotel opened in 1930, just as the Great Depression swept the country. After decades of struggle, it closed in 1957, and the Santa Fe Railway used the space as offices. By the 1990s the place was a wreck.

In stepped Arizona artist Tina Mion and her husband Allan Affeldt, a self-taught architect. In 1997 the couple bought the hotel and began a lengthy restoration. Today airy lobbies and lounges showcase contemporary Southwest artists, including Mion's own striking canvases. Guests play checkers, gather around the fireplace, or sprawl in nooks, book in hand. Guest rooms—named for famed past guests, including John Wayne, Gene Autry, and Mary Pickford—are comfortably cozy, with rustic Mexican and Southwest decor.

Room rates start at $99. Note that the train still rolls right behind the hotel; if you're in the back, you'll hear its rattle and whistle.

Even if you don't snag a room, try the hotel's Turquoise Room restaurant, where the artful dishes are worth every calorie. Don't miss the warm prickly-pear-cactus bread pudding—unless you order the pistachio-and-piñon pie instead. *La Posada, 303 E. 2nd St. (Rte. 66), Winslow, AZ 86047, 928-289-4366, www.laposada.org.*

brink of extinction, has been reintroduced to the area and is easily spied from Grand Canyon Village spring through early fall.

HOW TO GET IN TOUCH

Grand Canyon National Park, P.O. Box 129, Grand Canyon, AZ 86023, 928-638-7888, www.nps.gov/grca.

Xanterra Parks & Resorts, 6312 S. Fiddlers Green Circle, Ste. 600N, Greenwood Village, CO 80111, 888-297-2757 or same-day reservations 928-638-2631, www.grandcanyonlodges.com.

enjoy a classic new england vacation

VERMONT

New England has a harsh climate, a barren soil,
a rough and stormy coast, and yet we love it.

—AMERICAN STATESMAN HENRY CABOT LODGE (1850–1924)

4 A New England vacation is an immersion in nature, history, arts, and neighborliness. Along with curling up with a good book and canoeing lazily on a lake, you'll find plenty to tickle your brain and stretch your muscles. Then again, if you find yourself just standing in the general store chatting with someone you've never before met about nothing much at all, that's OK too.

The northeastern states offer picturesque towns where you can stroll down a classic main street, take a walk in the mountains, catch a concert on the town green, and visit a historic statehouse. A favorite spot is the corner of Vermont edging Canada and New Hampshire, which is known as the Northeast Kingdom. The barns are red, the mountains high enough for sweeping views, and the land cheap enough that craftspeople from artisan cheesemakers to woodworkers call it home.

With a few days—or the better part of a summer—you can station yourself in the historic town of St. Johnsbury (pop. 7,400), the cozy hilltop village of Craftsbury Common (graves in the village cemetery date from the early 1800s), a breezy cottage on Caspian Lake in Greensboro (the town still has no cell service), or the state capital, Montpelier.

From any of these, you're within a 30- to 45-minute drive of a dozen rural attractions. In the small town of Cabot, tours are offered daily in summer of the **Cabot Creamery** (2878 Main St., 800-837-4261, www.cabotcheese.coop, $2). In Danville, the **Great Corn Maze** (1404 Wheelock Rd., 802-748-1399, www.vermontcornmaze.com, $12) opens in late July. In Montpelier, you can tour the 1830s **Vermont State House** (115 State St., 802-828-2228, www.vtstatehouse.org) Monday through Saturday, July to October; audio or self-guided tours are

$PLURGE

A COZY COUNTRY INN

Visitors return year after year to Greensboro's historic **Highland Lodge** (802-533-2647, www.highlandlodge.com), a country inn with wide porches, a main building, and self-contained cottages. Summer rates run $285 for a double room and include breakfast and dinner daily, gratuities, and some recreational gear; single rates start at $160 and include the same.

OTHER CLASSIC NORTHEAST VACATION SPOTS

- **Adirondack lakes region, New York.** New York isn't technically part of New England, but we're claiming it anyway. Fish-rich lakes, rolling mountains, and charming antler chandeliers: How can you pass it up? *Adirondack Regional Tourism Council, 518-846-8016, www.visitadirondacks.com.*
- **Litchfield Hills, Connecticut.** Visiting the covered bridges, antiques shops, farmers markets, historic sites, and museums here can fill up a summer. From late August to mid-October, local fairs bring together racing pigs, country line dancing, fireworks, and quilt contests. *Western CT Visitors Bureau, 860-567-4506, www.litchfieldhills.com.*
- **Moosehead Lake, Maine.** Moosehead Lake is about nature hikes, boat rides, and the region's namesake antlered mammals, which outnumber humans three to one. Despite the odds, if you visit in late summer you may miss them altogether; they're most visible in May and June. *Moosehead Lake Region Chamber of Commerce, 888-876-2778, www.mooseheadlake.org.*

available at other times of year when the legislature is not meeting. And you could easily spend an entire day in St. Johnsbury, visiting the **Athenaeum** (1171 Main St., 802-748-8291, www.stjathenaeum.org), an art gallery, museum, and library, and the **Fairbanks Museum** (1302 Main St., 802-748-2372, www.fairbanksmuseum.org, $8), an engaging yet anachronistic cabinet of curiosities and planetarium dating from 1891.

Looking for more? A few minutes in front of the bulletin boards at The Willey's Store in Greensboro, the co-op in East Hardwick, or the town hall on Craftsbury Common will give you the update on local events. Young performers ages 10 through 18 tour the region as **Circus Smirkus** (802-533-7443, www.smirkus.org); most performances are in August but dates vary. Young thespians from **Get Thee to the Funnery camps** (www.vermontshakespeare.com) display their prowess with outdoor Shakespeare performances in Craftsbury Common, Hardwick, and St. Johnsbury—also in August. The **Bread and Puppet Theater** (802-525-3031, www.breadandpuppet.org) in Glover displays political satire with music, giant puppets, and street theater plays throughout the region. If that all seems too heady, there are always the cotton candy and greased pig races at the **Barton County Fair** (278 Roaring Brook Rd., 802-525-3555, www.orleanscountyfair.org), held in mid-August.

The mountains here are more enticing than daunting, which means outdoor activities are accessible to anyone who is reasonably fit. Cycling, golf, horse riding, llama trekking—even organized tree climbing—are on the options list. Hiking trails abound; if you're with children or want an easy path, check out the **Barr Hill Nature Preserve** (802-229-4425, www.nature.org).

Some sports and performances like those presented by Circus Smirkus and the Shakespeare camp are offered in summer only, but fall and winter too bring their charms, including autumn leaf viewing, and in winter, snowshoeing, cross-country, sleigh riding, dogsledding, and maple sugaring.

Among the area's least expensive lodging options are campsites in state parks (Vermont State Parks, 888-409-7579, www.vtstateparks.com) and at private campgrounds. Other value accommodations in the region include bed-and-breakfasts, mom-and-pop motels, and even chain outposts (these mostly are confined to the areas around I-91 and I-93). In addition, private owners often rent lakefront cottages suitable for families. The Northeast Kingdom Travel & Tourism Association can provide information on all of these options.

HOW TO GET IN TOUCH

Northeast Kingdom Travel & Tourism Association, 446 Rte. 114, East Burke, VT 05832, 800-884-8001, www.travelthekingdom.com.

follow the barbecue trail

FROM NORTH CAROLINA TO TEXAS

Grilling, broiling, barbecuing—whatever you want to call it—is an art, not just a matter of building a pyre and throwing on a piece of meat as a sacrifice to the gods of the stomach.

—CHEF AND AUTHOR JAMES BEARD, *BEARD ON FOOD* (1974)

5 No food seems more quintessentially American than barbecue. But despite our prowess with burgers, chicken breasts, and hot dogs on the grill, barbecuing has been a common cooking method around the world pretty much since humans first figured out how to strike a fire.

In modern-day America, what is meant by "barbecue" is likely determined by locality, says Steven Raichlen, James Beard Award–winning author of *Planet Barbecue, The Barbecue Bible,* and other popular books on grilling. In the Deep South, barbecued food is the result of a slow, prolonged cooking method. In Texas, it's smoked beef; in Kansas it's ribs with a sweet barbecue sauce or a dry rub grilled till the meat drips off the bone. In North Carolina, barbecue is pulled pork—though the fierce, decades-old battle between eastern-style (vinegar, no tomatoes) and western-style (vinegar, but with tomatoes) rages on.

To fully immerse yourself in barbecue, sample the fare and flavors on offer at a few favorite towns and fests where grilled beast—be it smoked, rubbed, pulled, slathered in sauce, or massaged with spice—is the main draw. If you're truly a 'cue fan, string the recommendations into a road trip. But beware: After five barbecue feasts in as many days, you may be in need of a giant salad.

$PLURGE

BARBECUE UNIVERSITY

For a splurge, sign up for Raichlen's Barbecue University, a three-day seminar held twice each summer at the Broadmoor Resort in Colorado Springs, Colorado. The per person $2,000 price includes three nights accommodations and meals—despite the cost, the course fills up quickly. *Broadmoor Resort, 800-634-7711, www.broadmoor.com.*

Kansas City, Kansas and Missouri. If there is a center of the American barbecue universe, it may well be Kansas City, straddling the Kansas-Missouri state line. As a staging center for western exploration, Kansas City was home to early meatpacking operations and stockyards; barbecue naturally followed. But it wasn't until the 1920s that a fellow named Henry Perry opened the first barbecue pit. Among the best loved of the city's more than one hundred barbecue joints are **Gates** (800-662-7427, www.gatesbbq.com), where you'll be greeted with a shouted "Hi, may I help you?"; **Fiorella's Jack Stack** (816-531-7427, www.jackstackbbq.com), for white tablecloth service; and the dignitary must-stop **Arthur Bryant's** (816-231-1123, www.arthurbryantsbbq.com); all have several locations around town.

Now entering its fourth decade, the annual **American Royal Barbecue Festival** (816-569-4021, www.arbbq.com), held in late September/early October, features 500 contestants and 20 acres of gluttony. Word from the wise: Get your $13 tickets in advance; festival lines are nuts.

Kansas City Convention & Visitors Association, 800-767-7700, www.visitkc.com.

Lexington, North Carolina. Lexington stakes its claim as "barbecue capital of the world" thanks to the 1919 establishment of the town's first pit-cooked barbecue tent. The furniture-manufacturing operations that were once the centerpiece of Lexington's economy have waned, but the town of 20,000 remains beloved for its coziness and two dozen barbecue restaurants, famed for pork—sliced, chopped, or pulled—served with coleslaw and hush puppies (beef and chicken dishes are also offered at some). Most are open any day you land there, though some are closed on Sunday. One of the largest and best known is **Lexington Barbecue No. 1** (10 Hwy. 29/70 S, 336-249-9814). For the full effect, come during the annual **Lexington Barbecue Festival** (www.barbecuefestival.com) in late October, held on Main Street near the historic county courthouse.

Lexington Area Chamber of Commerce, 336-248-5929, www.lexingtonchamber.net.

Lockhart, Texas. Located some 25 miles south of Austin, this tiny town of 14,000 on the historic Chisholm Trail boasts less than a handful of barbecue restaurants, but collectively they serve up 5,000 meals per week. Barbecued pork sausage is the specialty here, though you'll find chops and brisket as well. All the barbecue joints win raves, but if you must choose only one, make it **Kreuz** (pronounced KRITES) **Market** (619 N. Colorado St., 512-398-2361), where smoky brisket, peppered pork ribs, and jalapeño-cheese sausage win raves. Don't ask for sauce—they don't have it; but the sauerkraut is divine. The town's annual Chisholm Trail music and 'cue fest is held the second weekend in June.

Lockhart Chamber of Commerce, 512-398-2818, www.lockhart-tx.org or www.lockhartchamber.com.

Memphis, Tennessee. Debating where to find the best barbecue here is something of a city sport. With more than a hundred 'cue joints, there's

BARBECUE BACKGROUND

Nearly every culture claims an early form of 'cue, but the term "barbacoa" first appeared in print in Spain in the 1500s, says Steven Raichlen, author and host of public television's *Primal Grill* and *Barbecue University*. It referred to a wooden frame made with sticks—a primitive grill—used to slowly cook wild meats or seafood over a fire. "But in fact, people have been cooking meat with live fire for almost two million years," says Raichlen.

plenty to choose from. Often mentioned are **Rendezvous** (52 S. 2nd St., 901-523-2746), famed for its ribs since 1948; **Central BBQ** (2249 Central Ave., 901-272-9377), known for its slow-smoked ribs, pulled meat, and hot wings; **Corky's** (5259 Poplar Ave., 901-685-9744), seasoned with a dry rub, slathered in sauce, and slow cooked; and **Neely's** (670 Jefferson Ave., 901-521-9798), made famous by the Food Network's show *Down Home with the Neelys.* Also recommended? The funky **Blues City Café** (138 Beale St., 901-526-3637), where the ribs are flavored with a wet rub and slow cooked at 225°F, then drenched in a sweet barbecue sauce. They're worth every last calorie.

For the ultimate Memphis pig-out, check out the **World Championship Barbecue Contest** (800-745-3000, www.memphisinmay.org/bbq, tickets from $8), including barbecue tours and a chance to vote in the People's Pick. The weekend-long contest is held mid-month during the annual Memphis in May Festival.

Memphis Convention & Visitors Bureau, 888-633-9099, www.memphistravel.com.

St. Louis, Missouri. St. Louis is known for its barbecued spare ribs and reportedly leads the world in per capita consumption of barbecue sauce. The sauce is sweet; the ribs are trimmed to remove the fatty portion off the rack. But as far as the locals are concerned, you haven't tried St. Louis–style barbecue until you try the barbecued pork steaks, says Donna Andrews, spokesperson for the city's visitors bureau.

Among the city's famed 'cue joints are **Pappy's Smoke House** (3106 Olive St., 314-535-4340), known for its dry-rubbed, slow-smoked pork ribs; **Roper's Ribs** (6929 W. Florissant Ave., 314-381-6200), seasoned with a secret blend of spices and smoked over hickory; and **Smoki O's** (1545 N. Broadway, 314-621-8180), where the menu includes rib tips, crispy snoot (that would be pig and nostrils), and barbecue spaghetti.

The annual **Rib America Festival** (314-622-4550, www.ribamerica.com) featuring cook-offs and entertainment takes place in late May at the Soldier's Memorial in downtown; tickets cost $5.

St. Louis Convention & Visitors Commission, 800-325-7962, www.explorestlouis.com.

get to know thomas jefferson

CHARLOTTESVILLE, VIRGINIA

Educate and inform the whole mass of the people . . .
They are the only sure reliance for the preservation of our liberty.

—THOMAS JEFFERSON (1743–1826), 3RD U.S. PRESIDENT

6 George Washington gets honored as the father of our country, but Thomas Jefferson authored our Declaration of Independence and then nurtured our fledgling nation and nearly doubled its size through the Louisiana Purchase.

Jefferson was the ultimate American Renaissance man: visionary thinker, diplomat, gentleman farmer, architect, connoisseur of books and wine, slave owner, and antislavery activist—and yes, the third President of the United States. It's no small irony that Jefferson died on July 4, 1826—50 years to the day after the adoption of the Declaration of Independence.

If Christopher Hitchens's biography of Jefferson and the Ken Burns PBS special only tickled your interest, head to Charlottesville, Virginia. **Monticello** (931 Thomas Jefferson Pkwy., 434-984-9822, www.monticello.org, $22), Jefferson's gracious plantation home, stands atop a hill outside this friendly college town.

The guided 30-minute tour of the stately 18th-century brick home won't really give you enough time to check out the Great Clock that Jefferson himself designed, now in the Entrance Hall; the revolving bookstand in the Cabinet; or musical instruments in his Parlor. To get a fuller sense of the man, check out the visitor center, catch an architectural tour, and stroll the terraced vegetable gardens. All are included in the price of your ticket, though the two walking tours of the grounds are offered only April through October.

To continue your Jeffersonian quest, head down the hill to Charlottesville and "Mr. Jefferson's University"—the "Academical Village" that reflected Jefferson's passion for learning and formed the basis of the **University of Virginia** (434-924-0311, www.virginia.edu), which he founded in 1819. Today UVA is one of the country's top universities and a bustling home to more than 21,000 students. Now, as during Jefferson's day, the university's centerpiece is the **Rotunda** (near the intersection of University Ave. & McCormick Rd.), the domed library designed to recall Rome's Pantheon and set at the head of a lawn flanked by student quarters and classrooms. Free tours of the Rotunda are offered throughout the year except during Thanksgiving and Christmas breaks.

LIBRARY OF CONGRESS

One of the best places to get a sense of Thomas Jefferson is a building he never visited: the current Library of Congress in Washington, D.C. In 1814, when the British burned the Library of Congress, Jefferson owned what was said to be the largest private collection of books in the country. Despite his brilliance, Jefferson had fallen into debt, so he offered to sell his collection for whatever Congress wanted to pay; in 1815 Congress voted to buy nearly 6,500 volumes for $23,950.

Nearly two-thirds of those were destroyed in an 1851 fire; however, the records cataloging the original contents of Jefferson's library remain and, with a private grant, the Library of Congress is attempting to reassemble the original collection. An exhibit showcases some of Jefferson's former belongings, including a manuscript on crop rotation, *Memoirs of a Monticello Slave* by Isaac Jefferson, and the rough draft of the Declaration of Independence and the desk on which Jefferson wrote it.

The Library of Congress now contains more than 145 million items, including books in Braille, movie clips, musical scores, editorial cartoons by Herblock, Spiderman comics, and taped interviews with Elvis Presley. When you visit, set aside time to take in the spectacular floors and ceilings of the Great Hall in the Thomas Jefferson Building. *Library of Congress, Independence Ave. & 1st St. SE, Washington, DC, 202-707-8000, www.loc.gov, closed Sun.*

Also check out the nearby Small Special Collections Library in Harrison Institute, which holds early copies of the Declaration of Independence and other rare documents.

Be sure to save a day or evening for Charlottesville itself. Though the town's outer flanks are now home to all-too-familiar strip malls, the center retains a small-town artsy flavor with a touch of a hippie hangover. A free trolley links the UVA campus to downtown.

East Main Street long ago was closed to traffic, and on weekends and evenings this central promenade fills with crafts people, college students, and locals checking out the beaded earrings and necklaces sold on tables under the trees and the antiques and books in the storefront shops. When you tire of sightseeing, you'll find plenty of places to catch a coffee or a cocktail. Tuesdays, grab at three-course meal at **Maya** (633 W. Main St., 434-979-6292) for $12. On Wednesdays and Thursdays, **L'Etoile** (817 W. Main St., 434-979-7957) offers three-course dinners for $27; reservations recommended. **Miller's** (109 W. Main St., 434-971-8511) serves affordable pitchers of beer and pub food throughout the week. For a hearty, family-friendly traditional Southern lunch, served by waiters in period costume, the 200-year-old **Michie Tavern** (683 Thomas Jefferson Pkwy., 434-977-1234), between Charlottesville and Monticello, can't be beat. The buffet costs $16.25.

A word about lodging: Charlottesville's loyal alumni come streaming back for football and basketball games. When that happens, lodging prices skyrocket, as they do during other major university-related events. At other times you'll have a wide selection of bed-and-breakfasts and chain lodgings that often are a bit more atmospheric than the usual roadside stops.

If you arrive without a reservation, stop in at the Downtown Visitor Center (610 E. Main St., 434-293-6789, 9 a.m.–5 p.m.), which promises the best same-day rates from participating lodgings. One affordable option: the historic **Alexander House Inn** (1205 Monticello Rd., 434-327-6447, www.alexanderhouse.us), with both private and bunk lodgings. Rates run about $40 per person per night. Or try camping outside of town at **Misty Mountain Camp Resort** (888-647-8900, www.mistymountaincampresort.com), where rates begin at $25, or the **KOA Kampground** (434-296-9881, www.charlottesvillekoa.com), which operates mid-March to mid-November and has campsites from $26 and cabins from $50.

VIRGINIA PRESIDENTIAL HOMES

Virginia was birthplace to four of the first five U.S. Presidents, claiming eight Presidents in total. Several of their homes are open to the public:

- **Ash Lawn–Highland.** James Monroe, the fifth U.S. President, lived on this 535-acre plantation, which is still a working farm where cows, sheep, and peacocks are a hit with children. The farm often hosts arts performances. *Ash Lawn–Highland, 1000 James Monroe Pkwy., Charlottesville, 434-293-8000, www.al-h.us, $10.*
- **Berkeley Plantation.** This James River plantation was the seat of one of the foremost U.S. power families. Benjamin Harrison, a signer of the Declaration of Independence, was born here, as was his son, William Henry Harrison, the ninth President. In addition, the first official Thanksgiving was held here in 1619. Today's visitors see the 1,000-acre estate's 1726 Georgian-style mansion and expansive grounds. Daily period tours except on major holidays. *Berkeley Plantation, 12602 Harrison Landing Rd., Charles City, 888-466-6018, www.berkeleyplantation.com, $11.*
- **Montpelier.** This 2,650-acre estate in the Blue Ridge south of Orange was once the home of James and Dolley Madison. A 24-million-dollar renovation has restored the mansion to its 1809 appearance, when Madison returned from his term as the nation's fourth President. Tours of the mansion are offered daily. *Montpelier, 11407 Constitution Hwy., Montpelier Station, 540-672-2728, www.montpelier.org, $16.*
- **Mount Vernon.** Home to the first U.S. President, George Washington's riverside estate in Northern Virginia near Alexandria offers mansion and garden tours, encounters with costumed interpreters, and interactive and museum exhibitions (including his famous dentures). *Mount Vernon, 3200 Mount Vernon Memorial Hwy., Mount Vernon, 703-780-2000, www.mountvernon.org, $15.*

The countryside around Charlottesville offers numerous attractions as well. Should you cycle or wander the trails of the Thomas Jefferson Parkway? Canoe the nearby James River? Go hiking in Shenandoah National Park, or catch the views from the park's Skyline Drive on the spine of the Blue Ridge? Maybe visit nearby Ash Lawn–Highland, President James Monroe's home?

Or should you head for one of the dozens of local wineries (www.monticellowinetrail.com)? At some wineries, including **Mountfair** (4875 Fox Mountain Rd., Mountfair, 434-823-7605, www.mountfair.com), tastings are free. At others, such as **Cardinal Point** (9423 Batesville Rd., Afton, 540-456-8400, www.cardinalpointwinery.com), if you purchase wine by the bottle, your tasting fee (often as little as $4 per person) is discounted or waived. Three top vineyards—**Keswick Vineyards** (1575 Keswick Winery Dr., Keswick, 888-244-3341 or 434-244-3341, www.keswickvineyards.com), **Jefferson Vineyards** (1353 Thomas Jefferson Pkwy., Charlottesville, 800-272-3042 or 434-977-3042, www.jeffersonvineyards.com), and **Kluge Estate & Vineyards** (100 Grand Cru Dr., Charlottesville, 434-977-3895, www.klugeestate.com)—have joined together to offer a seasonal wine passport. It costs $10 per person and provides complimentary tastings at each vineyard as well as special discounts (savings of $10); it is available for purchase at any of the participating vineyards.

HOW TO GET IN TOUCH

Charlottesville Albemarle Convention & Visitors Bureau, 610 E. Main St., Charlottesville, VA 22902, 434-293-6789, www.pursuecharlottesville.com.

Skyline Drive and Shenandoah National Park, 540-999-3500, www.nps.gov/shen, $10–$15 per car.

celebrate american folk arts

NATIONWIDE

Well a simple kinda life never did me no harm
A raisin' me a family and workin' on a farm
My days are all filled with an easy country charm
Thank God I'm a country boy

—SONGWRITER JOHN DENVER, "THANK GOD I'M A COUNTRY BOY" (1974)

7 In this age of hip-hop, conceptual art, and global economics, it's fun—and maybe even essential—to nourish the music, storytelling, and art that seem thoroughly American in nature. Here are a few unique festivals where you can stomp your feet, play your fiddle, spin a few yarns, and enjoy the works of down-home, self-taught artists. In the process, you will help keep folk traditions from getting lost—and vacation in places where a dollar still buys more than a pack of gum.

Kentuck Festival, Alabama. If you've got an affection for the soulful works of self-taught artists like the late Jimmie Lee Sudduth and Howard Finster, head to Northport, Alabama, for this annual arts festival held the third week of each October. Along with paintings and other works by contemporary and traditional folk artists, you'll find crafts demonstrations, folk and gospel music, and of course, Southern food. A two-day pass costs $15; daily tickets are $10.

The festival is staged by the **Kentuck Museum** (503 Main Ave.), which showcases American craft artists. Stop in to see the Gallery Shop, artists-in-residence studios, and a new exhibition space.

For home-cooked meals, don't miss **City Cafe** (408 Main Ave., 205-758-9171). Lodging here is mostly chains, all located in nearby Tuscaloosa. Tip: Beware of football weekends, when lodgings fill up fast and prices can skyrocket.

Kentuck Festival, Kentucky Museum, 503 Main Ave., Northport, 205-758-1257, www.kentuck.org/festival; **Tuscaloosa Convention & Visitors Bureau** (including Northport), 800-538-8696, www.tcvb.org.

National Hollerin' Contest, North Carolina. Antique farm equipment, cars, and Carolina beach music are all part of the scene at the 40-plus-year-old National Hollerin' Contest held in Spivey's Corner, North Carolina. But the big attraction at this one-day event, held on the third Saturday of each June, is the hollerin' contests, held in several categories: whistlin', conch shell blowin', junior hollerin', teen hollerin', lady's callin', and finishing with the grand National Hollerin' Contest. Use 'em to call the kids, call your spouse, or call the critters—and keep this traditional 17th-century form of pre-cell communication alive. Admission is $5; to enter the contest, it'll cost you $10.

The town itself is not much more than a crossroads (pop. 450) a little more than an hour northeast of Fayetteville and south of Raleigh. The closest lodgings are in Dunn, where you'll find a couple chain hotels, as well as the **Barrington House B&B** (800-719-1674, www.barringtonhousenc.com, rooms from $80) and the **Simply Divine B&B** (910-892 2296, www.simplydivinebedandbreakfast.com, rooms from $99).

National Hollerin' Contest, www.hollerincontest.com; **Dunn Area Tourism Authority,** 910-892-3282, www.dunntourism.org.

National Storytelling Festival, Tennessee. Whether they're the family tales from your granny or the ghost stories from Scout camping trips, everybody loves a good yarn delivered with drama and flair. "It's something basic—in our bones," says Jimmy Neil Smith, founder of the International Storytelling Center in Jonesborough, Tennessee. Spoken stories can have even greater power than film because they allow you to fill in images from your own experience and imagination, he says.

That's the idea behind the National Storytelling Festival, staged by the center and held over a weekend early each October. From its early days in the 1970s when 100 people pulled up chairs around a wagon, the festival has grown to a tradition drawing 10,000 people to events over three days under five circus-like tents, with dozens of performances—from family friendly to bawdy. Tickets for the full festival start at $160 per adult; one-day tickets are also available starting at $50 for Sunday only.

A MOVEABLE CELEBRATION

Since the 1930s, the **National Folk Festival** (www.nationalfolkfestival.com)—organized by the National Council for Traditional Arts (www.ncta.net)—has wandered the nation, showcasing the nation's diverse cultural heritage via music, workshops, dance, and storytelling. The free three-day outdoor festival spends three years in each city before it moves on—often generating ongoing celebrations in its wake, including the **American Folk Festival** (207-992-2630, www.americanfolkfestival.com), held late each August in Bangor, Maine; and the **Richmond Folk Festival** (804-788-6466, www.richmondfolkfestival.org), held in Richmond, Virginia, in October. Beginning in 2011, the National Folk Festival will start a three-year run in Nashville, Tennessee (www.nashvillenff.org). Expect plenty of barbecue, country music, and multiethnic performances.

If October doesn't fit your schedule, time your trip for special events and summer weekly performances by storytellers-in-residence, starting at $10 per ticket.

Once the stomping grounds of Daniel Boone, Davy Crockett, and Andrew Johnson, Jonesborough is Tennessee's oldest town. As you would expect, there is plenty of lodging available in historic inns and bed-and-breakfasts. Among those establishments recommended are the 1793 **Hawley House B&B** (800-753-8869, www.hawleyhouse.com, rooms from $105) and the **AmericInn Lodge** (423-753-3100, www.americinn.com, rooms from $85), dating from the ripe old year of 2006.

National Storytelling Festival, 800-952-8392, www.storytellingcenter.net/festival; **Town of Jonesborough,** 866-401-4223, www.historicjonesborough.com.

party at mardi gras, dance at dawn in louisiana's cajun country

LAFAYETTE, LOUISIANA

Throw me something, Mister!

—MARDI GRAS REVELERS' CRY

8 What's the winter without the pre-Lenten Mardi Gras fetes that still thrive in Louisiana? Best known is the bacchanalia of New Orleans that culminates in the Fat Tuesday Carnival, that last wild fling before the repentance of Ash Wednesday. But just a couple of hours away, the Cajun Country of Acadiana celebrates in a family friendly way. Communities such as **Church Point** (www.churchpointmardigras.com), **Eunice** (www.eunice-la.com), and **Iota** (www.iotamardigras.com) maintain the medieval European tradition of Courir de Mardi Gras, when bands of horse riders romp through the countryside dressed in costumes, "begging" for the fixings to make gumbo. At the end of the day, they return to feast and dance.

Cajun Country's big city of **Lafayette** (pop. 115,000) combines spectacle with tradition in a free five-day festival of carnival rides, live music, fireworks, and, of course, parades—including a parade for dogs, a night parade, and a children's parade. Cries of "Throw me something, Mister!" are most likely to land you plastic beads and doubloons if you've got a cute kid or are hoisting a handmade sign indicating you're out-of-towners (such as "Family from Detroit"); unlike in New Orleans, revelers baring breasts and other body parts get arrested. Because Easter is a floating holiday, the dates for Mardi Gras and Lent vary but generally fall in February.

Whether you are in Cajun Country for Mardi Gras or visiting at another time of year, you'll find plenty of opportunities to experience the Cajun and Creole culture. Revel in the region's cuisine by ordering up a dish of étouffée, gumbo, bisque, or a home-cooked plate lunch—likely with a stew, fricassee, or smothered liver. In Lafayette, check

MORE TO DO IN CAJUN COUNTRY

- Visit the Jean Lafitte National Historical Park and Preserve Acadian Cultural Center (www.nps.gov/jela) in Lafayette.
- Take a swamp tour (www.lafayettetravel.com/attractions.aspx).
- Test your taste buds on the Tobasco factory tour on Avery Island (www.tobasco.com/tobasco_history/visit_avery_island.cfm).

out **Pat's Downtown** (107 E. Main St., 337-289-5270) or **Creole Lunch House** (713 12th St., 337-232-9929). Grab a po'boy from **Olde Tyme Grocery** (218 W. St. Mary Blvd., 337-235-8165) or boudin sausage from **Johnson's Boucaniere** (1111 St. John St., 337-269-8878). Don't miss a meal of crawfish, served during the crawfish fishing season that runs December through spring. The **Breaux Bridge Crawfish Festival** (337-332-6655, www.bbcrawfest.com) is usually early May; tickets $5–$10, depending on the day.

And then there's the music. Grab a fiddle and triangle, mix bluegrass with French and touches of German, Spanish, Scottish, Irish, Afro-Caribbean, and American Indian—an American mix if ever there was—and you're starting to hear the tunes. Throw in washboard, spoons, and a hefty touch of abandon, and you've got Zydeco in all its late night, foot-stomping glory. You'll find live music at restaurants and clubs at lunch and most nights—but always on weekends. Traditional venues for dinner and dancing include **Mulate's, The Original Cajun Restaurant** (325 W. Mills Ave., Breaux Bridge, 337-332-4648), **Prejean's Restaurant** (3480 I-49, N. Lafayette, 337-896-3247), and **Randol's Restaurant & Cajun Dancehall** (2320 Kaliste Saloom Rd., Lafayette, 337-981-7080). If you're out for music sans food, don't miss Lafayette's **Blue Moon Saloon** (215 E. Convent St., 337-234-2422, www.bluemoonpresents.com), on the back porch of the Blue Moon Guesthouse, where artists, politicians, and travelers kick up their heels and hoist a few, even when the weather turns chilly.

Whatever you do, drag yourself out of bed early on Saturday for Zydeco Breakfast at **Café des Amis** (140 E. Bridge St., Breaux Bridge, 337-332-5273). Or heck, just stay up all night. Breakfast and tunes start at 8:30, arrive by 7:30 to snag space.

Lafayette is a college town where lodging chains abound. For something unique, try the **Blue Moon Saloon & Guesthouse** (215 E. Convent St., 877-766-2583, www.bluemoonhostel.com) has both private rooms and hostel rooms available (beds in hostel rooms from $18). The aforementioned Blue Moon Saloon is out back, so if you're not up for music, bring your ear plugs. Or stay out of town in Breaux Bridge in an 1800s bayou cabin starting at $75 per night at **Bayou Cabins** (100 W. Mills Ave., 337-332-6158, www.bayoucabins.com).

HOW TO GET IN TOUCH

Lafayette Convention & Visitors Bureau, 800-346-1958, www.lafayettetravel.com.
Southwest Mardi Gras Association, www.gomardigras.com.

experience the wild and woolly

BLACK HILLS, SOUTH DAKOTA

Leave me alone and let me go to hell by my own route.

—FRONTIERSWOMAN CALAMITY JANE (1903)

9 The Black Hills region of South Dakota is both wild and woolly. Wild, as in home to Custer State Park, the nation's second largest state park, with 71,000 acres of open range, a twisting highway through miles of granite spires, and a 7,242-foot-high peak. Woolly, as in bison—1,300, give or take—and mammoths.

Add in Mount Rushmore, the Crazy Horse Monument, and the historic town of Deadwood, and you have to wonder if there's a more truly American place on the planet.

"It's different from the Rocky Mountains. They're kind of forbidding; you can't imagine climbing one. This is more intimate," says Nyla Griffith, a fourth-generation South Dakotan and former Deadwood city commissioner. "The Black Hills area is homey."

And so it is—if you stay out of the casinos and the badlands.

But let's start with the mammoths. The town of Hot Springs is the 21st-century home of the animated movie *Ice Age*'s Manny, the **Mammoth Site** (1800 U.S. 18 Bypass, 605-745-6017, www.mammothsite.com, $8). Actually, the 55 beasts here aren't woolly mammoths but rather Columbian mammoths, victims of a massive sinkhole that formed some 26,000 years ago. Scientists believe the sinkhole resembled a mud wallow—a favorite mammoth hangout. But once the mammoths waded into this particular pit, they were stuck—and preserved for visitors who come to tour the still working dig and exhibits.

Next stop: **Mount Rushmore** (Hwy. 244, near Keystone, 605-574-3171, www.nps.gov/moru), where 60-foot-high presidential faces were carved into the granite cliff beginning in the 1920s to draw tourists to the region. The place sounds hokey—until you see it and join a ranger-led tour explaining the phenomenal effort by sculptor Gutzon Borglum and those who worked with him to craft the monument during 14 years. Seventy years later, some three million visitors come each year to gaze into the faces of Washington, Lincoln, Jefferson, and Theodore Roosevelt. Even the cynical may feel a burst of patriotic swell.

If Mount Rushmore is a testament to American boldness, the **Crazy Horse Memorial** (12151 Avenue of the Chiefs, Crazy Horse, 605-673-4681, www.crazyhorsememorial.org, $27 per car) is witness to the nation's unflagging spirit of determination. In 1949—a few years after Rushmore's completion—the Lakota Indians of the Black Hills invited sculptor Korczak Ziolkowski to honor Native Americans, choosing as representative the great Indian chief hero Crazy Horse. Progress was and still is slow; Ziolkowski died in 1982, but his family carries on the effort. The monument will be 563 feet tall and 641 feet long once completed—still years away.

For a foray into the American past, head over to **Wall Drug** (510 Main St., Wall, 605-279-2175, www.walldrug.com), just off I-90 near Badlands National Park's Pinnacles Entrance. In the early Depression years, the drugstore put up billboards promising Free Ice Water to travelers. The place became a magnet, and over the years it's grown from a small shop to a department store of Western-abilia, with Stetsons, boots, mounted wildlife, a free kids play area, and homemade donuts worth every calorie.

Devotees of the HBO television series won't want to miss the town of **Deadwood** (800-999-1876, www.deadwood.org). Haven't seen the show? Go anyway. Despite the gambling halls—or maybe because of them—the cozy town feels strangely authentic. After all, Wild Bill Hickok—shot in a card game in 1876—is buried here in the Mount Moriah Cemetery, right next to Calamity Jane. Those days seem especially fresh each summer during Wild Bill Days in June, when free concerts spill into the streets and the cowboys compete in fast draw competitions, and during the Days of '76 rodeo each July.

The Black Hills' impressive man-made attractions are window dressing, however; the real star in this rugged part of the world is the land. **Wind Cave National Park** (26611 U.S. 385, Hot Springs, 605-745-4600, www.nps.gov/wica) encompasses more than 28,000 acres, home to bison,

CAMP IN A CABIN

National and state park cabins and lodges often book up quickly—and can be expensive. If you're looking for a less outdoorsy alternative to tent camping, check out the cabins offered at the many private campgrounds run by Kampgrounds of America, located in wilderness areas across the United States—and often just outside national parks.

But it's still camping. You'll need to bring sleeping bags or linens, towels, and toiletries. Cabin rates vary by location and demand. At the KOA grounds near Badlands National Park, for instance, a one-room, air-conditioned cabin without bath costs about $53 per night for two people in June; shared baths are located on the grounds. At the KOA grounds near Deadwood, a Kamping Kottage with bath and half kitchen costs about $125 per night for six people. Be sure to bring your own towels and linens. *Kampgrounds of America, 406-248-7444, www.koa.com.*

elk, pronghorn, and an intricate cave system. The park is free but a fee is charged for cave tours. The vast acreage of **Custer State Park** (13329 U.S. 16A, Custer, 605-255-4515, www.sdgfp.info/parks/regions/custer, $15 per car) stretches from bison and elk ranges to fish-rich lakes. You can catch a Jeep safari, pan for "gold," join a ranger walk, ride a horse, go fly-fishing. Or just rest your head in a park lodge, cabin, or campsite; cabins with electricity start at $45, campsites start at $16. Plan your visit for fall to catch the annual bison roundup and auction (yes, some bison sold at auction do end up in the freezer). But perhaps the most compelling landscape is that of **Badlands National Park** (Interior, 605-433-5361, www.nps.gov/badl, $15 per car), where a jagged wall of raw rock, banded with layers of color, separates miles and miles of north from south. As with all great landscapes, pictures—and words—don't come close.

HOW TO GET IN TOUCH

Black Hills Badlands & Lake Association, 605-355-3600, www.blackhillsbadlands.com.
South Dakota Tourism, 800-732-5682, www.travelsd.com.

follow the mission trail

CALIFORNIA

Always go forward, never turn back.

—FATHER JUNIPERO SERRA (1713–1784), FOUNDER OF THE CALIFORNIA MISSIONS

10 Father Junipero Serra was a man with a mission.

During the 1700s, the Spanish friar was assigned the daunting task of establishing Spain's foothold in the California frontier by creating a chain of missions, one day's horseback ride apart, up the Pacific coast.

For native Californians today, missions are something encountered in fourth grade, when all students, it seems, are assigned to write a report on them, draw one of them, and fashion a statue of Father Serra out of clay. After that, many think nothing more of them, even though the settlements started the state's major cities like San Diego, San Jose, and San Francisco.

But for a traveler, visiting missions offers an excuse for a road trip, a chance to explore history, and a journey to what were—and for many still are—spiritual outposts.

For Lynn Korleski Richardson, it was a bit of all three that inspired her pilgrimage. Several years ago, she and her husband packed up an RV and their dog to go on a quest to visit all 21 missions, from San Diego de Alcala in the south to San Francisco Solano in Sonoma in the north.

"It was a really great way to see California," she says.

It's hard to generalize about the missions. Three are state parks—La Purisima, San Francisco de Solano, and Santa Cruz—and while some are restored to their former glory—Carmel and Santa Inés, for example—others are ruins. Most have a statue of Father Serra, and there's usually a millstone sitting around too. Richardson's biggest surprise was the San Fernando Mission near Los Angeles, site of Bob Hope's grave. When his wife asked where he wanted to be buried, Richardson says, he answered: "Surprise me."

Richardson's mission mission took more than two weeks, but if you have time to just visit one, head to **Old Mission Santa Barbara** (2201 Laguna St., 805-682-4713, www.santabarbaramission.org), in the city of the same name. It's called the "queen of the missions" and one look explains why. Battered by earthquakes and fire, the twin-towered building has been reconstructed and

CALIFORNIA MISSIONS

- **1769:** Mission San Diego de Alcala, San Diego
- **1770:** Mission San Carlos Borroméo de Carmelo, Carmel
- **1771:** Mission San Antonio de Padua, Fort Hunter-Liggett
- **1771:** Mission San Gabriel Arcángel, San Gabriel
- **1772:** Mission San Luis Obispo, San Luis Obispo
- **1776:** Mission San Francisco de Asís, San Francisco
- **1776:** Mission San Juan Capistrano, San Juan Capistrano
- **1777:** Mission Santa Clara de Asís, Santa Clara
- **1782:** Mission San Buenaventura, Ventura
- **1786:** Mission Santa Barbara, Santa Barbara
- **1787:** Mission La Purisíma Concepción, Lompoco
- **1791:** Mission Santa Cruz, Santa Cruz
- **1791:** Mission Nuestra Señora de la Soledad, Soledad
- **1797:** Mission San José, Fremont
- **1797:** Mission San Juan Bautista, San Juan Bautista
- **1797:** Mission San Miguel de Arcángel, San Miguel
- **1797:** Mission San Fernando Rey de España, Mission Hills
- **1798:** Mission San Luis Rey de Francia, San Luis Rey
- **1804:** Mission Santa Inés, Solvang
- **1817:** Mission San Rafael Arcángel, San Rafael
- **1823:** Mission San Francisco Solano, Sonoma

restored several times since its founding in 1786. The mission is maintained by the Franciscan Order, and its water system is still used by the city of Santa Barbara. Its facade mixes Spanish style with Roman design—legend says it was inspired by a picture in a book on classical architecture.

Visitors should wander the rose-filled garden and cemetery, where American Indians, who built the original structure, are buried. For many Indians, the mission movement is not celebrated, as thousands died from disease and poor treatment. The cemetery also holds the grave of Juana María, featured in the award-winning children's book *Island of the Blue Dolphins*. The museum has period artifacts from swords to chess pieces and Mexican art.

The Spaniards meant the missions to be outposts of civilization, and that holds true in Santa Barbara. It would be a shame to come here without visiting a few area wineries, which were featured in the film *Sideways*. The **Fess Parker Winery** (6200 Foxen Canyon Rd., Los Olivos, 805-688-1545, www.fessparker.com) offers tastings from 10 a.m. to 5 p.m. daily. Come dinner, try **Brophy Bros** (119 Harbor Way, Santa Barbara, 805-966-4418), a seafood dive with stirring sunset views, clam chowder ($4.25), and beer-boiled shrimp ($8.95).

[$PLURGE: For a splurge, stay at the **Four Seasons Resort, The Biltmore** (1260 Channel Dr., 805-969-2261, www.fourseasons.com/santabarbara), which runs about

$425, and sip champagne overlooking the ocean at the Tydes restaurant.] A budget option is the original **Motel 6** (443 Corona Del Mar, 805-564-1392, www.motel6.com). Rooms once ran $6, but now fetch $80 and up.

Two other missions worth creating a trip around are the following:

- **La Purisima Mission, Lompoc.** Now a California park, about 60 miles from Santa Barbara, this site offers a chance to see what mission life was like 200-plus years ago. The park offers living history programs with costumed interpreters throughout the year, so you can watch weaving, potmaking, candlemaking, blacksmithing, and leatherwork—all tasks the original settlers performed.

  The building fell into ruins but was resurrected, first by the Civilian Conservation Corps in 1934 and then as a state park. In addition, there's a 5-acre garden with native and domestic plants typical for the time period, and a corral with burros, horses, longhorn cattle, and goats.

  Chain lodging can be found in the area, while **Angela's Restaurant** (115 S. J St., 805-737-0184) has tasty Mexican dishes—20 combo plates at $8.49 apiece. *La Purisima Mission State Historic Park, 2295 Purisima Rd., Lompoc, 805-733-3713, www.lapurisimamission.org, $6 per car.*

- **San Antonio de Padua, Fort Hunter-Liggett.** One of the most remote missions, this site is on a military post, Fort Hunter-Liggett, about 100 miles north of Lompoc. The third mission built—they weren't constructed in a neat geographic order south to north—it's said that San Antonio's the only one Father Serra might recognize today. Located in a valley filled with oak trees, it's owned by the Diocese of Monterey and is home to a tiny working parish.

  The museum ($5 donation) displays settlement artifacts, including a grape-stomping vat, wine cellar, and scale models. And a music room offers an audio tour with period music. Since it's located on a military base, drivers and all passengers older than 18 must show identification and proof of insurance. Fill your tank before coming, as nonmilitary visitors can purchase only five gallons of gas on the post.

  Despite its location on Army property, civilians can stay in the historic **Hacienda Guest Lodge** (831-386-2511, www.liggett.army.mil/sites/newcomers/lodging/lodging.asp), which was designed by famed architect Julia Morgan and constructed as a hunting lodge for William Randolph Hearst. Rooms from $45. *San Antonio de Padua, P.O. Box 803, End of Mission Rd., Jolon, 831-385-4478, www.missionsanantonio.net.*

HOW TO GET IN TOUCH

For more information about the California Missions, visit www.thecaliforniamissions.com.

take in a minor league game

DURHAM, NORTH CAROLINA

I like my players to be married and in debt. That's the way you motivate them.

—ERNIE BANKS, FORMER MINOR LEAGUE COACH

11 A handful of stars hit the headlines as soon as they hit the diamond. But most baseball players are more like Kevin Costner's *Bull Durham* character than New York superstar Alex Rodriguez. (And even A-Rod did a short stint in the minors with the Seattle Mariners' affiliate before moving to The Show.)

Minor leaguers are the true Boys of Summer, underdogs playing for dreams and love of the all-American pastime. (They also play for money. In his first contract season, a minor leaguer could earn a maximum of $1,100 per month in 2010, with $25 per day for meals while on the road.) On opening day, nearly 7,000 players may be listed on minor league rosters; historically, about 10 percent of minor leaguers will play at least one major league game.

A quick minor league primer: Minor League Baseball is composed of 251 clubs in the United States, Canada, Mexico, the Dominican Republic, and Venezuela. The league's highest level is Triple-A, where you're most likely to see the DiMaggios of the future. Down the rankings are Double-A, Class A Advanced, Class A, Class A Short Season, and Rookie. In total, the clubs will play more than 10,000 games each season.

But minor league ball isn't all about stats and standings—which is why more than 41 million fans catch a game each year. The parks are friendly and the ambience local—even if the rivalry is still intense. After all, some of these teams have been playing each other for a century; Minor League Baseball will celebrate its 110th season in 2011.

Comparatively speaking, a day at a minor league park is a bargain. About a hundred of the minor league teams offer free entry; the rest charge on average $7 per adult. For about $54, a family of four can take in a game—and that includes parking, four hot dogs, two sodas, two beers, and a program. With teams scattered across the continent, chances are good you can drive a short way and catch a game for an afternoon. Check on the Internet at http://web.minorleaguebaseball.com for information and schedules.

But why not go the whole *Bull Durham* route? The minor league action in Durham, North Carolina, will thrill you, while the city will charm you. The **Triple-A Durham Bulls** (919-687-6500, www.durhambulls.com) no longer play in the stadium where the 1988 film was set—they moved to the Durham Bulls Athletic Park in 1995, at 409 Blackwell Street—but you will still feel the same level of excitement. Tickets start at $7; the price varies with view and date of play.

Durham retains its tobacco town origins. Former brick warehouses have been transformed into lofts, boutiques, and craft breweries. Duke University, the school that tobacco built, boasts the stunning stone **Duke Chapel** (1 Chapel Dr., 919-681-9488, www.chapel.duke.edu), which offers periodic carillon and organ concerts, and the **Sarah P. Duke Gardens** (420 Anderson St., 919-684-3698, www.hr.duke.edu/dukegardens), where you can stroll among the flowers and watch students sun on the lawn. The university's **Nasher Museum of Art** (2001 Campus Dr., 919-684-5135, http://nasher.duke.edu/) houses special exhibitions as well as a permanent collection of Renaissance, classical, and African art.

MINOR LEAGUE MILESTONES

- **1901:** Minor League Baseball first formed as the National Association of Professional Baseball Leagues; 14 leagues and 96 clubs played the first season in 1902.
- **1921:** Agreement signed to allow major league teams to own minor league teams.
- **1933:** Joe DiMaggio plays his first pro season for San Francisco (Pacific Coast League).
- **1946:** Jackie Robinson debuts with the Montreal Royals (International League).
- **1954:** Joe Bauman becomes the greatest home-run hitter in pro-baseball history, hitting 72 for Roswell (NM) in the Longhorn League, a record that stood until Barry Bonds hit 73 for San Francisco in 2001.
- **1982:** The largest crowd in minor league history—65,666—watches an American Association game (and a giant fireworks show) at Denver's Mile High Stadium on July 4.
- **1999:** The NAPBL changes its name to Minor League Baseball.

Durham bubbles with a host of gourmet eateries, but for the real *Bull Durham* experience, don't miss **Bullock's Bar-B-Cue** (3330 Quebec Dr., 919-383-3211), a Carolina classic. Grab takeout, rent a copy of the movie at the video store, and spend your postgame hours steeped in Durham style.

Chain lodgings abound; for more ambience, check out bed-and-breakfasts like **Carol's Garden Inn** (2412 S. Alston Ave., 877-922-6777, www.carolsgardeninn.com), where rooms start at $85. **Eno River State Park** (919-383-1686, www.ncparks.gov) offers basic campsites a few miles from Durham.

HOW TO GET IN TOUCH

Durham Convention & Visitors Bureau, 101 E. Morgan St., Durham, NC 27701, www.durham-nc.com, 800-446-8604.

sleep in an american icon

CALIFORNIA & TENNESSEE

Don't throw the past away
You might need it some rainy day
Dreams can come true again
When everything old is new again

—SONGWRITER CAROLE BAYER SAGER, "EVERYTHING OLD IS NEW AGAIN" (1974)

12 In these fast-moving times, reinvention has become a way of life. It can also be a vacation when you book into a lighthouse, ship, or train turned hotel. You'll be sleeping in history—with modern conveniences.

***Chattanooga Choo-Choo,* Chattanooga, Tennessee.** Now a hundred years old, the *Chattanooga Choo-Choo*—inspiration for the Glenn Miller orchestra's 1940s classic, "Pardon Me Boys, Is That the Chattanooga Choo Choo?"—recently spent four million dollars sprucing up its guest rooms, gardens, and the Grand Dome Lobby.

Wait, isn't this a train? Well, yes and no. The steam locomotives that once ran through the city are now museum pieces. In 1973, the station terminal was transformed into a hotel that today encompasses restaurants, gardens, pools, and a model railroad. The hotel's 323 guest rooms are located in restored Victorian train cars and adjacent terminal buildings.

Rooms in the buildings start at $100 with advance purchase online, while sleeping in a train car starts around $155; all include wireless Internet access. No time for an overnight stay? Stop in for a taste of history at the Sweet Stop ice-cream shop, the Silver Diner eatery, or the Station House, where servers double as performers and sing for *your* supper.

Chattanooga Choo-Choo, 1400 Market St., 423-266-5000, www.choochoo.com; **Chattanooga Area Convention & Visitors Bureau,** 2 Broad St., Chattanooga, TN 37402, 800-322-3344, www.chattanoogafun.com.

***Delta King,* Sacramento, California.** Live your *Maverick* fantasies by spending a night aboard the *Delta King*. Born in 1927 as a river boat paddling the Sacramento River, the *Delta King* offered up booze, gambling, and jazz during the ten-hour trip from Sacramento to San Francisco—quite an excursion during Prohibition. The Great Depression brought the fun to a halt, and during World War II the *King* was drafted into service as a barracks, troop-transport, and hospital ship.

Afterward, the *King* became something of a derelict. In the mid-1980s the ship was stunningly restored with plenty of wood paneling and traditional decor. Since the late 1980s, the 285-foot paddle wheeler has made its home on the Sacramento River, moored at historic Old Sacramento as a hotel and restaurant. You can often catch a rate of about $100 per night including breakfast unless there's a special event on board. Alternative: Go for lunch, when a simple meal costs less than $10.

When you get off the boat, be sure to wander **Old Sacramento** (916-558-3912, www.oldsacramento.com), a 28-acre gold-mining historic district with raised wooden sidewalks and Old West flavor.

Delta King, 1000 Front St., 916-444-5464, www.deltaking.com; **Sacramento Convention & Visitors Bureau,** 1608 I St., Sacramento, CA 95814, 800-292-2334 or 916-264-7777, www.sacramentocvb.org.

***Delta Queen,* Chattanooga, Tennessee.** The *Delta King*'s sister ship, the *Delta Queen* enjoyed a more vaunted fate—at least for a while. Built and launched into service at the same time as the *King*, in 1947 the *Delta Queen* was sold, crated, and towed through the Panama Canal to New Orleans before she steamed under her own power to Pittsburgh for renovations.

From 1948 until 2008, the ship sailed the Mississippi as a tourist cruiser. In June 2009, the *Delta Queen* welcomed her first overnight guest as a hotel moored in Chattanooga. Rates start around $100 per night for a double, though a bunk room can cost about $20 less. Dinner and dancing are offered in the supper club, where a three-course fixed-price dinner costs $35.

Delta Queen, 100 River St., 423-468-4500, www.deltaqueenhotel.com; **Chattanooga Area Convention & Visitors Bureau,** 2 Broad St., Chattanooga, TN 37402, 800-322-3344, www.chattanoogafun.com.

***Queen Mary,* Long Beach, California.** When she was launched in the 1930s, the *Queen Mary* was the belle of the seas, carrying nearly 2,000 passengers at 28.5 knots as she steamed across the Atlantic Ocean. Like most ships of her day, she was pressed into military service during World War II. Once those days were behind her, the *Queen Mary* sailed once again in style—even hosting the Queen Mother. Her last voyage, in 1967, brought her to Long Beach, California, where she became a hotel.

An overnight stay starts around $100 for a double room. Alternatively, you can take a ship's tour; a two-hour self-guided tour costs about $25 and includes a walk-through show on ghostly onboard happenings.

Queen Mary, 1126 Queen's Hwy., 877-342-0738, www.queenmary.com; **Long Beach Area Convention & Visitors Bureau,** 1 World Trade Center, 800-452-7829, www.visitlongbeach.com.

Lighthouse hostels, northern California coast. Renting a lighthouse or staying in a lighthouse turned bed-and-breakfast sounds oh so romantic. It can also be oh so expensive. The northern California coast offers a cozy alternative: Lighthouse turned hostel. Hostelling International (HI) offers you two choices. And no, you don't have to be 20 to stay in one; and no, you don't necessarily have to sleep in a bunk.

At **Pigeon Point Lighthouse Hostel** (650-879-0633), 50 miles south of San Francisco, lodging isn't inside the 1872 lighthouse itself but in its shadow, in the former lighthouse keepers' quarters. Dorm rooms have six beds and cost $23–$25 per adult. Private rooms are available and cost $59–$68 for a single, $64–$76 for a double. The hostel makes a good base for exploring nearby redwood forests, as well as the breeding grounds for northern elephant seals at **Año Nuevo State Park** (650-879-20257, www.parks.ca.gov, $7).

About 25 miles south of San Francisco stands **Point Montara Lighthouse Hostel** (650-728-7177). Accommodations are in former Coast Guard quarters. Dorm rooms cost $23–$25 per person. Private rooms for one, two, or three people cost $63–$105. Set above a rugged coast, Point Montara offers convenient access to the picturesque town of Half Moon Bay.

Hostelling International Northern California Hostels, 415-863-1444, www.norcalhostels.org.

STAY IN A HOSTEL

Hostels aren't just for college-age kids anymore. Most—including more than a hundred in the United States—accept travelers of all ages, including families. "A lot of people who were familiar with hosteling in the 1960s and '70s came back to it as families or later in life," says Mark Vidalin, marketing director for Hostelling International (HI) USA.

Still, the majority of hostel guests fall between the ages of 18 and 30, Vidalin says. At HI hostels, guests under 18 are allowed, but they must be with a parent or guardian. Nonmembers may stay at most HI hostels, but they pay slightly more per night, and members may get priority during busy periods. An HI adult membership costs $28. HI hostels are listed at www.hiusa.org.

Not all hostels are members of HI. You can find listings and reviews and reserve non-HI hostels at www.bootsnall.com and www.hostels.com.

Baby boomers who haven't stayed in a hostel since college are in for a few surprises:

- Shared facilities have been expanded, often including a kitchen and laundry. Some hostels now offer private rooms as well as dorm accommodations.
- Nearly all have Internet access, and nearly all accept reservations.
- Sleeping bags typically aren't allowed; many if not most hostels now include sheets, soap, and towels with your stay.

But one thing hasn't changed: Waterproof shower shoes and a padlock for security are still a good idea.

visit the nation's capital

WASHINGTON, D.C.

I never forget that I live in a house owned by all the
American people and that I have been given their trust.

—PRESIDENT FRANKLIN DELANO ROOSEVELT (1938)

13 Taking in the sights of Washington, D.C., is always a worthy pursuit. Most of the renowned Smithsonian Institution museums—and many other monuments—are located on or near the National Mall, the 1.9-mile swathe of green running from the Capitol steps to the Lincoln Memorial. All sights are free, unless noted.

Start your visit with a tour of the **U.S. Capitol** (1st St. NE/SE, www.visitthecapitol.gov, closed Sun.), at the head of the National Mall. In late 2009 a new underground, three-level 621-million-dollar visitor center opened, complete with a restaurant and restrooms. Even if you aren't taking a tour of the Capitol, the center is worth a visit for its statues of 24 patriots formerly in the Capitol, an orientation film, and historic artifacts, including the pine platform on which President Lincoln's body lay in state. To tour the legislature, book in advance through the visitor center or through your congressperson; the visitor center has a limited number of same-day tickets. Weekday mornings are usually the least crowded times. Large daypacks and luggage are not allowed.

The west side of the Capitol faces the National Mall. A treasure trove of museums lines the stretch of Mall between 3rd and 14th Streets; all lie within walking distance. The East and West Buildings of the **National Gallery of Art** (Constitution Ave. bet. 3rd & 7th Sts. NW, www.nga.gov) contains a comprehensive collection of Western masterpieces. The National Gallery of Art is the only museum on the Mall that is not part of the Smithsonian Institution.

The **National Museum of the American Indian** (Independence Ave. & 4th St. SW, 202-633-6700, www.nmai.si.edu) stands opposite the National Gallery of Art East Building. Historical photographs, ethnographic displays, and exhibits trace the history of America's First People through their own eyes rather than those of the white settlers. Farther down the Mall stands the **National Air and Space Museum** (Independence Ave. & 6th St. SW, 202-633-2214, www.nasm.si.edu), home to airplanes, rockets, and space rocks, including the original 1903 Wright brothers flyer and the lunar module used in the Apollo program. Tours are offered daily at 10:30 a.m. and 1 p.m. The museum has an outpost near Dulles Airport, the **Steven F. Udvar-Hazy Center** (14390 Air and Space Museum Pkwy., Chantilly, VA, 703-572-4118), for larger aircraft and objects, including the space shuttle *Enterprise*.

Back on the Mall, the **National Museum of American History** (Constitution Ave. & 14th St. NW, http://americanhistory.si.edu) is home to Dorothy's "ruby slippers" from *The Wizard of Oz,* Julia Child's kitchen, and exhibits on the First Ladies.

Less visited by families, but worth the time, are a handful of Smithsonian art museums, the majority on the Mall:

- **American Art Museum.** Home to Albert Bierstadt's "Among the Sierra Nevada" and Georgia O'Keeffe's "Manhattan." *8th & F Sts. NW, 202-633-7970.*
- **Freer and Sackler Galleries.** Asian art. *1050 Independence Ave. SW, 202-633-1000.*
- **Hirshhorn Museum and Sculpture Gallery.** Modern art including works by Alex Katz, Alexander Calder, and David Smith. *Independence Ave. & 7th St. SW, 202-633-4674.*
- **National Museum of African Art.** Textiles, masks, and musical instruments. *950 Independence Ave. SW, 202-633-4600.*
- **National Portrait Gallery.** Showcase for Gilbert Stuart's most famous portrait of George Washington, plus portraits of revered Americans like singer Lena Horne and sports hero Yogi Berra. *800 F St. NW, 202-633-8300.*

The Mall is equally known for its iconic memorials. Walking west from 14th Street toward the Lincoln Memorial, you'll first pass the obelisk of the Washington Monument, honoring our nation's first President; the tributes to the soldiers of World War II, the Vietnam War, and the Korean War; and then the Reflecting Pool. South of the Washington Monument, the stately Thomas Jefferson Memorial overlooks the Tidal Basin, while the sprawling Franklin Delano Roosevelt Memorial lies hidden behind a screen of the basin's famous cherry blossom trees.

Beyond the National Mall, there are a few other sights every visitor to D.C. should see. The most famous house in America stands at 1600 Pennsylvania Avenue, NW: the **White House,** the office and residence of the President. Peer through the wrought-iron fence on its north or south side for quintessential views. The White House is a high-security zone—but it is possible to visit it if you make the request at least 30 days in advance through your congressperson. Details are available at www.whitehouse.gov. If you're unable to schedule a tour, visit the **White House Visitor Center** (corner of 15th & E Sts., NW), which has many exhibits featuring White House artifacts.

One of the Washington area's most moving sights lies just across the Potomac River in Arlington, Virginia. **Arlington National Cemetery** (214 McNair Rd., 703-607-8000, www.arlingtoncemetery.org) is a grim testament to the fact that freedom is earned with a staggering price. Set on a wooded hillside, the cemetery is home to the Tomb of the Unknowns, honoring fallen unidentified soldiers from World War I, World War II, the Korean War, and the Vietnam War; and the grave site of John F. Kennedy, one of the two U.S. Presidents buried here. Many visitors reach the cemetery

$PLURGE

FIND OUT WHO IS WATCHING YOU

Recent years have seen a revolution in news delivery, as cable TV, blogs, and the Internet have played growing roles in informing the public of local, national, and global events. The **Newseum** (555 Pennsylvania Ave. NW, 888-639-7386, www.newseum.com, $19.95)—the museum of news, journalism, and media—explores both the past and future of the news in a series of programs, exhibits, and events. You can see Tim Russert's NBC office, learn about presidential pets, and discover how the FBI's 10 Most Wanted list got started. Between films, photographs, and an interactive newsroom where you decide how to cover the day's news, you'll need several hours.

Check out the "watchers" you don't read about—except in the novels of John Le Carré and Vince Flynn—at the **International Spy Museum** (800 F St. NW, 202-393-7798, www.spymuseum.org, $18). Find out what it takes to be a spy, see the historic tools of the trade, and learn the price of traitors. The museum is especially eerie on Fridays and Saturdays, when it's open at night. Children's programs are also offered.

by walking across Memorial Bridge, behind the Lincoln Memorial, but you can also take the Metro, the D.C.-area subway.

Another painful, but worthy, lesson comes back in Washington at the **Holocaust Memorial Museum** (100 Raoul Wallenberg Pl. SW, 202-488-0400, www.ushmm.org), where the heart-wrenching permanent exhibit offers a stark reminder of the consequences of cruelty. During summer months, reserving (free) timed tickets is advised.

When it comes time to chow down, hit one of the popular **happy hour deals,** where you'll find discounted drinks and eats from 4:30 or 5 p.m. to around 7 p.m. Monday through Friday. Offers change regularly; see http://washington.org/visiting/experience-dc/foodie-experience/happy-hours-cheap-eats for an up-to-date list.

Now, about lodging. As in other business cities, you'll often find the best hotel deals on weekends, especially during the winter. Laura Boyd, a frequent visitor, recommends the website bedandbreakfast.com for well-located lodgings at value prices. For other alternatives, check out lodging across the Potomac River in historic Alexandria, Virginia (703-746-3301, http://visitalexandriava.com), a short Metro ride away.

HOW TO GET IN TOUCH

Destination D.C., 901 7th St. NW, Washington, DC 20001, 202-789-7000, www.washington.org.
National Mall and Memorial Parks, www.nps.gov/nama.
Smithsonian Institution museums, www.si.edu.

learn the culture of the first americans

NATIONWIDE

Don't be afraid to cry. It will free your mind of sorrowful thoughts.

—HOPI PROVERB

14 It wasn't so long ago that Native American "culture" was confined to the movies and Indian reservations. But in recent years, the artwork and traditions of America's first peoples have become more appreciated—and more accessible. Pueblos once closed to outsiders now offer tours. Powwows showcasing drummers and dancers in traditional costumes draw thousands of non-Indian visitors. Major museums dedicated to the art of the First Americans have opened.

Tribes themselves have become major players on the national tourism scene, developing hotels decorated with traditional crafts and interpretive centers featuring storytellers and crafts. On some longer tours, tribal members escort visitors into Indian lands.

Attend a powwow. A parade of tribal peoples in fringed and feathered dress starts the ceremonial gathering. But this is far more than movie-style spectacle; tribal gatherings often are a combination of heritage celebration, dance contest, drum competition, social get-together, and marketplace. They are also a sacred tradition. Dancers move in the clockwise pattern of the sun, their circle representing the unity of life. Ornaments and regalia may honor an event in the wearer's life or a special religious tradition.

The Gathering of Nations (505-836-2810, www.gatheringofnations.com) in Albuquerque, New Mexico, is one of the largest and best known powwows. Each April, this three-day event draws 75,000 people to partake in dances, ceremonies, crafts, traditional foods, and the Miss Indian World Talent Presentation and Show. Tickets start at $19. Non-Indians are welcome, but you'll want to know the etiquette: Stand for the entry of the eagle staff. Don't point with your finger. Never touch any regalia or ornamentation.

Visit the Mesa Verde cliff dwellings. For more than 600 years, ancestral Puebloans—also called Anasazi—made their homes in what is now **Mesa Verde National Park** (www.nps.gov/meve, 970-529-4465). Simple shelters on mesa tops gave way to sometimes elaborate stone villages of a hundred-plus rooms carved into the sandstone cliffs below. By around 1300 these people moved away, but the 4,800 or so sites they left behind—including the 150-room Cliff Palace—can be seen by visitors to the Four Corners region, where Colorado, New Mexico, Arizona, and Utah meet.

To do the place justice, you'll want at least a couple of days. Your best bet is to visit between April and October. The park—an hour from Cortez, Colorado—is open year-round but some facilities are closed in winter, when tours are more limited. You can visit the archaeological museum and some sites on your own, but the Cliff Palace, Balcony House, and Spruce Tree House can only be visited on a ranger-led tour (additional nominal fee).

Park entry costs $10–$15, depending on the time of year. Bare campsites and base camps outfitted with a canvas tent and cots are available at Morefield Campground. Far View Lodge is

$PLURGE

TAKE A TRIBAL TOUR

Expert-led tours are rarely the least expensive way to visit any place, but seeing Native American sites through the eyes of a local tribesman may be worth the splurge.

- **Billie Swamp Safari, Florida Everglades.** Here, on the 2,200-acre Big Cypress Preserve, members of the Seminole Tribe offer tours by swamp buggy and airboat through the swamplands and hammocks. Overnight visitors get the full immersion, with campfire storytelling, an after-dark tour of the swamp, and a stay in a traditional open-air chickee, a thatched dwelling without running water or electricity.

  Entrance to the Billie Swamp Safari is free. Daytime activities, including swamp buggy and airboat tours and wildlife shows, are ticketed à la carte at prices beginning at $8. Day packages including all activities start at $43 for adults. Overnight packages cost about $100 per person.

  The tribe's nearby Ah-Tah-Thi-Ki Museum is home to more than 5,000 square feet of exhibits and artifacts. *Billie Swamp Safari, 800-949-6101, www.swampsafari.net.*
- **Goulding's Lodge, Monument Valley, Arizona.** From this lodge located 170 miles north of Flagstaff, Arizona, Navajo guides lead half- and full-day tours of Monument Valley that visit petroglyphs, hogans, stone arches, and Anasazi ruins. Tours start at around $40 per adult. An original trading post has been transformed into a museum. The restaurant serves Navajo and American dishes. Campsites are available from $25; cabins are also available. *Goulding's Lodge, 435-727-3231, www.gouldings.com.*
- **Lodgepole Gallery and Tipi Village, near Browning, Montana.** A half-day cultural history tour for four people with a historian and artist who is also a Blackfeet tribal member costs $100. The excursion includes stops at a medicine lodge, tipi ring, and buffalo jump. You can also spend the night in a tipi ($65 for two people; bring your own sleeping bag) and dine on traditional foods like elk and buffalo. Horseback riding, art workshops, and lectures are also offered. *Lodgepole Gallery and Tipi Village, www.blackfeetculturecamp.com.*

open late April to mid-October. All park lodging and dining facilities are run by **Aramark** (800-449-2288, www.visitmesaverde.com).

The Mesa Verde area is a treasure trove of Native American sites, and if you've got time you may also want to visit the ruins of the Lowry Pueblo, which exhibits two cultural traditions; Ute Mountain Tribal Park, where tribe members guide all tours; the Anasazi Heritage Center, a museum that's home to three million artifacts; the Cortez Cultural Center, an interpretive center with exhibits and gallery; and the Crow Canyon Archaeological Center, which offers one-day programs with a tour of an archaeological site. You'll find visitor information to all online at www.swcolo.org.

NATIVE AMERICAN MUSEUMS

The number of museums dedicated to Native American culture and those with significant collections have increased in recent years. The following are among the many worth visiting:

- **Heard Museum, Phoenix, Arizona.** Expansive historical exhibits plus a stunning selection of Kachina dolls. *Heard Museum, 2301 N. Central Ave., 602-252-8344, www.heard.org, $12.*
- **Museum of Anthropology, Vancouver, B.C.** Changing exhibits but a wide-ranging display of masks and objects from Canada's First Peoples. *Museum of Anthropology, 6393 NW Marine Dr., 604-822-5087, www.moa.ubc.ca, $14.*
- **National Museum of the American Indian, Washington, D.C.** Historical photographs, ethnographic displays, and exhibits trace the history of America's First People through their own eyes. *National Museum of the American Indian, Independence Ave. & 4th St. SW, 202-633-6700, www.nmai.si.edu.*

ride historic rails

NATIONWIDE

It would be difficult, indeed, to overestimate the transcendent importance of the part the railroad has played in making the Nation what it is to-day.

—AUTHOR CHARLES FREDERICK CARTER, *WHEN RAILROADS WERE NEW* (1910)

15 From the time the first rail ties were laid down in the early 1830s, railways made remote areas of the United States accessible, kick-starting settlement and tourism from coast to coast. Though interstates and air carriers have since taken over the job, a handful of historic train routes remain.

As you chug up a mountain on a narrow-gauge rail, you get that sense of what an adventure such a ride must have been more than a century ago, when so much of the country was untamed and, to most people, unknown.

"Today's diesels and the electric locomotives don't have anywhere near the drama and romance of the old steam engines," laments science writer Stuart Brown, a longtime railway enthusiast.

Neither, unfortunately, do many up-to-date lodgings. Thankfully, many historic trains are set in woodsy areas where campsites are plentiful—and wallet friendly. Leave the iPod and other modern-day gadgets at home and prepare to truly step back in time aboard these wondrous marvels of transportation.

Mount Washington Cog Railway, New Hampshire. The British may have pioneered the steam engine, but Americans built the first mountain-climbing cog railway. In 1869, when the Mount Washington Railway opened as a tourist attraction in the White Mountains, it was an engineering

AMTRAK & RAIL CANADA

Today's commuter rails and long-distance trains do not offer the glamour of rail travel gone by, but they still offer one of the great luxuries of train travel: watching the scenery go by. Promotional sales make it affordable as well.

- **Amtrak.** Though the railway's routes are more limited than in olden days, you can still roll from north to south and across the United States. *Amtrak, www.amtrak.com.*
- **Rail Canada.** The railway offers trips from coast to coast; for the ultimate trip, book a cross-country winter jaunt on a train with a glass-domed car. *Rail Canada, www.viarail.ca.*

MORE HISTORIC RAILWAY EXCURSIONS

- **Copper Canyon, Mexico.** Opened in the 1960s after nearly a century of construction, the **Copper Canyon Railway** (www.mexicoscoppercanyon.com, www.visitmexico.com)—the adventurous Chihuahua-al-Pacifico or El Chepe—links the Pacific coast with the desert interior via 390 miles of track in northwest Mexico.
- **Durango, Colorado.** Using reproductions and restored trains from the 1880s, the **Durango & Silverton Narrow Gauge Railroad** (479 Main Ave., 970-247-2733, www.durangotrain.com) offers year-round service through some of the Rockies' most beautiful landscapes.
- **Roanoke, Virginia.** The **Virginia Museum of Transportation** (303 Norfolk Ave. SW, 540-342-5670, www.vmt.org) is home to a remarkable collection of vintage locomotives, while the nearby **O. Winston Link Museum** (101 Shenandoah Ave., 540-982-5465, www.linkmuseum.org) features stunning railway images by the late photographer that will transform the way you think of trains.
- **San Francisco, California.** The Market Street Railway uses genuine early 20th-century cable cars, and streetcars carry commuters and visitors over the West Coast city's famous hills as part of the San Francisco Municipal Railroad. Single rides cost $5. Learn about both types of railcars at the **San Francisco Railway Museum** (77 Steuart St., 415-974-1948, www.streetcar.org, closed Mon.).

coup: 3 miles of track leading up the 6,288-foot-high granite face of the highest mountain in the Northeast. At a 37-degree angle, it remains the second steepest railway in the world—and the only one built entirely on a trestle.

True to the original cars, the railway's reproduction wooden cars feature open windows, so beware: Even in midsummer the temperature as you ascend the mountain can go from warm to chilly to downright arctic—bring a jacket just in case. Mount Washington features some of the planet's most extreme weather, as documented and monitored since 1932 by the Mount Washington Observatory, which maintains an interesting mountaintop **museum** (www.mountwashington.org, $3).

The three-hour round-trip ride runs May through November and includes enough time at the top to check out the views and the museum, grab lunch, and listen to the hikers who have made the trek on foot.

Beyond the railway, the beauty of the White Mountains beckons. Local outfitters can help you plan and execute kayaking, mountain biking, fishing, and horseback riding adventures. Or just bring your own gear or stick with hiking; the views are free.

So are the more than two dozen historic covered bridges strewn about the countryside. This isn't Madison County, but the romance is just as rich.

The museum at the base of the Mount Washington Cog Railway is free; a ride on the rail costs $62. For information about camping, lodging, state parks, outdoor recreation, and covered bridges, see www.visitwhitemountains.com.

Mount Washington Cog Railway, Base Rd., Bretton Woods, 800-922-8825, www.thecog.com.

White Pass & Yukon Route, Alaska. When a gold claim was registered at the Yukon's Klondike River in 1896, droves of prospectors surged to Skagway, Alaska, the closest seaport. From there, prospectors faced a daunting overland trek across the steep peaks of the Coast Mountains separating Alaska and British Columbia. The solution: The White Pass & Yukon Route railway, a 110-mile engineering marvel requiring tens of thousands of laborers and 450 tons of explosives, and completed in just 26 months.

The first 67.5 miles of the narrow-gauge rail route now operate as a tourist attraction from May to September.

The 3.5-hour round-trip White Pass excursion is popular with cruisers but costs $110. For a less expensive option, book the railway's hiker drop-off service to the trailheads for day hikes to Denver Glacier or Laughton, starting at $31.50 round-trip (reservations required). At either trailhead, you can stay overnight in a railcar turned cabin run by the Forest Service. The town has a hostel and several campgrounds.

Much of Skagway forms part of **Klondike Gold Rush National Historical Park** (907-983-2921, www.nps.gov/klgo)—which means free ranger-led walking tours of the town and maintained trails for day hikes and longer hauls along the 33-mile Chilkoot Trail, tracing the onetime path of the prospectors. The park's visitor center is open May through late September. After you've seen the exhibits about the hardships of building the railway, you'll be grateful it's all in the past.

White Pass & Yukon Route, 231 2nd Ave., Skagway, 800-343-7373, www.wpyr.com; **Skagway Visitor Center,** 907-983-2854, www.skagway.com.

revisit the cold war

WHITE SULPHUR SPRINGS, WEST VIRGINIA

We don't propose to sit here in our rocking chair with our hands folded and let the Communists set up any government in the Western Hemisphere.

—PRESIDENT LYNDON BAINES JOHNSON (1965)

16 Between spy novels and movies, the Cold War sometimes seems like a figment of pop culture. But Americans of a certain generation remember all too well the nuclear bomb drills of the 1960s. Berlin was divided by the wall. American warheads were pointed at Russian warheads and vice versa. When the Soviets placed warhead-armed missiles in Cuba just 90 miles from the Florida coast in 1962, American schools began training children in Cold War safety measures.

You can recall those treacherous days on a **bunker tour** (300 W. Main St., 800-624-6070 or 304-536-7810, www.greenbrier.com/site/bunker.aspx, $30) at the Greenbrier Resort in White Sulphur Springs, West Virginia.

The bunker was designed to shield key members of Congress. The resort—a longtime favorite of the posh and the powerful, including Presidents and industrial barons—offered easy access from Washington (a train still rolls right to its gates) but was far enough to avoid nuclear fallout in the event of an attack on the capital. And who would expect a secret government hideout on the grounds of an exclusive resort?

A 25-ton door of steel and concrete would secure the powerful 720 feet underground. Congressional leaders would sleep in dormitory bunks and subsist on freeze-dried beef, breathe filtered air, and drink from an underground water tank. The 112,544-square-foot hutch feels grim—just like the times they were built for. Reservations are required for the 90-minute tour and children under the age of 10 are not admitted.

$PLURGE

WHITE-WATER RAFTING

West Virginia is famous for its white-water rafting, especially along the New and Gauley Rivers northwest of White Sulphur Springs. The water typically is wildest in spring, and unless you're a white-water expert, you'll need to join an organized trip—usually around $100 per adult. You'll find tamer—and cheaper—alternatives at the **Greenbrier River Campground** (800-775-2203, www.greenbrierriver.com), where a river tube, shuttle ride, and life jacket costs $17.50. Tent campsites here start at $21.50; RV sites are also available. If you'd prefer to stay inside, check out the **Dawson Inn** (2625 Lawn Rd., Dawson, 877-332-3349) where rooms start at $63 a night.

MORE COLD WAR ATTRACTIONS

In recent years, a number of formerly closed Cold War government sites have opened to tours. Group sizes are limited, and most require advance reservations. Here are few worth considering:

- **Minuteman Missile National Historic Site.** Located in the heart of South Dakota's Black Hills, this site offers tours Monday through Friday in winter and Monday through Saturday in summer. Visitors with limited time can take a peek at a Minuteman II missile; those with deeper interest can sign up for a 90-minute guided tour of the living quarters, the underground launch control center, and the launch facility. Tours are free but reservations are required. *Minuteman Missile National Historic Site, 605-433-5552, www.nps.gov/mimi.*
- **Nike Hercules Missile Site.** Set in the Florida Everglades, this site was a reaction to the Cuban missile crisis that put the world on edge. For years the government denied its existence. Guided driving tours of the site are now offered on weekends during winter months only; the tours are free with park admission. You must have a car; reservations are recommended. *Nike Hercules Missile Site, 305-242-7700, www.nps.gov/ever/planyourvisit/nikemissle.htm.*
- **Nike Missile Site.** This site in San Francisco's Golden Gate Recreation Area is one of the 288 Nike missile sites built by the U.S. Army as the last defense against a Soviet nuclear attack. Guided tours are offered Wednesday through Friday in the afternoons. On the first Saturday of each month, docents share real-life experiences from Nike missile sites. *Nike Missile Site, 415-331-1453, www.nps.gov/goga/nike-missile-site.htm.*

The tour is a bit of a splurge, but thankfully the surrounding countryside is filled with parks, scenic byways, and cozy small towns, which means there's plenty to check out that's free or cheap.

Want to open the car windows and let the countryside roll by? The Greenbrier Valley is home to five designated scenic byways, including the **Farm Heritage Road** that passes fields and barns little changed in the past 200 years, and the **Lower Greenbrier River Byway,** which follows its namesake waterway through the town of Alderson, home to a restored Chesapeake & Ohio Railroad depot and a historic arched bridge. Information for both is available at http://wvcommerce.org/travel/gettinghere/wvbyways/newgreenbrier.aspx.

You can also toodle along U.S. 60, known as the **Midland Trail** (www.midlandtrail.com), a national scenic byway stretching 180 miles from White Sulphur Springs to the Kentucky–Ohio–West Virginia border. Just 10 miles from White Sulphur Springs lies the cozy colonial-era town of Lewisburg; its downtown, filled with shops and galleries, has been named one of a dozen Distinctive Destinations by the National Trust for Historical Preservation. Be sure to drop in for homemade soups and pastries plus a chicken BLT for lunch or roasted pork shank for dinner at the **Stardust Café** (102 E. Washington St., 304-647-3663).

Just north of town on Fairview Road is **Lost World Caverns** (304-645-6677, www.lostworldcaverns.com, $12 self-guided tour), a natural underground cave system that is home to the 30-ton stalactite dubbed the Snow Chandelier and the 28-foot stalagmite called the War Club.

For more natural pursuits, check out the nearby 5,100-acre **Greenbrier State Forest** (304-536-1944, www.greenbriersf.com) in Caldwell, with 13 miles of hiking and biking trail, plus an archery court, horseshoes, and a pool. Cabins start at $66 per night, depending on the season, campsites at $20. The 79-mile **Greenbrier River Trail** (www.greenbrierrivertrail.com) along a former railroad right-of-way is popular with hikers and bikers.

HOW TO GET IN TOUCH

Greenbrier County Convention & Visitors Bureau, 540 N. Jefferson St., Ste. N, Lewisburg, WV 24901, 800-833-2068, www.greenbrierwv.com.

take a road trip

NATIONWIDE

See the USA in Your Chevrolet

—COMMERCIAL JINGLE (1949)

17 As a nation, we've done it by Conestoga wagon, VW minibus, and the family SUV, and it's been memorialized in movies as iconic as *National Lampoon's Vacation* and *Little Miss Sunshine.* No vacation is more truly American than a road trip. But a journey can be much more than motorized sightseeing. It's a time for bonding and accumulating junk-food wrappers on the floorboard. Planned right it offers a chance to experience parts of the country too often bypassed when traveling via interstates and airplanes. It's a rite of passage, a tradition everyone should experience at least once.

Both co-authors of this book have passed thousands of hours on highways and country roads. Jane Wooldridge once took 28 days to drive a zigzaggy 5,000 miles from Miami to Seattle, relying on e-mailed tips from strangers to choose her route. Larry Bleiberg has done his share of transcontinental travel: wheeling it from Virginia to Idaho, Kentucky to British Columbia, and each time emerging from the car bleary-eyed but a little smarter about his country—and himself. Road trips develop themes and theme songs. Even decades later, when Johnny Cash's "Folsom Prison Blues" comes on the radio, Larry still flashes back to a middle-of-the-night drive across West Virginia with his younger brother.

A trip shouldn't be aimless wandering. It needs a goal, a purpose, an excuse to take you off the main routes and fill your mind with memories. Here are three ideas around which to structure a road trip.

Lake Superior Route. Circle one of the world's largest inland seas on a fascinating two-nation vacation that will cover more than 1,100 miles. Tip: Remember to bring your passport, as you'll need it to reenter the United States. Going clockwise from Duluth, Minnesota, you'll hit Thunder Bay, Ontario, home to one of the largest populations of Finns outside Helsinki. Have a bargain meal of Finnish pancakes or smoked salmon at the **Hoito Restaurant** (314 Bay St., 807-345-6323). You'll love the lake scenery along the north shore, then stop to gawk at the giant Canada goose statue in Wawa, Ontario, and finally watch ships slip through the locks at Sault Ste. Marie. Back in Michigan, consider a side trip to car-free Mackinac Island, if only for free samples of fudge at its famous shops. Then it's across the Upper Peninsula, with sites like **Pictured Rocks National**

Lakeshore (906-387-3700, www.nps.gov/piro) and into Wisconsin, for a detour to the **Apostle Islands** (715-779-3397, www.nps.gov/apis).

North of Superior Tourism Association, 920 Tungsten St., Ste. 206, Thunder Bay, ON P7B 5Z6, Canada, 800-265-3951, www.lakesuperiorcircletour.info.

Pacific Coast Highway. This route can take you all the way from San Diego to northern California–and beyond. Pick a section or drive it all. Central California offers Santa Barbara, the unforgettable Big Sur coastline, and Monterey. You can get your fill of sightseeing at places like San Simeon's **Hearst Castle** (750 Hearst Castle Rd., 805-927-2020, www.hearstcastle.org) and San Jose's **Winchester Mystery House** (525 S. Winchester Blvd., 408-247-2101, www.winchestermysteryhouse.com). And everyone, it seems, wants to stop at San Luis Obispo's **Madonna Inn** (100 Madonna Rd., 805-543-3000, www.madonnainn.com), many to take a peek at the waterfall urinal in the men's bathroom.

North of San Francisco, you'll find dramatic coastline at **Point Reyes National Seashore** (415-464-5100, www.nps.gov/pore) and fun strolling in towns like **Mendocino** and **Fort Bragg.** If possible, drive the route north to south, so you can have an unobstructed view of the ocean.

California Travel & Tourism Commission, P.O. Box 1499, Sacramento, CA 95812, 877-225-4367, www.visitcalifornia.com.

Pony Express National Historic Trail. Wending from St. Joseph, Missouri, to Sacramento, California, this 2,000-mile trail passes through several distinct geographic zones: the Great Plains, the Rocky Mountains, the Salt Lake Desert, and the Sierra Nevada.

RULES OF THE ROAD

- Put someone in charge of music and bring plenty of it. If your car doesn't have a plug for an MP3 player, get a radio transmitter. You don't want to be stuck listening to the same CDs again and again and again.
- Bring a cooler packed with water and healthy snacks. But don't neglect the unhealthy ones, too. Part of the charm of a road trip is nibbling on Swedish Fish, beef jerky, or boiled peanuts.
- Make plenty of stops. If a historical marker or an unusual store catches your attention, pull over and take a look. But limit your visits to obvious tourist traps. They can break a budget quickly.
- If you're going to play DVDs for younger travelers, at least pack a few about the area you're visiting. An educational video about the Oregon Trail has much more meaning when you're actually driving the route.
- Pull over when you're tired, or switch drivers. It's not a race to a finish line. The going is the goal.

Pony Express riders typically covered about 75 miles a day—you'll be able to do that before lunch, and still have time to explore the **Pony Express Home Station No. 1** (106 S. 8th St., 800-752-3965) in Marysville, Kansas; the original barn forms part of a museum open mid-April to October. Consider finding a motel in Kearney, Nebraska (rooms at the Microtel Inn & Suites run about $75; 104 W. Talmadge Rd., 308-698-3003, www.microtelinn.com) or keep going—you're the driver.

You'll want to hit places like **Chimney Rock National Historic Site** (308-586-2581, www.nebraskahistory.org/sites/rock) in Bayard, Nebraska, which once signaled the start of the wide-open frontier, and you'll feel that way even now. Soon the flat plains will give way to Wyoming's mountains. Plan to stop at the **Fort Laramie National Historic Site** (307-837-2221, www.nps.gov/fola), an early 19th-century former fur-trading post turned military outpost, and then make sure to visit the road trip icon, **Little America travel center** (Exit 68 off I-80, 888-652-9042, www.littleamerica.com/wyoming). Once just a giant truck stop, it's now a destination itself, with a motel and restaurants. Rooms run about $80.

For a real adventure, detour on to Utah's **Pony Express Trail National Back Country Byway** (800-748-4361, www.byways.org/explore/byways/68993), a route that traces well-maintained gravel and dirt roads across endless vistas of U.S. Bureau of Land Management property, skirting the southern edge of the Salt Lake Desert. Be sure to top off your gas tank before driving this desolate 130-mile byway. After that adventure you deserve a good night's sleep. Head back to I-80 and West Wendover, Nevada, which has chain motels and a few casinos.

Stop next at **Sand Springs Station,** near Fallon, Nevada. Look for historical markers and ATVs climbing a 500-foot dune. Bunk down in Reno at a bargain hotel like the **Hawthorn Suites** (2050 Market St., Reno, 775-786-2500, www.hawthorn.com) for less than $70, or check for last-minute deals at a casino hotel. Before turning in, enjoy a memorable meal at the **Santa Fe Hotel** (235 Lake St., 775-323-1891), which serves Basque cuisine. A family-style lamb chop dinner runs $14.

Now, it's on to California and **Old Sacramento** (916-442-7644, www.oldsacramento.com), where you can commemorate your journey with a photo in front of the Pony Express Statue at Second and J Streets.

Pony Express National Historic Trail, 324 S. State St., Ste. 200, Salt Lake City, UT 84111, 801-741-1012, www.nps.gov/poex; **XP Pony Express Home Station,** www.xphomestation.com.

see new york on the cheap

NEW YORK CITY

And New York is the most beautiful city in the world? It is not far from it.

—ESSAYIST AND POET EZRA POUND, "PATRIA MIA" (1912)

18 New York is the city that best captures America's go-go spirit. And not surprisingly, it also ranks as one of the country's most expensive destinations—but it doesn't have to be. Many of its less known attractions are cheap or even free. So is walking the streets—as long as you keep your wallet securely in your pocket. Here are some favorite New York values:

- **Brooklyn Heights Promenade.** The promenade offers unparalleled views of the city, encompassing the Brooklyn Bridge and Staten Island. This esplanade atop the Brooklyn-Queens Expressway is also one of New York's most romantic spots, especially at sunset. *Bet. Montague & Middagh Sts., Brooklyn.*
- **Central Park.** New York City's backyard is big (843 acres) and historic—sheep once grazed in the 150-plus-year-old green space. On any weekend you'll find joggers circling the reservoir and children climbing on the Alice-in-Wonderland bronze statue at East 74th Street near the Conservatory Water; in summer, would-be Boys of Summer throng the sports diamonds. Some of Central Park's freebies are well known: Holiday concerts on the Great Lawn and at the Naumberg Bandshell; Shakespeare in the Park performances at the Delacorte Theater; the John Lennon Memorial near the park entrance at 72nd Street and Central Park West. Others are often overlooked, including the 18th-century Dairy (now a history center), the Conservatory Garden at East 105th Street, and the catch-and-release fishing program at the Harlem Meer. A few park attractions charge modest fees, including the **Carousel** (212-879-0244, $2), the **Central Park Zoo** (212-439-6500, $10), and, in winter, the **Wollman Ice Skating Rink** (212-439-6900, Nov.–March, $14). *www.centralparknyc.org, www.centralpark.com.*
- **The Cloisters.** The entrance ticket to the Metropolitan Museum of Art also includes same-day entry to the Cloisters in Fort Tryon Park at Manhattan's north end. The Cloisters is what it sounds: a medieval cloister constructed from architectural elements gleaned from various structures in Europe dating from the 12th to 15th centuries. The artworks—chalices, tombs, stained-glass windows, tapestries, and more—hail primarily from the same period. (Hint: Admission prices at the Met are suggestions only; you should pay the full amount, but if you're really strapped you can pay less.) *The Cloisters, 99 Margaret Corbin Dr.,*

SLEEPING ON THE CHEAP

Though a number of shared-bathroom and value-conscious lodgings have opened in New York and other hot tourist areas in recent years, an increasingly popular option is to rent an apartment or time-share—especially if you're traveling with a family or several couples.

What you'll get: more space for your buck. Sometimes you'll save 50 percent or more over a hotel. In New York, vrbo.com recently listed a two-bedroom apartment in midtown Manhattan for $275 a night and a four-bedroom East Side townhouse for $600 a night. What you'll likely give up: room service, daily maid service, and, in many cases, 24-hour support.

Lodgings are available through a variety of websites in metro and tourist-friendly areas around the globe. Some websites put you directly in touch with the property owner, who has the final responsibility for delivering the property as promised. Other websites offer only properties that are professionally managed by an on-site company, which means you may have some backup if the property isn't quite as advertised, or if something goes wrong. Be sure to check out any guarantees. Note that some cities are considering bans on rentals of less than a week.

Ask plenty of questions when looking at listed properties because each is individually owned. Are linens included? Is there a minimum rental required? Does the property have a full kitchen or just a refrigerator? What is the cancellation policy? Is the unit suitable for small children or those with mobility issues? Are there any additional fees beyond the per-night rate? What about parking?

The following sites on the Internet are good places to start your search:

- www.homeaway.com: Owned by the same company as vrbo.com, including properties from individuals and some management companies.
- www.hotels.com: Click on the "condos" tab to see city and resort rentals.
- Hyatt Vacation Club: These resort time-shares are available for nonowners; visit www.hyatt.com; under brands search for Hyatt Vacation Club.
- Marriott Vacation Club: Resort time-shares available for nonowners; search from www.marriott.com.
- www.vacationroost.com: Specializes in ski and beach destinations.
- www.vrbo.com: One of the largest websites, offering tens of thousands of units, mostly offered by individual owners. (Vrbo stands for "vacation rentals by owner.")
- www.zonder.com: All properties listed are professionally managed.

212-923-3700. Metropolitan Museum of Art, 1000 5th Ave., 212-535-7710, www.metmuseum.org.

- **Free museum days.** A number of New York City museums and gardens are free one evening a week or month, including the **Museum of Modern Art** (11 W. 53rd St., 212-708-9400, www.moma.org, Fri. 4 p.m.–8 p.m.), the **Morgan Library** (225 Madison Ave., 212-685-0008, www.themorgan.org, Fri. 7 p.m.–9 p.m.), and the **Whitney Museum** (945 Madison Ave., 212-570-3600, www.whitney.org, donation, Fri. 6 p.m.–9 p.m.).

- **Free walking tours.** The **Central Park Conservancy** (212-360-2726, www.centralpark nyc.org) offers free walking tours of the park, exploring its history, ecology, and design; each tour lasts 60 to 90 minutes. Neighborhood development groups offer free walking tours as well: **Village Alliance** (212-777-2173, www.villagealliance.org, summer only), **Lower East Side Business Improvement District** (866-224-0206, www.lowereastside ny.com, 2-hr. tour of Orchard St. April–summer), **Grand Central Partnership** (212-883-2420, www.grandcentralpartnership.org, 90-min. tour of Grand Central Terminal and neighborhood Fri. 12:30 p.m.; meet at 120 Park Ave. in sculpture court), and **Municipal Arts Society** (http://mas.org, 90-min. tour Tues. 12:30 p.m.; meet at Downtown Information Center, 55 Exchange Pl., Ste. 401, bring photo ID, donation).
- **New York Federal Reserve Museum.** The fortress-like New York Federal Reserve is actually open to the public—or at least parts of it are, with advance reservation. Its museum hosts exhibitions on the history of money and how the Fed works; it's even possible to visit the gold vault on a free scheduled tour. Requests must be made in advance. *New York Federal Reserve, 33 Liberty St., 212-720-6130, www.newyorkfed.org.*
- **Staten Island Ferry.** The Staten Island Ferry is one of the world's great rides—and it's free. Some 20 million people per year make the journey between Lower Manhattan and Staten Island, the city's most suburban borough. For most tourists, though, the destination isn't Staten Island but the hour-long round-trip ride itself, with views of Ellis Island, the Statue of Liberty, and the Lower Manhattan skyline. *Staten Island Ferry, 4 South St. (Manhattan), 1 Bay St. (Staten Island), www.siferry.com.*

Other "cheap trip" tips to keep in mind when visiting New York City:

- Hotels are typically cheaper on weekends and in the coldest winter months. The days just before Thanksgiving and Christmas also yield bargains. Discount travel websites like travel zoo.com and hotels.com can lead you to lodging values.
- For meal deals, check online at www.nycgo.com for special dining weeks when fixed-price meals are offered at many local restaurants. Delis dotted around the city offer great value, and often, some of the best comfort food in the city.
- For theater tickets, check out the TKTS booths in Times Square, South Street Seaport, and downtown Brooklyn. You're unlikely to find tickets to the hottest shows but consider the off-Broadway shows, where the drama is often inventive and edgy, and the prices cheaper.

HOW TO GET IN TOUCH

NYC & Company, www.nycgo.com.

hear cowboy poetry

ELKO, NEVADA

There were poems about dyin' a'horseback.
Poems about shootin' a bear.
There even were poems about ol' beat up cowpokes
bemoanin' the loss of their hair.

—BAXTER BLACK, COWBOY POET AND LARGE-ANIMAL VET,
"ON THE EDGE OF COMMON SENSE" (1985)

19 The West may be tamed, but the romance of the resilient, self-reliant, and rugged cowboy lives on—and not just in the movies or the local Western bar. The United States remains one of the top beef-producing countries in the world, with more than 93 million cows, according to the U.S. Department of Agriculture. And though today's cowboys have access to advanced animal husbandry techniques, iPods, and the Internet, much of the farming requires wide, open spaces and a man on horseback.

From Florida to California, cowboy traditions are celebrated at rodeos, fairs, and cattle drives. But if you want to understand the soul of the men (and women) who ride the range, the **National Cowboy Poetry Gathering** is the place.

COW-CULTURE FACTS

- Despite doctors' orders to lay off the red meat, consumers chow down more than 27 billion pounds of U.S. beef per year.
- In 2010, the United States was home to 93.7 million cows—about a third the number of people.
- The top U.S. states for cattle farming (by number of cows) are, in order, Texas, Nebraska, Kansas, Oklahoma, and California.
- The world's largest cattle ranch, Anna Creek Station in South Australia, is bigger than Israel.
- A 1,000-pound cow produces about 80 pounds of manure per day (according to the U.S. Department of Agriculture).

For a week each January since 1985, cowboy poets, storytellers, and musicians gather in Elko, Nevada, for musical performances, poetry readings, sing-alongs, and workshops for young writers. The gathering is organized by the Western Folklife Center, headquartered in the Pioneer Hotel; tickets start at $20 per event.

Elko, a place that seems like a long way from anywhere, was chosen for the gathering for just that reason, explains Ryan T. Bell, a cowboy, author, and frequent contributor to *Western Horseman* magazine. "This is the epicenter of ranching—of buckaroo culture and Basque immigration, and that's about as cowboy as it gets." The festival is set in the

BUCKIN' BRONCOS

If your heart is set on bucking broncos and barrel races, consider these rodeos:

- **Calgary Stampede.** Held each July in Calgary, Alberta, Canada, the Calgary Stampede is one of the continent's best known cowboy events. The one-million-dollar purse draws top contestants in bull riding, barrel racing, steer wrestling, and wild-pony racing. If that's not enough to get your pulse beating, check out the chuck wagon races. Musical acts, a grandstand show, and a carnival midway are all part of the action, along with diet-defying food favorites like deep-fried jellybeans and pizza on a stick. Standing room tickets start at $12 per show, $15 in the evening. If you're staying several days, check out the ticket packages. Tip: Don't miss the free line-dance lessons each Friday night at **Ranchman's** (9615 MacLeod Trail S, 403-253-1100, www.ranchmans.com). *Calgary Stampede, 800-661-1260, http://calgarystampede.com.*
- **Houston Livestock Show and Rodeo.** Headliners such as Gene Autry, Elvis Presley, and Kenny Chesney have all taken the stage at this 75-plus-year-old event held each March in Houston, Texas. Along with rodeo events like mutton busting, a calf scramble, and Xtreme bull riding, the 20-day show includes a barbecue contest, trail rides, horse show, and livestock exhibitions and auction; some events take place the week before the main rodeo. Tickets start at $16. *Houston Livestock Show and Rodeo, 832-667-1000, www.rodeohouston.com.*
- **Oklahoma State Prison Rodeo.** In one of the nation's most unusual cowboy events, inmates at the state penitentiary in McAlester, Oklahoma, compete in a two-day extravaganza of steer wrestling, bareback riding, and calf-roping contests. August. *Oklahoma State Prison Rodeo, McAlester, 918-423-2550, www.mcalester.org.*

winter months because that's the off-season for cowboys. "If it were in the summertime, there ain't no working cowboy that would take time to go to this event," he explains.

Elko—that's what the cowboys call the festival—"still feels very homemade. It doesn't have much pomp and circumstance," says Bell. Even the well-known poets just sit in the audience, get up and deliver their rhymes, and then sit back down. Poets may read their own work, but often they perform classics—works by the late Badger Clark and by living poets including Wally McRae, Ross Knox, and Joel Nelson.

Then it's a scurry to jump a shuttle—eight venues are scattered around town—before ending the day in the **Stockman's Hotel and Casino** (340 Commercial St., 775-738-5141, www.elkocasinos.com) or the **Pioneer Saloon** (Pioneer Hotel, 501 Railroad St.), dancing, kicking back brew, and, of course, telling the tales of life on the range.

Most poetry events are held in the evenings, which leaves days free for checking out wildlife and Western art exhibits at the **Northeastern Nevada Museum** (1515 Idaho St., 775-738-3418, www.museumelko.org, closed Mon., $5), snowsledding and snowmobile tours in the Ruby Mountains, a drive to **Lamoille Canyon,** and a visit to the 1875 **Sherman Station homestead** (14th & Idaho Sts., 775-738-7135).

Lodging during the Poetry Gathering starts at around $50 per night. Chain motels are probably your best bet; in January, camping is out of the question even for hearty souls. Popular budget options include the **Thunderbird Motel** (345 Idaho St., 775-738-7115) and Stockman's (see opposite)—which is sure to be rowdy.

HOW TO GET IN TOUCH

Elko Convention & Visitors Authority, 700 Moren Way, Elko, NV 89801, 800-248-3556, www.elkocva.com.

Western Folklife Center, 501 Railroad St., Elko, 775-738-7508, www.westernfolklife.org.

sail into history aboard the *victory chimes*

ROCKLAND, MAINE

I love the poetry of motion, the challenge of it. And the nature. I just love it.

—JOHN DICKEY, AVID SAILOR AND GUEST ABOARD THE *VICTORY CHIMES*

20 When launched in 1900, she was America's largest commercial sailing vessel built to haul cargo along the eastern seaboard. The *Victory Chimes* has seen a few upgrades since then—including electricity and indoor plumbing. And she's swapped cargo: Instead of hauling lumber and rum barrels, the *Chimes* now transports vacationers on three- to six-day summer sails among the 3,000 islands of Maine's Penobscot Bay.

On a fine day you'll find yourself traveling courtesy of the same lusty winds that brought the pilgrims to the New World. Though the *Chimes* carries a yawl boat—a motorized mini-tug that gets it in and out of harbors and through the islands on still days—the real power comes from the sails hoisted from her triple masts. On a foggy day—and in Maine, there are plenty of them—you'll sail through the mists, trusting your fate to the elements (and the well-schooled captain, who has radar on board).

Don't go looking for the spa, the pool, or the gourmet restaurant. "It's a bit like camping," says the captain, Kip Files. The tight cabins offer just enough space for sleeping and storing a small duffle, and enough light for reading. Except in the "honeymoon" suite, the toilets are down a hall or up a wide wooden ladder. The showers are in their own cozy cabins off the deck.

HISTORY OF THE *VICTORY CHIMES*

Built in Bethel, Delaware, in 1900, the *Victory Chimes* originally was dubbed *Edwin & Maude*, after the children of her first captain. In her early decades, the ship carried lumber and fertilizer. During World War II, she was drafted into service to check offshore magnetic antisubmarine devices—a role difficult for a metal ship, but fitting for this wooden vessel. By the time the war ended, faster steam-powered ships took over the merchant transport trade; in the 1950s the ship was rechristened the *Victory Chimes* and moved to Maine as a windjammer ship.

Among her private owners was Domino's Pizza founder Tom Monahan. When Monahan decided to sell the *Chimes* in the late 1990s, the most likely buyer was Japanese. Then the ship's captain, Kip Files, put together a plan to purchase the ship with fellow captain Paul DeGaeta to maintain the *Chimes*' American heritage.

The 132-foot wooden ship—designated a national historic landmark—carries a maximum of 40 passengers. Most pitch in to help the crew with the sails at the beginning of each day—after fortification with fresh-brewed coffee, fruit, hearty eggs, and biscuits baked in the snug galley—and again at day's end. Between, you'll go where the winds take you. Cappy—yes, the crew really calls him that—plots the daily course based on weather and the length of the trip. Most days begin with a ride via the yawl boat into the town at the previous night's anchorage, where you might walk to a century-old lighthouse, visit a general store, or stroll through a small artists gallery.

But the best part of the day is spent on board—reading, chatting with fellow passengers, scanning for porpoises and whales, and watching the craggy coast roll by. Even on a foggy day, the trip takes on an air of romance, and you may well believe that you've slipped into the maritime past. Until the next meal, that is, when the cheery crew serves up homemade soup, fresh salads, lobster, corn on the cob, or a heaping tray of pork in barbecue sauce. Just don't count the calories; you're on vacation, after all.

The *Victory Chimes* sails from Rockland, in Maine's mid-coast region, from June through late September. Three-day sails start at $450 per person and include three generous family-style meals daily plus hors d'oeuvres each evening; guests bring their own sodas and alcoholic beverages that can be iced in the cooler. Veterans and their families and those celebrating birthdays and anniversaries get a discount. Dress is extremely casual; anything fancier than jeans is overkill. Because this is a historic vessel, there are no accommodations for those with disabilities.

Children are allowed, though the trip may not be suitable for very young children who can't navigate the stairs, or those who go stir-crazy without TV.

MAINE WINDJAMMER FLEET

A dozen classic sailing ships called windjammers compose the Maine Windjammer Association; a few additional ships sail the waters as well. Most are based in the towns of Rockport, Rockland, and Camden.

Each ship is individually owned. Some date from the 1800s; a few were built as windjammer cruisers. Each has her own character and hosts occasional specialty cruises for families, photographers, lighthouse enthusiasts, and more; the historic *Stephen Taber*, for instance, features wine weekends.

Each season the fleet gathers for parades, races, and holiday celebrations; dates vary by year. *Maine Windjammer Association, 800-807-9463, www.sailmainecoast.com.*

HOW TO GET IN TOUCH

Victory Chimes, 800-745-5651, www.victorychimes.com.

MidCoast Chamber Council, 800-787-4284, www.mainesmidcoast.com.

honor the struggle for civil rights

BIRMINGHAM, ALABAMA

We know through painful experience that freedom is never voluntarily given by the oppressor, it must be demanded by the oppressed.

—DR. MARTIN LUTHER KING, JR., "LETTER FROM A BIRMINGHAM JAIL" (1963)

21 Key events in the civil rights movement occurred throughout the South, but perhaps none with such notoriety as those that unfolded in Birmingham, Alabama. "The most segregated city in America," that's what Birmingham was dubbed in the 1950s. Bathrooms, water fountains, restaurants, movies, and streetcars all had separate sections for blacks and whites—if blacks were allowed at all. Ku Klux Klan cross burnings and bombings were common. When the U.S. Supreme Court banned school segregation in 1954, Alabama simply ignored the ruling.

The **Birmingham Civil Rights Institute** (520 16th St. N, 205-328-9696 ext. 203, www.bcri.org, $12, free on Sun.) focuses on the struggle for civil rights . . . and forms the centerpiece of a getaway to this friendly (and affordable) Southern city. The photos, personal testaments, and news accounts memorialized in the institute are painful to read, hear, and watch—but a critical part of U.S. history. Here are the bars of the jail cell from which Dr. Martin Luther King, Jr., wrote his "Letter from a Birmingham Jail" and a blackened carcass of a bus replicating one ridden by Freedom Riders firebombed in 1961. Most chilling, perhaps, are exhibits recalling the 1963 rally by thousands of schoolchildren—a peaceful protest turned ugly when Police Chief Bull Connor turned water cannon and attack dogs on the crowd. Images of the conflict were shown around the world, and within days, segregation in Birmingham officially ended.

The institute is the centerpiece of Birmingham's Civil Rights District. Across the street lies both the **Kelly Ingram Park** (6th Ave. N & 16th St.), where Connor attacked the protesters, and the **16th Street Baptist Church** (1530 6th Ave. N, 205-251-9402), where a Sunday morning bombing in 1963 killed four young girls. Entry to both is free; an audio tour of Kelly Ingram Park, available at the Civil Rights Institute, runs $5.

Found within walking distance of the institute are both the **Alabama Jazz Hall of Fame** (1631 4th Ave. N, 205-254-2731, www.jazzhall.com, self-guided tours $2), in the historic Carver Theatre, and the **Fourth Avenue Business District** (4th Ave. N bet. 15th & 18th Sts.), once the hub of black commerce.

MORE CIVIL RIGHTS SITES BEYOND BIRMINGHAM

CivilRightsTravel.com (created by co-author Larry Bleiberg) notes the following as must-see civil rights sites:

- **Central High School.** Three years after the Supreme Court outlawed segregated schools, nine brave students in 1957 tried to enroll in Little Rock, Arkansas' white public high school. An angry mob fought them, so President Eisenhower sent in federal troops. The story is told at a moving National Park Service site. Call ahead for a tour of the high school, which is still operating. *Central High School, 2120 Daisy Bates Dr., Little Rock, 501-374-1957, www.nps.gov/chsc.*
- **International Civil Rights Center & Museum.** Four freshmen at North Carolina A&T State University sat down at a "Whites' Only" Woolworth's lunch counter in 1960. Their sit-in sparked similar protests throughout the region, and six months later, Woolworth's backed down. This new museum occupies the former store and documents the students' pivotal role in history. *International Civil Rights Center & Museum, 134 S. Elm St., Greensboro, 336-274-9199, www.sitinmovement.org, $8.*
- **Lowndes County Interpretive Center.** The nation was shocked on March 7, 1965, when lawmen attacked voting rights marchers on the Edmund Pettus Bridge in Selma, Alabama, a day that came to be known as "Bloody Sunday." Two weeks later, a federal judged cleared the way for the protest march to Montgomery. This National Park Service visitor center, located along the Selma to Montgomery National Historic Trail, tells the story of the march, which led to passage of the National Voting Rights Act. *Lowndes County Interpretive Center, 7001 U.S. 80W, Hayneville, 334-877-1984, www.nps.gov/semo.*
- **Martin Luther King, Jr., National Historic Site.** Martin Luther King, Jr., personified the civil rights movement through the 1950s and '60s. Discover his story in the preserved Sweet Auburn neighborhood of Atlanta, Georgia, which was the center of African-American life. Admission is free, but you will need to register to tour his birth home. *Martin Luther King, Jr., National Historic Site, 450 Auburn Ave. NE, Atlanta, 404-331-5190, www.nps.gov/malu.*
- **National Civil Rights Museum.** Dr. King's life came to an end at the Lorraine Motel in Memphis, Tennessee. The assassination site is carefully preserved at this ambitious museum, including King's motel room, number 306, and the adjacent guesthouse, where James Earl Ray allegedly shot Dr. King from a bathroom window. *National Civil Rights Museum, 450 Mulberry St., Memphis, 901-521-9699, www.civilrightsmuseum.org, $13.*
- **Rosa Parks Museum.** When a middle-aged seamstress in Montgomery, Alabama, refused to yield her bus seat to a white passenger in December 1955, history was forever changed. This eponymous museum literally puts you on a bus to witness the event. *Rosa Parks Museum, 252 Montgomery St., Montgomery, 334-241-8615, http://montgomery.troy.edu/rosaparks/museum/, $6.*

Today, Birmingham is a far different place—a neighborly city where fried okra meets tapas, and both Indycar *and* NASCAR coexist with the largest municipal art museum in the Southeast.

You'll find the **Birmingham Museum of Art** at 2000 Rev. Abraham Woods, Jr. Boulevard (205-254-2565, www.artsbma.org). If you've got an hour or more, call local folk hero Joe Minter and his wife Hilda (205-322-7370) and ask if they can show you **Joe's African Village,** filled with artworks inspired by found objects. (Tours are free but you may want to buy Joe's book, *To You Through Me.*) Or make your own iron art throughout the year and during the annual Stokin' the Fire barbecue and festival each August at the **Sloss Furnace National Historic Landmark** (20 32nd St. N, 205-324-1911, www.slossfurnaces.com).

When you're done, grab a sandwich and some tunes at the **Garage Café** (2304 10th Terr. S, 205-322-3220), noted by visitors and *GQ* magazine for its music, food, and antiques for sale. And don't miss a chance to giggle at "Vulcan," the bare-bottomed statue that lords over the city.

However you decide to spend your time, you won't be bored. As Dilcy Hilley of the city's tourism bureau puts it, "Funky is our middle name."

As in all cities, lodging isn't exactly cheap, but it's less expensive than in Atlanta or New York, and on a quiet weekend you might well snag a value rate of $109 at the hip **Aloft Birmingham Soho Square** (1903 29th Ave. S, Homewood, 205-874-8055, www.starwoodhotels.com). Or you could opt for a country-meets-city getaway and stay about 15 minutes away in **Oak Mountain State Park** (200 Terrace Dr., Pelham, 800-252-7275, www.alapark.com/oakmountain), where campsites start at $14 per night. Bring your friends and rent a cabin for six; prices start at $110 per night.

HOW TO GET IN TOUCH

Greater Birmingham Convention & Visitors Bureau, 2200 9th Ave. N, Birmingham, AL 35203, 800-458-8085, www.birminghamal.org.

meet me at the fair

DALLAS, TEXAS

Our State Fair is a great state fair,
Don't miss it, don't even be late.

—SONGWRITING DUO RODGERS AND HAMMERSTEIN, "OUR STATE FAIR" (1945)

22 Even if you never saw the iconic (and some might say, corny) 1945 movie *State Fair*, you know that a great state fair offers as fine a slice of American life as it does rhubarb-and-strawberry pie. Once you have duly admired the calves and piglets raised by 4-H groups, ogled the giant squash, complimented the homemade jams, strolled the midway, and tried to win a giant stuffed bear at the balloon pop, you'll want to take in a musical act, ranging from once-famous pop stars to fiddlers to big-name country stars. And if you can't get kissed atop the Ferris wheel, why, you're clearly with the wrong date!

Taking in all a state fair has to offer can take a couple of days at least, which is just enough time for you to get your fill of corndogs and cotton candy. Just be sure to ride the whirl-a-gig before you hit the barbecue stand. And bring the Pepto.

One of the nation's biggest fairs is, naturally, in Texas, drawing close to two million people to the 277-acre Fair Park near downtown Dallas. Most everything at the State Fair of Texas is supersize, from the 212-foot-tall Texas Star Ferris wheel to livestock exhibitions featuring about 8,000 animals to Big Tex, a 52-foot-tall iconic cowboy figure topped by a 75-gallon hat that greets fairgoers with a hearty "Howdy folks."

The 120-plus-year-old fair takes place from late September to mid-October and lasts 24 days, so you will have plenty of time to visit. If you plan your trip right, you can catch one of the hotly contested football games that occur while the fair is going on, including the University of Texas–Oklahoma University game.

Recent years have brought celebrity chef appearances along with name entertainment and jazz concerts in the wine garden. Ticket prices change yearly, but expect to pay less than $20 per day for an adult and less for children and seniors. Check for promotions that offer half-price rides on less crowded weekdays, and look for widely available discount coupons at area grocery stores and fast-food restaurants.

Most of the fair's events and shows are free once you get inside. Don't miss the pig races, BMX bike show, and the nightly parade. Take stock of your surroundings as you revel in the activities: The fairground boasts the nation's largest collection of art deco exposition buildings, built for the 1936 Texas Centennial Exposition.

POPULAR STATE FAIRS

The United States is a nation of fairgoers: About 40 million visitors show up at the country's top 50 fairs—an assortment of state fairs, rodeos, county fairs, exhibitions, and more—according to the website carnivalwarehouse.com, which tracks this kind of data. Of the state fairs on the "top 50" list, the State Fair of Texas drew the highest number of visitors in 2010, but here are a few other stand outs:

- **California State Fair.** If the tractor pull, harness racing, and demolition derby aren't enough to get you to the California State Fair, the Dachshund Derby or the Karaoke Contest just might do it. California celebrates its reputation for the unconventional with the Weird, Wild and Wacky Zone with a Twisted Cabaret, hypnotist, and an exhibition highlighting some of the state's strangest museums. A brewfest, farmers market, agriculture exhibitions, and midway round out fair offerings. The fair is held in late July. Tickets cost $12; concerts are free with entry. *California State Fair, 1600 Exposition Blvd., Sacramento, 916-263-3247, www.bigfun.org.*
- **Great New York State Fair.** Along with traditional pursuits like lumberjack demonstrations and butter-sculpting contests, this fair that dates from 1841 throws in contemporary twists including world-class wines, text-messaging speed contests, women's boxing matches, and live culinary demonstrations by star chefs, such as Bobby Flay. Tickets cost $10; concert tickets cost more, but they include fair entry. *Great New York State Fair, 581 State Fair Blvd., Syracuse, 800-475-3247, www.nysfair.org.*
- **Iowa State Fair.** The corny movie *State Fair* was, naturally enough, inspired by the Iowa State Fair, which has been in staged since 1854. Today, more than one million fairgoers gather each August at the 400-acre fairgrounds in Des Moines to celebrate agriculture, music, classic fair culture, and the Butter Cow—yes, a life-size cow statue in wood, wire, and steel mesh covered in more than 600 pounds of pure cream Iowa butter. General admission costs $10. *Iowa State Fair, E. 30th St. & E. University Ave., Des Moines, 515-262-3111, www.iowastatefair.com.*
- **Minnesota State Fair.** This state fair—where President Theodore Roosevelt issued his "speak softly and carry a big stick" edict—features marching bands, fiddlers, talent contests, livestock shows, equestrian events, and more. In recent years performers such as Bonnie Raitt, REO Speedwagon, Lynyrd Skynyrd, and the *Prairie Home Companion*'s Garrison Keillor have taken to the stage. Admission costs $11, with discounts offered on some days. Some concerts and performances cost extra. *Minnesota State Fair, 1265 Snelling Ave. N, St. Paul, 651-288-4400, www.mnstatefair.org.*

And bring an appetite for outrageous offerings: The State Fair of Texas is famous for its long menu of creative fried delicacies, including fried banana splits, deep-fried lattes, and fried butter. There is also a slew of more mundane but no less delicious items. Be sure to sample the Blue Bell ice cream and Fletcher's corny dog, says *Dallas Morning News* travel editor Mary Ellen Botter.

The fairgrounds are on the DART light-rail line, which lets you avoid the hassle and expense of parking (usually about $10).

For an affordable lodging option, try the pet-friendly **Belmont Hotel Dallas** (901 Fort Worth Ave., 800-951-2997, www.belmontdallas.com) with rooftop dining and individually decorated casitas and rooms. During fair season rooms start at $109. The closest campground is about 17 miles away: **Texan RV Ranch** (1961 Lone Star Rd., Mansfield, 866-348-3978, www.rvparksdallasfortworth.com) has tent sites starting at $15, RV sites at $32.

HOW TO GET IN TOUCH

State Fair of Texas, 3921 Martin Luther King Blvd. (U.S. 30), Dallas, TX 75210, 214-565-9931, www.bigtex.com.

catch the country stars of tomorrow

NASHVILLE, TENNESSEE

I wish I was in Nashville, guitar on my back
Maybe someday I will ride in the back of a big Cadillac

—SINGER/SONGWRITER DON WILLIAMS, "WISH I WAS IN NASHVILLE" (1974)

23 No music speaks to the American heart quite like country music, and even devotees of Mozart and hard-core Stones fans can appreciate country's tales of broken hearts, cheating lovers, and revenge . . . and the joys of everyday life.

Nashville is the heart and soul of country music—history, songwriting, publishing, and, yes, performance. It's certainly the best place going to get an earful of the hits that have yet to make the airwaves. On any Friday afternoon, you can stroll along Lower Broadway in downtown and catch live performances in a dozen bars by would-be stars singing tunes of money burned and romance spurned. (The songs and performers get better as the hour gets later . . . especially if you've had a few beers.) Tom Adkinson, "an almost lifelong Nashvillian," says the following places are must-visits:

- **Legends Corner.** A classic, with country album covers on the wall, live music on stage, and cold beer on the table. Ages 21 and over after 6 p.m. No cover charge. *Legends Corner, 428 Broadway, 615-248-6334, www.legendscorner.com.*
- **Robert's Western World.** How can you beat a place that sells burgers, beer, and boots in the middle of an afternoon while a would-be country star croons about the hazards of hangovers? Free and open to all ages until 10 p.m.; must be 21 to stay or enter after 10 p.m. No cover charge. *Robert's Western World, 416B Broadway, 615-244-9552, www.robertswesternworld.com.*
- **Tootsie's Orchid Lounge.** This 50-year-old beer joint was popular with country music stars (including Kris Kristofferson, Willie Nelson, and Patsy Cline) when the Grand Ole Opry was just across an alley in the Ryman Auditorium. Movies filmed here include *Coal Miner's Daughter*. *Tootsie's Orchid Lounge, 422 Broadway, 615-726-0463, www.tootsies.net.*

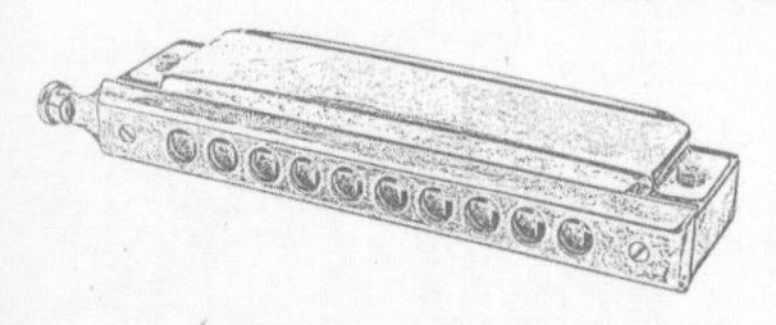

When your own heart gets a little too achy—and it's still before 5:30 p.m. any day except Sunday—wander into **Gruhn Guitars**

NASHVILLE MUST-SEE SITES

- **Belle Meade Plantation.** Home to an antebellum mansion that evolved greatly from its original 1820 two-story federal-style appearance, this plantation holds a revered place in Thoroughbred horse-racing history. *Belle Meade Plantation, 5025 Harding Pike, 615-356-0501, www.bellemeadeplantation.com, $16.*
- **Country Music Hall of Fame and Museum.** This Smithsonian-caliber museum explains the multifaceted history of country music through artifacts, photos, film, lectures, and performances. It operates Historic RCA Studio B, nearby on Music Row, where Elvis Presley recorded 162 songs. *Country Music Hall of Fame and Museum, 222 5th Ave. S, 615-416-2001, www.countrymusichalloffame.org, $19.99.*
- **Grand Ole Opry and Museum.** The Opry still broadcasts before a live audience from its high-tech home a few miles from downtown; its museum pays homage to the show and its stars. Performance prices vary but generally start at $39 for adults, $29 ages 4–11. *Grand Ole Opry and Museum, 2804 Opryland Dr., 800-733-6779 or 615-871-6779, www.opry.com, tours $15.*
- **The Hermitage.** Andrew Jackson lived here before and after his tenure as the seventh U.S. President. A successful farmer, he transformed the small farm he purchased in 1804 into a prosperous 1,000-acre plantation where he raised cotton and racehorses. *The Hermitage, 4580 Rachel's Ln., 615-889-2941, www.thehermitage.com, $17.*
- **The Parthenon.** This full-size reproduction of the 1,500-year-old temple in Athens, Greece, was built in 1897 for the Tennessee Centennial Exposition. Originally wooden, it was rebuilt in masonry in 1925. *The Parthenon, Centennial Park, 2600 West End Ave., 615-862-8431, www.nashville.gov/Parthenon, $6.*
- **Ryman Auditorium.** Built in 1892, the Ryman hosted Sarah Bernhardt, Charlie Chaplin, and W. C. Fields before becoming the home of the Grand Ole Opry from 1943 to 1974. A restoration in 1994 made it one of the world's best performance venues again; concert prices vary. *Ryman Auditorium, 116 5th Ave. N, 615-889-3060, www.ryman.com, tours $13.*

(400 Broadway, 615-256-2033, www.gruhn.com), one of the world's best known shops for vintage guitars. Even if you're not a country fan you'll be wowed by the vintage inventory that has passed through here: a Stromberg G-3 once owned by Ranger Doug of Riders in the Sky ($30,000), a Gretsch guitar once owned by Dan Fogelberg ($80,000), and Buddy Holly's personal Magnatone amp ($87,500).

For the best of what's to come, head to the snug **Bluebird Café** (4104 Hillsboro Pike, 615-383-1461, www.bluebirdcafe.com) in the city's Green Hills neighborhood. Every night this unimposing little storefront hosts two shows where songwriters, both new and quite accomplished, try out their works in progress and where future stars often get their start. The food is simple (chicken fingers, barbecue), the place is always packed, and reservations are highly recommended. Wear your jeans; everyone else will. Most nights there's no cover charge for the early show, but you'll need

HOW NASHVILLE BECAME MUSIC CITY

Nashville has always been musically inclined; by the early 1800s, religious music publishing was a thriving business, and the famed Ryman Auditorium opened in 1892, soon hosting performances by Italian tenor Enrico Caruso, conductor John Philip Sousa, and the Vienna Orchestra. But it was the 1925 launch of radio station WSM and its broadcast called the Grand Ole Opry that drew the music publishers, recording studios, and entertainment offices of today's Music Row. The many artists who have recorded in Nashville include Patsy Cline, Buddy Holly, Johnny Cash, Dolly Parton, and even Bob Dylan. The tradition continues today with stars such as Billy Ray Cyrus and Shania Twain.

to pay $7–$12 for late shows. All shows have a $7 minimum food/drink charge. A word of advice: This is a place to listen to music, not talk with your pals.

For a fix of Mozart, head to the new 123-million-dollar **Schermerhorn Symphony Center** (1 Symphony Pl., 615-687-6500, www.nashvillesymphony.org; temporarily closed due to large-scale flooding of Nashville in May 2010), home to the Nashville Symphony.

HOW TO GET IN TOUCH

Nashville Convention & Visitors Bureau, 800-657-6910, www.visitmusiccity.com.

take in prairie culture

COTTONWOOD FALLS & COUNCIL GROVE, KANSAS

It is the sweet, simple things of life which are the real ones after all.

—AUTHOR LAURA INGALLS WILDER (1917)

24 The word "prairie" brings to mind the waving, golden wheat of the song "America the Beautiful," the adventure of crossing wide spaces in a covered wagon, the hardships of farming a stubborn land, and living miles from your nearest neighbor. And who can't help but think of prairie dogs, those sandy-colored sentries poised to alert their fellows to the slightest danger?

The grasslands that once stretched across the North American continent's midsection from the north to Texas have, in many places, given way to cities and highways and farm fields. But a few places offer a glimpse into the prairie in its pioneer state—including the landscape surrounding Council Grove, Kansas.

A drive through the rolling farm fields south of Council Grove—be mindful of speed traps, where the limit drops to 10 miles an hour when you least expect it—brings you to **Tallgrass Prairie National Preserve** (2480 Hwy. 177, W of Strong City, 620-273-8494, www.nps.gov/tapr), a fitting place to start your prairie exploration.

The grass isn't nearly as tall as many visitors expect, park rangers acknowledge, though in the right conditions it can grow to 6 or 8 feet. But it's not the height of the grasses on these 11,000 rolling acres but the ecosystem here that gives the preserve its name. The land here is too dry for forest, too wet for desert, supporting instead the grasses where elk, deer, and bison once grazed. In recent months a small herd of bison has been reintroduced to this preserve for the first time in more than 140 years.

The ranch turned park was the 1880s homestead of Stephen Jones, built at a time when the land switched from open public access to private ownership. The government paid 40 cents for every 16

$PLURGE

ABOVE IT ALL

Plan ahead to join one of the monthly overnight wagon train trips that take place on specified weekends in summer. The trips are something of a splurge—$190 per adult, less for those under 21—and include the trail ride, overnight camping, and meals. Alternatively, you can get a taste of the trail experience by joining up just for dinner, entertainment, and a 15-minute wagon ride for $40. *Flint Hills Overland Wagon Train, 316-321-6300, www.wagontrainkansas.com.*

LITTLE HOUSE ON THE PRAIRIE

Laura Ingalls Wilder's (1867–1957) much loved Little House series of books about life on the prairie still inspires legions of fans, enticing them to visit the various sites featured in the books.

Laura was born in Pepin, Wisconsin, where a reproduction of the Little House in the Big Woods stands today. The **Laura Ingalls Wilder Historical Museum** (306 3rd St., 715-442-2142, mid-May–mid-Oct.) hosts the annual **Laura Ingalls Wilder Days** (800-442-3011, www.pepinwisconsin.com) in September.

When Laura was a toddler, the Ingalls family lived for several months near Independence, Kansas. Their **log cabin** (off U.S. 75, 620-289-4238, www.littlehouseontheprairie.com, donation) has been reconstructed at the original site, some 13 miles southwest of Independence.

Walnut Grove, Minnesota, is home to Plum Creek and Laura's childhood home. The **Laura Ingalls Wilder Museum** (330 8th St., 800-528-7280, www.walnutgrove.org, closed winter, $4) details her family history. The town hosts a series of **Wilder Pageant** (888-859-3102, $12) performances each July.

After the grasshopper plagues hit Plum Creek in the 1870s, Laura's family moved to Burr Oak, Iowa. The **Laura Ingalls Wilder Park and Museum** (3603 236th Ave., 563-735-5916, www.lauraingallswilder.us, $7) commemorates this early part of Laura's life.

By 1880, the family had moved again, this time to De Smet, South Dakota, where Pa Ingalls claimed the **Ingalls Homestead** (20812 Homestead Rd., 800-776-3594, www.ingallshomestead.com, closed winter, $10), where Laura grew to young adulthood. Today it offers wagon rides, camping, and prairie exhibits.

Laura's home in Mansfield, Missouri, where she wrote her Little House books, is home to the **Laura Ingalls Wilder Home and Museum** (3068 Hwy. A, 417-924-3626, www.lauraingallswilderhome.com, $8).

feet of wall a rancher put in—about 80 percent of the cost. Jones's barn and home are still standing; the one-room schoolhouse he built stands a short stroll away.

The preserve is open year-round, but the best time to come is May through October, when free ranger-led bus tours are offered at 11 a.m. and 3 p.m. (call for reservations). Spring is prime time for the 150 bird species that live or migrate through here, among them cattle egret, red-tailed hawk, prairie-chicken, and ruby-throated hummingbird.

Though easy hiking trails cross the land, there's no camping or lodging at the preserve; for that you'll need to drive about 5 miles to **Cottonwood Falls,** where the city office (220 Broadway St., 620-273-6666, www.cottonwoodfallskansas.com) can direct you to local campgrounds, mom-and-pop motels, and bed-and-breakfasts.

While in Cottonwood Falls, don't miss the surprisingly elegant 1873 **French Renaissance–style county hall** (318 Broadway, 620-273-8469, free weekdays, $3 for weekend tours) at the head of Broadway. You should also check out the collection of American Indian artifacts at the **Roniger Museum** (Courthouse Sq., 620-273-6310, closed Mon. & Thurs., donation); galleries such as **The Fiber Factory** (209 Broadway, 620-273-8686), filled with shawls and scarves made on turn-of-the-20th-century looms; and **Humble Clay Studio** (325 Broadway, 620-366-1840), where artist Larry Matson spins masterful clay works. The studio is open in summers but Matson meet you other times of the year at his shop by appointment.

Historic **Council Grove,** an 1860s way station along the Santa Fe Trail, lies about a half-hour drive north of Cottonwood Falls. You can easily spend a half day or more checking out the town's historic sites—the 270-year-old trunk of an oak that served as a post office and message board for travelers; the **"Last Chance Store"** (W. Main St.), which dates from the mid-19th century and doubled as a polling place; the 1860s **Terwilliger Home** (803 W. Main St., 620-767-7986), the last house in town wagons passed as they headed west (now a bakery and restaurant). The **Hayes House** (112 W. Main St., 620-767-5911) serves much of the same fare today as when it opened in 1857—brisket, crispy chicken, and peach pie—making it the oldest continuously operated restaurant west of the Mississippi.

But one of the best reasons to hang out in Council Grove is that it's a sweet and friendly place where people will say hello to you on the street, ask how your day has gone, and point you in a good direction. If you've gotten hit with one of those speed-trap tickets, the friendliness is an especially comforting salve.

HOW TO GET IN TOUCH

Council Grove Chamber of Commerce, 207 W. Main St., Council Grove, KS 66846, 800-732-9211 or 620-767-5413, www.councilgrove.com.

Flint Hills Tourism Coalition, 866-660-2622, http://kansasflinthills.travel.

discover kentucky bourbon

BARDSTOWN, KENTUCKY

What's a good bourbon? You look for balance and you look for cleanliness, and you look for something that's enjoyable.

—BILL SAMUELS, JR., PRESIDENT OF MAKER'S MARK DISTILLERY SINCE 1975

25 Ireland has whisky, Mexico, tequila. The United States' claim to high-proof fame is a smooth, smoky, slightly sweet drink with roots in rural Kentucky.

"We don't have many products that we completely call our own, but we have a rich history with bourbon," says Zane Lamprey, host of the television show *Three Sheets* on the Fine Living network. "It's a taste of America."

In the last 20 years, bourbon distilleries have opened their doors to the touring public. That coincides with renewed interest in bourbon, which has buffed its image with new single-batch and ultra-premium products.

At most distilleries, visitors see granaries where corn, wheat, barley, and rye are stored. (By an act of Congress, bourbon has to be at least 51 percent corn liquor.) They also visit mash tanks where the grains are mixed with Kentucky limestone filtered water. When the fermented mixture is ready several days later, it's a clear liquid called "white dog," which is poured into white-oak barrels, with the insides charred, and left to age inside warehouses for a half dozen years or more. All this fills the air with wonderful smells of toasted bread, yeasty beer, and a rich vanilla-honey scent.

You can get a good taste for the spirit by basing in historic **Bardstown,** which calls itself the "bourbon capital of the world," and is about an hour south of Louisville.

A great place to start your bourbon pilgrimage is **Heaven Hill Distilleries** (1311 Gilkey Run Rd., 502-337-1000, www.bourbonheritagecenter.com). Its multimillion-dollar Bourbon Heritage Center offers several tours ranging from a quick video and museum run-through to bus tours and a $25 behind-the-scenes tour that lasts 2.5 hours. It includes guided tastings of ultra-premium brands and finishes in the "Taste of Heaven" room that seats 20 and resembles the inside of a giant whiskey barrel.

"This is really Bourbon Tasting 101," says tour guide Lynne Grant. "If you're really nice to me, we'll let people taste William Heavenhill." The 225-bottle limited edition runs $500 a bottle and is sampled by the thimbleful.

KENTUCKY BOURBON TRAIL

The major bourbon distilleries have teamed up to create a Kentucky Bourbon Trail, linking six distilleries in the region. Bourbon fanciers can get a free passport and have it stamped at each site they visit. Fill the book, and send it in for a free T-shirt. *www.kybourbontrail.com.*

- **Buffalo Trace Distillery,** 113 Great Buffalo Trace, Frankfort, KY 40601, 800-654-8471, www.buffalotrace.com. Not officially part of the Bourbon Trail, but offers tours.
- **Four Roses Distillery,** 1224 Bonds Mill Rd., Lawrenceburg, KY 40342, 502-839-3436, www.fourroses.us. Mon.–Sat. 9 a.m.–3 p.m. Tours start on the hour.
- **Heaven Hill Distilleries,** 1311 Gilkey Run Rd., Bardstown, KY 40004, 502-337-1000, www.bourbonheritagecenter.com. Tues.–Sat. 10 a.m.–5 p.m. & Sun. 12 p.m.–4 p.m. March–Dec. The last tour starts one hour before closing.
- **Jim Beam,** 526 Happy Hollow Rd., Clermont, KY 40110, 502-543-9877, www.jimbeam .com. Mon.–Sat. 9 a.m.–4 p.m. & Sun. 1 p.m.–4 p.m.
- **Maker's Mark Distillery,** 3350 Burks Spring Rd., Loretto, KY 40037, 270-865-2099, www.makersmark.com. Mon.–Sat. 10:30 a.m.–3:30 p.m. & Sun. 1:30 p.m.–3:30 p.m. March–Dec.
- **Wild Turkey,** 1525 Tyrone Rd., Lawrenceburg, KY 40342, 502-839-2182, www.wildtur keybourbon.com. Mon.–Sat. 9 a.m.–2:30 p.m. No tastings.
- **Woodford Reserve,** 7855 McCracken Pike, Versailles, KY 40383, 859-879-1812, www .woodfordreserve.com. Tours run $5 and include a shot glass.

Also popular is Heaven Hill Distilleries' $3 **Spirit of Bourbon bus tour,** which visits Bardstown sites like the houses of Distillers' Row, William Heavenhill's original limestone spring, and Jim Beam's home. You'll hear about the antics of moonshiners, like the one who was chased by agents into a church. But when they caught him, his moonshine had disappeared. Only later did someone discover where he had hidden it: the baptismal fount.

Also in Bardstown, the **Oscar Getz Museum of Whiskey History** (114 N. 5th St., 502-348-2999, www.whiskeymuseum.com) features old stills, vintage bourbon bottles, and artifacts from pre-colonial days to the present. You'll learn about medicinal whiskey, the only thing distilleries were legally able to make during Prohibition.

Bardstown has a range of chain and small motels. If you're interested in bunking down in a place with a more interesting backstory, check out the **Jailer's Inn Bed and Breakfast Inn** (111 W. Stephen Foster Ave., 800-948-5551, www.jailersinn.com), where you'll pay from $80 a night to sleep in a former poky. [$PLURGE: For a splurge, dine aboard the 1940s vintage dining cars of **My Old Kentucky Dinner Train** (602 N. 3rd St., 866-801-3463 or 502-348-7300, www.rjcor man.com) while it makes a two-hour excursion through the Kentucky countryside; the meals run $74.95 for dinner, and $15 less for lunch.]

LOUISVILLE'S URBAN BOURBON TRAIL

Kentucky's largest city has a concentration of restaurants and bars devoted to bourbon. Its new Urban Bourbon Trail highlights nine bars and restaurants that have more than 50 different labels available to taste, and trained staff to help visitors detect the different notes and flavors. You can even sample bourbon-flavored cuisine from chocolate truffles to grilled shrimp.

One spot, the **Old Seelbach Bar** (500 S. 4th St., 502-585-3200) is a cozy retreat in a hotel F. Scott Fitzgerald mentioned in *The Great Gatsby,* while **Maker's Mark Bourbon House & Lounge** (446 S. 4th St., 502-568-9009) has more than 60 bourbons on offer. If you visit all nine stops and get a passport stamped, you can send it in for a free T-shirt. But don't try to do it all in one day! *www.justaddbourbon.com.*

Outside Bardstown are several must-visit sites. The first is a cooperage. The spirit wouldn't be possible without oak barrels; in fact, it would just be moonshine. **Kentucky Cooperage** (712 E. Main St., 270-692-4674, www.independentstavecompany.com) makes up to 1,800 barrels a day in Lebanon. Visitors watch the barrels constructed and see the charring process that gives bourbon its dark color and rich flavor. Tours are offered Monday through Friday from 9:30 a.m. to 1 p.m. and last about 45 minutes.

Finally, **Maker's Mark** (3350 Burks Spring Rd., 270-865-2099, www.makersmark.com) in Loretto should be on every bourbon tourist's list. It's on the National Register of Historic Places and is the oldest Kentucky distillery site still in use, dating from 1805, although the Samuels family—distillers since the late 1700s—didn't purchase it until 1953. It's a pretty sight, with black wooden distillery buildings with red shutters scattered around manicured grounds. A highlight is dipping your own souvenir bottle in red sealing wax, which costs $18.95 for a pint. [$PLURGE: **For a splurge, you could pick up a liter for $44.95, which has a private label and is signed by distillery president Bill Samuels, Jr., and his son Rob.**]

HOW TO GET IN TOUCH

Bardstown–Nelson County Tourist & Convention Commission, 1 Court Sq., Bardstown, KY 40004, 800-638-4877, www.visitbardstown.com.

shop the world's longest yard sale

MICHIGAN TO ALABAMA

Three dollars and it only transports matter?!

—CARTOON CHARACTER HOMER SIMPSON, SHOPPING AT A YARD SALE

26 Imagine if the offerings of eBay were spread out over hundreds of miles of highway. You could drive all day, stopping to examine antique four-poster beds and vintage vinyl record albums. How about a two-headed stuffed squirrel, a manhole cover, or a practically new socket wrench set? The possibilities are endless, and without a doubt, you'd discover something you just have to take home.

Once a year this extravagant display of commerce is offered for your shopping and gawking pleasure along 654 miles (and growing) of highway from Michigan to Alabama. The 127 Corridor Sale, as it's called, brings tens of thousands of visitors to tiny places like Russell Springs, Kentucky. From the first Thursday in August through Sunday, little towns and county seats have bumper-to-bumper traffic, but no one seems to mind.

"It's like an Easter egg hunt," says Jami Nathan, who has helped organize the sale in West Unity, Ohio. "People go and look for little things that you can't get in a store: antique post cards, buttons, first edition books that sellers don't know they have. The hidden treasure."

Like so many success stories, the sale began as a dream and a crazy idea. Mike Walker, a Tennessee county official, was searching for a way to lure visitors off the interstates and into his home

SHOPPING TIPS FOR THE ULTIMATE YARD SALE

- Haggle. Any marked price is just a suggestion. Try offering half, and see what happens. Be ready to walk away.
- If you really like something, buy it. You'll probably never see the same thing again. And you're unlikely to turn around and drive dozens of miles back to buy it.
- Be prepared to haul things home. Many shoppers rent U-Hauls or come with trucks and vans filled with packing materials.
- Consider becoming a seller. Some of the merchandise you'll see was purchased during a previous sale. That box of antique tools you found for $1. What if you clean it up and try to sell it for $25? It happens all the time.

of Jamestown. Just about every place has a festival, he knew. That wouldn't get much attention. But how about an outdoor sale? (To this day, Walker thinks "yard sale" sounds too common.) He got a few towns in Tennessee and Kentucky to participate and wrangled a small grant from each state to help publicize the effort. And like that baseball field in Iowa, he learned that if you build it, they will come.

"The first year I had people counting the types of cars coming through. We had 40 something states and Canada represented. It was amazing," he says, before admitting the obvious. "I probably misjudged how many people enjoy outdoor sales."

Since then, the sale has grown like kudzu every year, creeping down into Georgia and Alabama, and up across Kentucky and Ohio. It recently reached Michigan, and is marching north. It's just a matter of time before it goes international, making its way into Ontario, Canada.

Todd Burnett, a Tennessee circuit judge, has been selling at the sale for years. He and his father even bought property along Highway 127 and constructed a warehouse to store their merchandise. He says the people are what makes the experience so enjoyable.

Part of the fun is haggling and hearing the story of an antique: how it belonged to someone's great-grandmother and was passed down through the generations. "Sometimes it's true, sometimes it's not," Burnett says with a laugh. But it makes a good story to go along with your purchase.

The challenge for a visitor is how to take in this shopping spectacular. There's no way you can see it all, so don't even try. The whole idea is to browse and talk to the sellers.

Many people build their visits around **Jamestown,** the sale's spiritual home. Lodging here and in most the towns along the sale route is limited, so it makes sense to reserve a room months in advance. If you want to stay in Jamestown, consider the **Wildwood Lodge B&B** (3636 Pickett Park Hwy., 931-879-9454, www.twlakes.net/~wildwoodbed), where rooms begin at $95 during the sale. Some visitors find hotels 25 miles away, and Burnett has even let stranded travelers sleep in his parking lot.

If you set up base in Jamestown, take one day to drive south, perhaps 30 miles out and 30 back. That approach maximizes your gawking opportunities because sellers set up on both sides of the road, and you'll get a chance to take a long look on the west side in the morning and on the east side when you return in the evening. The next day you could head north.

Some people like to build a mini road trip along Highway 127. Experienced shoppers suggest not trying to tackle more than 50 or 75 miles a day, making a reservation at a preselected town up the road. A good place to start might be **West Unity,** Ohio, near the northern end of the sale. There's camping at **Harrison Lake State Park** (26246 Harrison

Lake Rd., Fayette, 419-237-2593, www.dnr.state.oh.us/parks) from $16 a night and cottages from $75, or motels in nearby Montpelier. Similar types of accommodation can be found at many of the towns you'll encounter as you continue moving south until your budget, car storage space, or the sale runs out.

As for where to stop, that's up to you. Many sellers congregate in tent cities, creating mini flea markets, and a chance to maximize your shopping in one place. But between towns, you'll also see lone sellers. They're less likely to be professional dealers, and you might have a better chance at finding bargains.

Dining, you'll soon discover, is almost as much a treat as the shopping. Local vendors spend weeks preparing for the crowd, readying fried apple pies and barbecue dinners. The sale crosses through small Amish and Mennonite communities in Tennessee, so you can pick up delicacies like apple butter, honey, and freshly baked bread. Not only are they tasty but also consider them necessary fuel to power long days of shopping.

HOW TO GET IN TOUCH

Fentress County Chamber of Commerce, 114 Central Ave. W, P.O. Box 1294, Jamestown, TN 38556, 800-327-3945, www.127sale.com.

see where the midshipmen train

ANNAPOLIS, MARYLAND

*It follows that as certain as that night succeeds the day,
that without a decisive naval force we can do nothing definitive,
and with it, everything honorable and glorious.*

—GEN. GEORGE WASHINGTON, IN A LETTER TO THE MARQUIS DE LAFAYETTE (1781)

27 Annapolis is about two things: the sea and American history. Often, they intertwine. Since 1845, the U.S. Naval Academy has trained undergraduate men—and now women—here, and the sight of uniformed midshipmen walking around the 18th-century seaport town is a reminder of the service they give to the country.

The free (and recently renovated) **Naval Academy Museum** (Preble Hall, 410-293-2108, www.usna.edu/museum) traces the naval history through exhibitions, documents, flags, paintings, and ship models. For information about the academy itself, catch a 75-minute tour ($9.50)—arranged conveniently to end right outside the museum (try to go around noon, when the midshipmen stand in formation for uniform inspection before lunch). The tour begins at the **Armel-Leftwich Visitor Center** (52 King George St., 410-293-8687, www.navyonline.com), located at the academy's Gate 1, one block from the Annapolis City Dock. All visitors 16 and over must have a photo ID; only vehicles with handicapped tags are allowed on academy grounds.

Even if you don't take a tour, you'll likely glimpse midshipmen strolling across the bricks—don't call them cobblestones—as you wander the city's historic district, home to more 18th-century brick buildings than any other U.S. city. Stop in at the **1774 Hammond-Harwood House** (19 Maryland Ave., 410-263-4683, www.hammondharwoodhouse.org, guided tours, $6), dubbed the "most beautiful doorway in America," for a glimpse into Georgian life. Check out the **Maryland State House** (100 State Circle, 410-974-3400, www.msa.md.gov/msa/mdstatehouse/html/home.html), the nation's oldest state house in continuous legislative use and the national capitol from November 1783 to August 1784. Free tours are offered daily except Thanksgiving and New Year's Day; closed Christmas.

If you're up for more history and houses, you've got plenty of options, including the **Charles Carroll House** (107 Duke of Gloucester St., 410-269-1737, www.charlescarrollhouse.com, open limited days), which belonged to the only Catholic signer of the Declaration of Independence, and the **William Paca House and Garden** (186 Prince George St., 410-990-4538, www.annapolis.org, $8). But if your feet are worn or you're ready for a break, take to the water.

You can catch an excursion on a schooner, take a kayak tour, or rent an electric boat. For a wallet-friendly alternative, take a **water taxi** (410-263-0033, www.watermarkcruises.com). Rides cost $2–$6, depending on your destination. (One popular route runs from City Dock to Eastport's restaurant row.) [$PLURGE: **If your timing is right and you're up for a splurge, tours to the 1875 Thomas Point Shoal Lighthouse are offered on specific weekend dates for $70; reservations are required. The trips leave from the Annapolis Maritime Museum (723 2nd St., Eastport, 410-295-0104, www.amaritime.org).**] Set in an old oyster packing plant, the museum is worth a visit for its displays about the life of watermen and the seafood industry of years past.

Or you could just watch the boating scene from land. Annapolis is known as the sailing capital of America, and each Wednesday night during summer a hundred-plus sailboats race through the bay; first gun is at 6:05 p.m. (410-263-9270, www.annapolisyc.com). Any day, don't miss the yachtie fave, **Boatyard Bar & Grill** (400 4th St., Eastport, 410-216-6206), hailed by *Sail Magazine* as one of the world's top ten sailing bars. Remarkably, it's family friendly.

More dining recommendations: afternoon tea at the historic **Reynolds Tavern** (7 Church Circle, 410-295-9555) and steamed crabs at either **Cantler's Riverside Inn** (458 Forest Beach Rd., 410-757-1311) or the South River side **Mike's Crab House** (3030 Riva Rd., 410-956-2784) in nearby Riva. And if you venture to **Chick & Ruth's Delly** (165 Main St., 410-269-6737) for breakfast, don't be late: At 8:30 sharp each weekday (9:30 weekends), patrons stand and deliver the Pledge of Allegiance.

Lodging-wise, what you pay will depend on when you visit. Summer weekends are prime time for weekenders from Washington; event weekends at the Naval Academy also mean high prices. Chain lodgings found a few miles outside of town can be a price-savvy option. Bed-and-breakfasts in town start at $125; for information check out www.annapolisbandb.com. The **SpringHill Suites** (189 Admiral Cochrane Dr., 443-321-2500, www.marriott.com) offers rooms from $139. At the style-savvy **Aloft Hotel** (1741 W. Nursery Rd., Linthicum, 410-691-6969, www.alofthotelbwi.com) at BWI Airport, rooms start at $89.

SEE THE CADETS IN ACTION

The U.S. Military Academy at West Point—the Army training ground for Robert E. Lee, Douglas MacArthur, and George S. Patton, among others—may also be visited via guided tours ($11–$13). The academy is located at Highland Falls, New York, about 40 miles north of New York City. Tours must be booked through www.westpointtours.com or 845-938-2638.

HOW TO GET IN TOUCH

Annapolis & Anne Arundel County Conference & Visitors Bureau, 888-302-2852, www.visitannapolis.org.

eat pie

UPPER MIDWEST

Vegetables are a must on a diet.
I suggest carrot cake, zucchini bread, and pumpkin pie.

—JIM DAVIS, "GARFIELD" CARTOONIST

28 Whether sweet or tart, flaky or crusty, pie is an American tradition. Apple pie, sure. But how about huckleberry or banana cream? It's hard to go wrong with choices like these.

So why not build a vacation around pie? Think of it as a cultural field trip. A tasty journey through the heartland. Because truth is that despite the abundance of celebrity chefs on both coasts, you've got to head to the upper Midwest for your pie fix. "You find Germans and Scandinavians there," says Minneapolis food writer Carla Waldemar. And, she notes, "they're good bakers."

A word of advice: Order ice cream on the side. You don't want to get up from the table hungry.

Start your pie quest two hours east of Minneapolis in the tiny town of **Osseo,** Wisconsin, where you'll find **Norske Nook** (13804 7th St., 715-597-3069, www.norskenook.com) and an introduction to the dilemma you'll face on this trip. What to order? The obvious choice is sour-cream raisin, a meringue concoction on graham cracker crust that is legendary. But not so fast. This Norwegian outpost has won national pie awards for choices like its double-crust baked strawberry. Then there's "Dutch" (strudel-topped) peach melba, nut-topped pies like pecan stout, and whipped-topped wonders like coconut pineapple dream. All cost $3.29 a slice. Other locations of this shop can be found in Hayward, Rice Lake, and Eau Claire, Wisconsin.

Head 25 miles north to **Eau Claire,** where you can work off a few calories hiking or biking the **Chippewa River State Trail** (715-232-1242, http://dnr.wi.gov/Org/land/parks/specific/chiprivertrail/), a rail line turned park that mostly parallels the Chippewa River and is now part of a 37-mile hiking system. Use of the trail is free within the city of Eau Claire; otherwise you'll need to purchase a day pass ($4).

Now head north 180 miles to the Lake Superior coast. You'll be rewarded with stunning scenery and, in **Bayfield,** the **Candy Shoppe** (217 Rittenhouse Ave., 715-779-3668), which uses local berries and

WORLD'S BEST DONUTS

Finally, if you need a little variety in your treats, Grand Marais is home to the **World's Best Donuts** (10 E. Wisconsin St., 218-387-1345, www.worldsbestdonutsmn.com). It's a grand claim perhaps, but they clearly know their doughnuts, which start at 75 cents or $6 for a dozen.

apples to make exceptional pies. Choose wisely because the pies are only sold whole ($11). Also try the wine bread, a pastry with fruit and cheese that resembles coffee cake.

Bayfield is the jumping-off point to visit the **Apostle Islands National Lakeshore** (visitor center, 415 Washington Ave., 715-779-3397, www.nps.gov/apis); all 21 islands are only accessible by private boat/kayak, by ferry (Madeline only), or by excursion boat (Apostle Islands Cruise Service, 715-779-3925). If it's berry season (June–Sept.), you can pick your own to help tide you over for the next leg of the trip. Visit http://bayfield.org/orchards_and_berry_farms_berry_schedule.php for a list of orchards and berry farms. Spend the night in Bayfield at the **Seagull Bay Motel** (325 S. 7th St., 715-779-5558, www.seagullbay.com), which offers lake views and rooms from $75.

Now it's time to head 125 miles west to Minnesota's Highway 61, which could be called the national "pieway." In the town of **Two Harbors,** you'll find pie, and some debate. Betty's Pies has long been a regional favorite, but many local residents swear by upstarts like Rustic Inn Café & Gifts. Try them both and decide for yourself.

Betty's Pies (1633 Hwy. 61, 877-269-7494 or 218-834-3367, www.bettyspies.com) began as a smoked fish shack in the 1950s. It eventually expanded its offerings, and became a local legend. Now it bakes 300 pies a day during the summer, and offers next-day shipping on Internet orders. You can't go wrong with Great Lakes Crunch with apples, blueberries, raspberries, rhubarb, and strawberries. Slices run around $4. For something unique (or horrifying), try the Polar Pie Shake ($6.25), a slice of pie dropped into a blender with ice cream and milk.

Outside of Two Harbors, you'll find about two dozen made-from-scratch choices at the **Rustic Inn Café & Gifts** (2773 Hwy. 61, 218-834-2488). The restaurant is nearly a century old, and it still features log walls, birch floors, and checkered tablecloths. The berry pies are popular, of course, but don't overlook the five-layer chocolate or caramel apple pecan. Slices run around $5.

Take a serving and head over to **Gooseberry Falls State Park** (3206 Hwy. 61, Two Harbors, 218-834-3855, www.dnr.state.mn.us/state_parks/gooseberry_falls) for hiking to the namesake series of falls on the Gooseberry River. If you don't want to camp, try **Superior Shores Resort** (1521 Superior Shores Dr., Two Harbors, 800-242-1988 or 218-834-5671, www.superiorshores.com), with rooms beginning at $79 on weekdays during the summer high season.

For your final destination, head 75 miles north to **Grand Marais.** The name-says-it-all **Pie Place** (2017 W. Hwy. 61, 218-387-1513, http://northshorepieplace.com, closed Mon.) is a ramshackle house known for leisurely service and great pie. For this final stop, choose whatever slice you want. But both the frozen banana split and maple apple cream come highly recommended. Slices run $5.95.

CHAPTER 2

into the wild

Sometimes it seems as if the nation has been covered in asphalt. The landscape, you're convinced, holds nothing more than highways, drive-thrus, and strip malls. When that feeling hits, it's time to head out of town. Because as photographers (and philosophers) have often maintained, when you change your location, you change your perspective, too.

In just a day, you can find yourself marveling at waterfalls, kayaking with dolphins, or zipping through trees. You can gasp at the wonders of nature and geology, and quite literally find yourself alone in the wilderness—a place where deadlines and career highlights don't matter. When you're moving under your own power—by foot, paddle, or with the kick of a flipper—you won't go as far as you would in a minivan or SUV, but you'll see so much more. And when you arrive, you'll know instinctively that life is simpler, yet infinitely more complex, than you ever imagined.

How does this magic happen? There were no committee meetings to design the whale shark, the largest fish on the planet. No flow chart organizes the elaborate ecosystem of a rain forest. And caves were formed without benefit of architects and interior decorators. But as you spend time in and around these wonders of nature, you'll feel connected to the world around you, and part of something much bigger than a towering interstate interchange.

Perhaps you once found yourself in the wilds of South Dakota or some other isolated area, far from the city lights, and looked up to the sky on a moonless night and saw the Milky Way in all its glory, the heavens filled with constellations, novas, and glittering stars beyond counting—even beyond comprehension. The band of light was so dense that it did, really, look milky. That moment filled you with awe—and with a strangely tangible sense of self.

And revelations like that are what these "wild" adventures offer.

hop a ferry to alaska

ALASKA

Never before this had I been embosomed in scenery so hopelessly beyond description.

—NATURALIST JOHN MUIR, ON A VISIT TO ALASKA ABOARD THE STEAMER *DAKOTA* (1879)

29 Alaska's marine highway is a street like no other. It's a place where eagles nest, glaciers calve, and whales breach. The imaginary road is navigated by state-run ferries (called "Blue Canoes"), linking communities along the Inside Passage, and out to the far end of the Aleutian Islands.

The 3,500-mile Alaska Marine Highway System also offers a way for visitors to experience the grandeur of the Last Frontier. However, with a choice of more than 30 routes, a trip takes time and planning. If you bring a car aboard and reserve sleeping rooms, you could easily spend as much on your rustic adventure as you might on a traditional cruise vacation, which includes unlimited meals and entertainment. Each experience has its pluses but is different. The Alaska you see from a cruise ship will be carefully packaged. And shore excursions, which last just a few hours, can cost hundreds of dollars a person.

Taking the Alaska State Ferry as a walk-on passenger, though, makes the trip affordable and allows you to hop on and off the boat and spend time seeing Alaska's rich coastal heritage, both scenic and cultural. Depending on ferry schedules, you may spend a day or two camping by the sea, or staying in a rustic bed-and-breakfast.

Even years later, passenger Wes Lafortune says he can still remember awakening early one morning when the ferry captain alerted the ship to an orca swimming just a few hundred feet away. "It was misty and the whale started breaching straight out of the water," he says. "It was very still and quiet and quite dramatic. It was one of those 'This is why we went on this trip' experiences."

The marine highway is essentially composed of four sections—the Inside Passage, the Cross Gulf Route, Prince William Sound to Kodiak Island, and the Aleutian Chain—with popular routes branching off the main north-south Inside Passage route that parallels Alaska's southeast coast, linking Bellingham, Washington, with Skagway, Alaska. A nonstop trip from Bellingham to Skagway takes 67 hours and costs $363 per adult, with rates cut by about half for passengers under 12. It's an additional $478 for a passenger car, while bicycles and kayaks cost about $60.

The base fare does not include accommodations. Cabins begin at $333 for a two-berth room for the Bellingham to Skagway run. If you'd like to save that money, there are two free options: You can pitch a pup tent on the ferry's back deck, which is heated, or sleep on reclining chairs in

$PLURGE

SEE THE BEARS

With few roads and millions of acres of wilderness, touring doesn't come cheap in Alaska. That said, some experiences are worth the expense.

How about seeing bears in the wild? From Wrangell, many commercial guides offer a six-hour round-trip excursion to the **Anan Creek Wildlife Viewing Site,** 30 miles south of town. A boat brings you deep into the Tongass National Forest to a half-mile boardwalk and protected observatory site where you can spend a few hours watching wild bears jostle each other and fish pink salmon out of a creek. Tours offered by **Alaska Waters** (800-347-4462 or 907-874-2378, www.alaskawaters.com) run $265.

the public area in an impromptu slumber party with fellow passengers, a colorful mix of rugged Alaskans, international travelers, and U.S. vacationers.

If you stay on the main Inside Passage route, the first leg of your adventure—Bellingham to Ketchikan, Alaska—will take 40 hours, providing plenty of time to get acquainted with the ship. Often park rangers are on board to interpret the stunning Inside Passage scenery, easily visible from the ship's solarium. There also may be nature movies shown on board. For meals, you can bring a cooler or purchase meals in the cafeteria, which features Alaska seafood along with burgers and snacks.

Ketchikan, like many coastal Alaska cities, can resemble a theme park when a cruise ship is in port, but as soon as the passengers are gone, the town relaxes and you will too. Take in sites like the **Totem Heritage Center** (601 Deermount St., 907-225-5900). Book a room at **Captain's Quarters B&B** (325 Lund St., 907-225-4912, www.captainsquartersbb.com, from $105 in season), or, to really save, a bed at the **First United Methodist Church hostel** (400 Main St., 907-225-3319, www.ktnumc.com/hostel/index.html) runs $20 in single-sex dormitories. For a memorable meal, **Diaz Café** (335 Stedman St., 907-225-2257) is a city favorite with its Filipino-Alaska seafood dishes.

Make your next ferry stop one of the small communities rarely visited by cruise ships. In Wrangell, for example, you can visit Petroglyph Beach to view ancient rock carvings. Base yourself at the **Stikine Inn** (107 Front St., 888-874-3388 or 907-874-3388), with rooms from about $85.

Now reboard the ferry and head to Juneau. The state capital has an only-in-Alaska urban buzz. Make the 13-mile trip to the **Mendenhall Glacier Visitor Center** (8510 Mendenhall Loop Rd., Juneau, 907-789-0097, www.fs.fed.us/r10/tongass/districts/mendenhall/), where trails let you explore as much as you would

CANADA'S FERRYLAND

British Columbia's extensive ferry system might seem to cover the same ground as that of Alaska, but the two are as different as the United States and Canada.

The bulk of BC's ferry traffic travels a main artery connecting the city of Vancouver to Vancouver Island. Thousands of cars will make the crossing in a day, and if you're trying to go on a holiday weekend, be prepared to wait for hours. But for a more relaxed look at the province, consider driving the Sunshine Coast circle tour, a clockwise sweep through coastal scenery, harborside villages, art studios, restaurants, and inns.

From Vancouver, take the ferry to Nanaimo on Vancouver Island, and head north, meandering along the Island Highway to take in the rugged Pacific Northwest scenery. In **Comox,** you'll connect to an 80-minute ferry ride across the Georgia Strait to **Powell River** on the Sunshine Coast, so named because its weather patterns defy the typical gray Pacific Northwest forecast. You can get a cozy room at the **Herondell B&B** (RR 1, Black Point 29, Powell River, 604-487-9538, www.herondell.com) for just $60 Canadian.

From there, you can slowly work your way southeast on Highway 101 to **Saltery Bay** and then take a 50-minute ferry to **Earls Cove.** Along the way keep alert for purple banners marking local galleries and studios. In **Gibsons,** make sure to stop for fresh-from-the-wharf seafood at **Smitty's Oyster House** (643 School Road Wharf, Lower Gibsons, 604-886-4665). The road runs out at **Langdale,** where you'll catch a 40-minute ferry back to Horseshoe Bay in Vancouver's North Shore. The ferries should run about $175 Canadian for two passengers and a vehicle, but discounts are often available. *BC Ferries, 1112 Fort St., Victoria, BC V8V 4V2, Canada, 888-223-3779 or 250-381-1401, www.bcferries.com.*

like. You can take a bus for $14 round-trip (907-789-5460, www.mightygreattrips.com). For a basic room from $95 in high season, try the **Driftwood Lodge** (435 W. Willoughby Ave., 907-586-2280, www.driftwoodalaska.com). If you just need a bed until you catch the ferry, the **Juneau International Hostel** (614 Harris St., 907-586-9559, www.juneauhostel.net) has single-sex dorm rooms from $10.

Skagway's another fascinating stop. The heart of this former gold-rush town is now designated as **Klondike Gold Rush National Historical Park** (907-983-2921, www.nps.gov/klgo), and you can take free, ranger-led walking tours. From here, you can drive into Canada's Yukon and then back to the States. But if you've gone car free, simply grab a ferry back to Washington State, or hop another ferry for more adventures on the edge of the Last Frontier.

HOW TO GET IN TOUCH

Alaska Marine Highway System, P.O. Box 112505, 6858 Glacier Hwy., Juneau, AK 99811, 800-642-0066, www.dot.state.ak.us/amhs.

kayak with dolphins

BAJA CALIFORNIA

Man has always assumed that he was more intelligent than dolphins because he had achieved so much . . . But conversely, the dolphins had always believed that they were far more intelligent than man . . . for precisely the same reason.

—DOUGLAS ADAMS (1952–2001), AUTHOR OF THE HITCHHIKER'S GUIDE TO THE GALAXY SERIES

30 Traveling in a kayak is like being a water bug. With little effort you skim along the surface, quiet and unassuming, taking in incredible views from the waterline.

That's how you can explore the Sea of Cortés off the coast of the Mexican state of Baja California Sur. For four glorious days you'll paddle through pods of dolphins and pass sunning sea lions. If you're lucky you may encounter whales. You'll spend your nights on a desert island, eating grilled fish and sipping margaritas prepared by guides. If this sounds like a dream trip way out of your budget, don't worry. It runs about $1,000.

The trip, offered by Sea Kayak Adventures, leaves from the historic, seaside town of Loreto. Just off the coast lies Mexico's half-million-acre Loreto Bay National Marine Park, a UNESCO World Heritage site. The reserve is protected from commercial trawlers, which means habitat and food are preserved for sea mammals, including dolphins, thousands and thousands of dolphins.

You're bound to see common dolphins. "A woefully inappropriate name for them," says Nancy Mertz, co-owner of Sea Kayak Adventures. "They should be called the wonderful dolphin, the exceptional dolphin. Yesterday my husband and I went out and saw them. They were leaping and spiraling, and their tails were splashing down. There were babies traveling along."

The basic six-night tour includes four days of camping and kayaking and two nights in a hotel. It runs $995 per adult, plus a $25 park fee, and $20 to rent snorkeling gear and a wet suit.

The kayaking is geared for beginners. Before the group leaves shore, guides make sure everyone is comfortable paddling. The two-person boats weigh about 200

$PLURGE

THAR SHE BLOWS

If you're wild about whales, you'll probably want to try a more elaborate Sea Kayak Adventures expedition. A ten-day Sea of Cortés/Gray Whale combo trip will let you see the behemoths up close. The whales give birth in nearby Magdalena Bay, and it's possible to kayak right up to them. A trip with motorboat support, which means you won't have to carry all your gear, runs $1,895.

pounds and include foam-padded seats and adjustable backrests. Then the adventure starts. The first day's destination is a cactus-studded island just a few miles off-shore, which will serve as a base camp. On the way, the water is usually glassy calm, leaving plenty of time to look out for seabirds, like brown pelicans, gannets, and terns. But soon guests will likely encounter sea creatures. "We've seen so many," says Glen Stickle, a Canadian who has visited Baja nearly a dozen times. "Whales, dolphins, mantas."

Once the tour party makes landfall, it's time to set up camp in a cove rimmed with white-sand beaches. Participants help pitch the tents, but everything's provided, including sleeping pads, sleeping bags, linens, and camp seats. The bathroom is a unique kayak potty, a pit toilet of sorts that sits in a boat discreetly placed away from camp. When the tour group leaves the island, it takes the waste with them. This is camping—the islands are home to scorpions and tarantulas and you're likely to encounter a few during your stay—but, it's hardly roughing it. Cocktails are always served before dinner, which might be Mexican-style fish, chicken mole, or tortilla soup; dessert might be chocolate cake or mango cobbler. All equipment, food, and gear are carried in the kayaks.

GREAT SEA KAYAKING TRIPS

Here are a few more favorite trips in which to see the sea from eye level:

- **Channel Islands, California.** These isolated islands off Santa Barbara and Ventura are sometimes called America's Galápagos. They make for an incredible kayaking adventure. You'll paddle through sea caves and camp in one of the least-visited national parks. Two-day trips cost $290. *Aqua Sports, 111 Verona Ave., Goleta, CA 93117, 800-773-2309 or 805-968-7231, www.islandkayaking.com.*
- **San Juan Islands, Washington.** The rocky, forested San Juans are perfect for a kayaker: They're ringed with coves, and many are separated by just a few miles of paddling. Try a three-day tour from San Juan Island on which you'll camp on uninhabited islands and be sure to see orcas and bald eagles. The trip runs $549. *Outdoor Odysseys, 86 Cedar St., Friday Harbor, WA 98250, 800-647-4621 or 360-378-3533, www.outdoorodysseys.com.*
- **Penobscot Bay, Maine.** You can camp or check into inns as you paddle your way up this beautiful Maine coast. Although the scenery is rugged, you're never far from a lobster pound where you can order an incredible meal at a bargain price. A two-day overnight trip runs about $300. *Maine Kayak, 113 Huddle Rd., New Harbor, ME 04554, 866-624-6352 or 207-948-5194, www.mainekayak.com.*

Over the next couple days, depending on the weather, the tour group may switch between the two principal islands, Isla Danzante and Isla Carmen. When you're not paddling, guides often lead island hikes or snorkeling expeditions, taking in views of the nearly 900 species of fish that live in the park. "You just go in the water, you put your head under, and there are fish," Stickle says. It's not unusual to see octopus, pufferfish, sea stars, sea horses, angelfish, or thick schools of sardines.

Back in camp, you can relive your adventure while flipping through a field guide. Along with everything else, the guides bring along a portable library.

HOW TO GET IN TOUCH

Sea Kayak Adventures, Inc., P.O. Box 3862, Coeur d'Alene, ID 83816, 800-616-1943, www.seakayakadventures.com.

go underground

SEQUOIA & KINGS CANYON NATIONAL PARKS, CALIFORNIA

I looked on, I thought, I reflected, I admired,
in a state of stupefaction not altogether unmingled with fear!

—AUTHOR JULES VERNE, *JOURNEY TO THE CENTER OF THE EARTH* (1864)

31 For the claustrophobic or even vaguely timid, clambering up a rock face and along a narrow ledge tucked beneath the earth with only a headlamp for light can be downright nerve-racking. It can also be exhilarating.

In Sequoia National Park's **Crystal Cave,** a six-hour-plus *Journey to the Center of the Earth*–type wild cave tour leads you through hip-hugging crevices and along crags dozens of feet above needle-sharp stalagmites. Yet the views surrounding Solstice Lake, a glassy 40-foot-deep underground pond surrounded by knobby crystal formations, make the wriggling, clawing, and near hyperventilating moments worth the effort.

The association offers gentle 45-minute tours ($13) suitable for children several times daily; two 90-minute tours are also offered on specified days in summer and cost $20. [$PLURGE: **Crystal Cave's wild cave tour is the most rugged way to see what lies beneath this majestic forest in the California highlands—and at $135, a splurge. The tours are offered only a few times per year and must be booked well in advance through the Sequoia Natural History Association; the minimum age is 16.**] Purchase all cave tour tickets at the Foothills or Lodgepole Visitor Centers in Sequoia National Park.

Sequoia and adjacent Kings Canyon National Parks ($20 per car, pass good for both parks) are located about a four-hour drive east from San Francisco. Even California residents will want to make this a multiday trip in order to drive the majestic Generals Highway through the towering trees and catch a guided ranger walk through the giant redwoods. Allow at least an extra overnight for Kings Canyon's Zumwalt Meadow, flanked by granite domes that naturalist John Muir called "a rival to Yosemite."

The two parks boast a wide selection of campgrounds with sites starting at $12 a night; some are available only in summer. Only **Dorset Creek** and **Lodgepole** accept reservations (877-444-6777, www.recreation.gov); the others are first come, first served.

Lodgingwise, affordable options can be found in Kings Canyon: At the **John Muir Lodge,** winter rates start at $69; at the historic **Grant Grove Cabins,** a collection of rustic cabins and permanent tents, summer rates start at $62 (book both at 866-522-6966, www.sequoia-kingscanyon

.com). Just on the edge of Kings Canyon, located in Sequoia National Forest and accessed via the Generals Highway, **Montecito Lake Resort** (800-843-8677, www.montecitosequoia.com) has rooms starting at $49 in winter, $89 in spring; it offers weeklong summer family camps.

HOW TO GET IN TOUCH

Sequoia and Kings Canyon National Parks, 559-565-3341, www.nps.gov/seki.
Sequoia Natural History Association, 559-565-3759, www.sequoiahistory.org.

$PLURGE

MORE WILD CAVE TOURS

Turns out plenty of people are into the Jules Verne act—so many that such wild cave tours are now offered at multiple locations around the country and book up well in advance.

Wild cave tours generally qualify as a splurge. The price includes experienced guides and equipment unless otherwise noted. Unless you yourself are fully trained, you don't want to do this on your own, and even then, you should take an experienced buddy. Young participants generally must be at least 14 or 16; all participants need to be fit. The following caves have wild cave tours:

- **Carlsbad Caverns National Park, Carlsbad, New Mexico.** Four-hour Spider Cave tour, $20. *Carlsbad Caverns National Park, 877-444-6777, www.nps.gov/cave.*
- **Longhorn Cavern State Park, Burnet, Texas.** 1.5-hour tours, $40; equipment rental an additional $20. *Longhorn Cavern State Park, 830-958-2283, www.longhorncaverns.com.*
- **Mammoth Cave National Park, Mammoth Cave, Kentucky.** Six-hour tour, $48. *Mammoth Cave National Park, 270-758-2180, www.nps.gov/maca.*
- **Organ Cave, Greenbrier County, West Virginia.** A variety of wild cave tours, from two hours to overnight, from $40. Some of the tours are open to children 8 and older. *Organ Cave, 304-645-7600, www.organcave.com.*
- **Rat's Nest Cave, Canmore Caverns, near Calgary, Alberta, Canada.** A variety of four-hour tours, from $110. *Canmore Caverns, 877-317-1178, www.canmorecavetours.com.*

Most of these caverns also offer general tours that are reasonably priced and suitable for children. Some have light shows and scripted spiels; others are led by geologist guides who explain the slow science behind cave formations. All reveal a world so unlike that above ground that they may well be worth a stop—even if you've gone underground before.

track the gray wolf

CENTRAL IDAHO

He who cannot howl, will not find his pack.

—POET LAUREATE CHARLES SIMIC, "AX" (1971)

32 In this era of GPS and Google Earth, it's hard to imagine that some things still remain hidden. Consider *Canis lupus.* The only sure way to find a wolf in the wilderness is to track it, step by step, finding its footprints, measuring its gait, and, most memorably, listening to its haunting howl in the middle of the night.

These skills, once essential to Native American hunters and pioneer explorers, are still taught by Wilderness Awareness. Every summer, this outdoor educator teaches how to track down one of nature's greatest hunters from a base camp in central Idaho.

Wolves were reintroduced in the region in the mid-1990s, a move some still consider controversial. Since then the population has grown from 200 to about 1,000. Limited hunting is now allowed. But the tracking classes are about honoring the predator, not harvesting it.

A weeklong adult tracking program is offered every summer and runs $895, which includes food, instruction, and transportation from the Boise, Idaho, airport. The class camps about 100 miles and three hours north of Boise, west of the Sawtooth Range, and at the south edge of Frank Church River of No Return Wilderness. It's an area of rolling hills of ponderosa pine forest, intermingled with wide, flat open meadows. Perhaps most notable, a number of dirt Forest Service roads weave through the region offering likely spots to find wolf tracks.

Accommodations are glorified car camping and a cook prepares meals. Students help with nightly clean up and must bring a tent and sleeping bag. Daily lessons are determined by the wolves. Every morning, instructors base the day's activities on the animals' likely location, and students self-select into groups. Several people might hike 15 miles to a ridge where tracks suggest wolves may be found. Another group might head out for a few hours to watch a herd of several hundred elk, which serve as a source of food for the pack. Along the way, instructors will stop to note tracks or examine wolf droppings to determine what the carnivores have been eating.

Students are urged to participate, not just listen. Experienced trackers might measure the paw prints, while others examine the setting in an attempt to recreate the wolf's path and activity.

A CENTER FOR WOLVES

Once common throughout much of the United States, the gray wolf now is only found in a handful of the lower 48 states, including Minnesota, where the wolf population is estimated to number 2,000 to 3,000. Established 25 years ago in northern Minnesota, in Ely, the International Wolf Center welcomes visitors to its interpretive center. Live exhibits at this educational resource offer a chance to study the impressive predators.

Special programs allow you to enrich your inner wolf. A wolf-tracking experience takes guests off site to locate a radio-collared wolf. Guests learn the basics of tracking and how to use telemetry equipment. And an evening program teaches you how to howl like a wolf, and then takes you to the woods to call out to a pack. Admission: $8.50; programs cost an additional $8.50. *International Wolf Center, 1396 Hwy. 169, Ely, MN 55731, 218-365-4695, www.wolf.org.*

"We want to put together this whole story of how wolves are moving," says Emily Gibson, the adult program director and lead instructor. "What's the energy? Is it just walking along and biding its time, or is it running or chasing something?" Over the course of a week, students enter the wolves' world. "It's amazing to me to see the transformation that happens to people, the way their eyes light up and the way they're more connected to the natural world, and to themselves."

Although there are no guarantees, groups usually see wildlife, including elk, bears, moose, deer, mountain lions, river otters, beavers, foxes, coyotes, and *sometimes* wolves. Student Jackie Aaron, a yoga instructor from Florida, was drawn to the class out of a fascination with wolves, and not tracking. Still, she found the class moved her in unexpected ways. One afternoon, a Native American woman visited the class and suddenly began singing about the animal they were tracking. "When that elder sang that wolf honoring song, I wasn't the only one that had tears in my eyes," Jackie says. "It wasn't a planned thing. It was the epitome of going with the flow in a really healthy way."

Ultimately, the experience adds up to much more than the mechanics of stalking a wild creature. Jackie heard wolves howling on her first and last nights, but she never saw the mysterious creatures. Did she feel cheated? Not at all. "Just because you can't see it, doesn't mean you can't feel its presence palpably. I didn't need someone to tell me that the wolves were around."

Nearly a year later, Jackie says she cherishes the memories. "I saw something in my journal that said I'm really glad I did this for myself," she recalls. "There are some vacations that are restful and there are some that are nourishing for the spirit."

HOW TO GET IN TOUCH

Wilderness Awareness School, P.O. Box 219, PMB 137, Duvall, WA 98019, 425-788-1301, www.wildernessawareness.org.

strap on the snowshoes

NATIONWIDE

The first fall of snow is not only an event, it is a magical event. You go to bed in one kind of a world and wake up in another quite different, and if this is not enchantment then where is it to be found?

—AUTHOR J. B. PRIESTLEY, *APES AND ANGELS: A BOOK OF ESSAYS* (1928)

33 If you can walk, you can snowshoe. Experts confirm it: "It's a little like hiking in the snow, but with big feet," says Sue Leslie, whose octogenarian mother still snowshoes.

All you need is snow and a good pair of lightweight modern snowshoes to enjoy the glory of countryside so freshly powdered that the only footprints you'll see are those left by the squirrels. "You can do it off your back porch," says Andy Brown, a snowshoe enthusiast who lives in Vermont. "You can take the walks you like during the summer, but enjoy them in a way that has been transformed for the winter." And you won't need pricey lift tickets or hours of lessons beforehand.

No snow in your back yard? That's where out-of-the-way and less ritzy snow-sports centers come in. Some have groomed slopes, professional lifts, and lodges; others are less formal, with trails across public lands and simple lifts. Accommodations typically cost far less than at the upscale resorts likely to grace the cover of upscale travel magazines—often in bunkhouses, local motels, and owner-rented cabins. You often can rent snowshoes at local sports shops for $10–$20 per day.

Here are three venues that rate as relative bargains:

Mount Baker, Washington. The Mount Baker Scenic Byway (aka Rte. 542) provides access to many popular snowshoeing trails into **Mount Baker–Snoqualmie National Forest** in the North Cascades. Access to most is free, although a few require a Northwest Forest Pass ($5 per day), sold locally in and around Bellingham. Snowshoe rentals are available for about $20 per day from local ski shops. The **Mount Baker Ranger District** (360-856-5700) and the **Mount Baker Ski Area** (360-734-6771, www.mtbaker.us), a private downhill ski center, can provide information on area snowshoeing. Cabin and chalet rentals abound. The Whatcom County Parks department rents six rustic cabins at **Silver Lake** (360-599-2776, www.co.whatcom.wa.us/parks/silverlake/cabins.jsp) that sleep four to six people and cost $78 to $105 per night (bedding not provided).

Mount Baker–Snoqualmie National Forest, 425-783-6000, www.fs.fed.us/r6/mbs/; **Bellingham Whatcom County Tourism,** 360-671-3990, www.bellingham.org; **Washington State Tourism,** 800-544-1800, www.experiencewa.com.

Taos, New Mexico. The area around Taos is best known for its Native American culture and desert landscapes hauntingly reflected in the works of the late painter Georgia O'Keeffe. But its location in the Sangre de Cristo Mountains in the southernmost Rockies means this is also snow country. For locals and visitors alike, the 1.5 million acres of Carson National Forest offer plenty of free trails and meadows for snowshoeing. The region boasts two upscale resorts: **Taos Ski Valley** (www.skitaos.org) and **Angel Fire** (www.angelfireresort.com). But for more solitude (and cheaper prices), visitors head to **Sipapu Ski and Summer Resort** (800-587-2240, www.sipapunm.com), founded by Sue Leslie's family, 20 miles southeast of Taos. Even in winter, overnight rates start at $24 for a dorm room and $44 for a double cabin; other accommodation types are also available. For something less rustic, try **El Pueblo Lodge** (575-758-8700, www.elpueblolodge.com, rooms from $89) in the historic district of Taos.

Taos County Chamber of Commerce, 575-751-8800, www.taoschamber.com; **Carson National Forest,** 575-758-6200, www.fs.fed.us/r3/carson/; **New Mexico Tourism Department,** 505-827-7400, www.newmexico.org.

White Mountains, New Hampshire. Part of the Appalachian chain, the White Mountains are considered New England's most rugged peaks. A popular hiking destination in the summer, the mountains also attract cold-loving hikers: In winter, snowshoers can sign up for free or low-cost hikes led by naturalists from the **Appalachian Mountain Club** (603-466-2727, www.outdoors.org). Options include a family-friendly two-night lodge-to-hut snowshoe trip from AMC's Highland Lodge to Lonesome Lake ($206, all meals and gear included) to moonlit snowshoe tours (specific dates) offered free to guests at Joe Dodge Lodge (bunk space from $62 per night per person; specials offered) at Pinkham Notch. Guests can bring their own snowshoes or rent them and arrange self-guided snowshoe hikes through AMC's hut system, where sleeping space starts at $35 per night per person.

New Hampshire Division of Travel & Tourism Development, 603-271-2665, www.visitnh.gov; **White Mountains Attractions Association,** 800-346-3687, www.visitwhitemountains.com.

HISTORY OF SNOWSHOEING

Like many sports, tromping around in the snow likely started out as a matter of survival. According to the U.S. Snowshoe Association, the practice of snowshoeing dates back a good 6,000 years or so to Asia. White ash frames laced with rawhide were the norm until the 1970s, when aluminum and other man-made materials became common. By the 1990s, advances such as step-in bindings had transformed snowshoeing into a bona fide sport, involving about three million Americans by 2010, per the Outdoor Industry Association.

chase butterflies

MORELIA, MEXICO

The butterfly counts not months but moments, and has time enough.

—RABINDRANATH TAGORE, INDIAN AUTHOR AND NOBEL LAUREATE (1861–1941)

34 The monarch butterfly is amazing. It weighs just a few grams, but migrates thousands of miles, following a route it has never traveled before—and with incredible reliability. Researchers can predict within a few days when flocks of butterflies will be passing through a specific area. For example, on about September 10, you'll find them in Lawrence, Kansas. The insects travel about 30 miles a day, so several weeks later you can expect to see them in Eagle Pass, Texas.

But to truly appreciate the scope of the migration one must visit the butterflies' winter home near Morelia, Mexico—both the nature reserve and the city have been named UNESCO World Heritage sites. The reserve's five sanctuaries lie in mountains about 75 miles northwest of Mexico City. Every winter, nearly a billion orange-and-black monarchs fill these forests. These insects are four generations removed from the previous year's visitors, yet somehow they know to come here.

Guide Luis Miguel Lopez Alanis says visitors are astounded when they first visit. "Imagine ten butterflies spinning around your head. Now try to imagine 100. Now try to imagine 10,000. Now try to imagine one million. It goes beyond understanding. It's something you've never seen anywhere."

Lopez Alanis, who works for **Mex Mich Guides** (www.mmg.com.mx), leads trips to the area from Morelia, a colonial city of about 750,000, about two hours from the sanctuaries. Daylong group tours to see the monarchs run about $50 and include transportation, lunch, and a guided visit. You can book it directly with tour companies or through hotels or the tourist office.

If you base in Morelia, **Hotel de la Soledad** (Ignacio Zaragoza 90, Col. Centro, fax 877-315-8785, www.hoteldelasoledad.com, rooms from $80) is a pretty choice built around a tranquil interior garden. Some visitors opt to stay closer to the sanctuaries in small mountain towns, but English is not widely spoken there. The town of **Zitácuaro** is home to the **Villa Monarca Inn** (Carretara Toluca-Morelia km 103.5, 52-715-153-5346, www.villamonarca.com), which runs about $80 a night; or for clean, basic accommodations, try the **Rosales del Valle Hotel** (Ave. Revolución Sur, 52-715-153-1293, www.allmexicohotels.com/michoacan/zitacuaro) for about $30 per night. For dinner, **Rancho San Cayetano**'s dining room (Carretera a Huetamo km. 2.3, 52-715-153-1926, www.ranchosancayetano.com) is recommended, but inexpensive options abound in the city center, too.

If you're not on a tour, you can hire a licensed guide in Zitácuaro or at the sanctuaries. From Zitácuaro, it's less than an hour's drive on maintained, well-marked gravel roads to the two most popular sanctuaries, Rosario and Sierra Chincua. At the **Rosario sanctuary,** visitors find stands at the entrance selling tasty quesadillas. Then they may face a walk of about ten minutes, or more than an hour up and down mountains that top out at 10,000 feet—the otherwise predictable butterflies vary their locale based on weather conditions. The trail, which has wooden steps at steep areas, leads past fir, oak, and pine trees. At **Sierra Chincua sanctuary,** it's possible to rent a horse to ride part of the way in. Remember, though, there will still be some walking, and you'll have to hire another horse if you want to ride out.

If the trip in is long, there may be some grumbling, guide Lopez Alanis says. But on the return, everyone is silent, overwhelmed by the experience. No two visits are alike. On windy or cool days the butterflies cling to trees and might look just like browning leaves. But on warm sunny days, the sky explodes with color and activity. "It's very, very variable," says Lopez Alanis. "If you visit the monarchs ten times, each time you will see them in a different mood."

HOW TO GET IN TOUCH

Michoacán tourism office in Morelia (Secretaria Estatal de Turismo), Government Palace, Av. Madero 63, C.P. 58000 Mexico, 52-443-317-7805, e-mail: sectur@michoacan.gob.mx, www.turismomichoacan.gob.mx.

BUTTERFLIES U.S.A.

The monarchs wintering in Mexico come from throughout the United States, east of the Rockies, and as far north as Canada. It's possible to catch them on their epic road trip south at festivals throughout the country. Perhaps the most impressive is in Lawrence, home to the University of Kansas and Monarch Watch (1200 Sunnyside Ave., 888-824-4464 or 785-864-4441, www.monarchwatch.org), an international research group. On the second Saturday in September, the organization invites the public to help intercept monarchs and tag them with fingernail-size coded labels that help researchers learn more about their habits.

"We put them through butterfly school and teach how to catch them," says Chip Taylor, director of the group. "They come back hours later with smiles on their face because they've had a good time swinging a net."

In recent years, the event has attracted more than 500 people, and tagged more than 3,000 butterflies. If the outing coincides with a Kansas football game, visitors might have trouble getting a room, but Taylor can guarantee there will be butterflies. "I can predict it to within two or three days anywhere on the continent. There's a pattern here, and the pattern is very, very predictable."

For lodging consider the **Eldridge Hotel** (701 Massachusetts St., 800-527-0909, www.eldridgehotel.com), a campus classic with rooms starting at about $95 a night.

pitch a tent by the sea

NATIONWIDE

The sea does not reward those who are too anxious, too greedy, or too impatient. One should lie empty, open, choiceless as a beach—waiting for a gift from the sea.

—ANNE MORROW LINDBERGH, *GIFT FROM THE SEA* (1955)

35 The sea is one of nature's palliatives, and even if you aren't much of an angler or sailor, simply sitting on the strand listening to the waves kiss the shore is a pleasure in itself. Why not stay overnight?

Beachside campsites dotted across the country and continent offer a budget-friendly way to enjoy the surf. Some are as busy as small cities; others offer quiet coves where you're almost alone. If sleeping on the ground isn't for you, take heart: Some sites have permanent tents and cabins.

Florida Keys. Some of the most beautiful and serene beachside campgrounds in the United States are in the Florida Keys, the string of islands linked to the tip of the Florida peninsula by 127 miles of blacktop called the Overseas Highway. Wading birds, pelicans, crabs, and other seaside creatures thrive in these warm protected waters, popular with kayakers, snorkelers, and anglers. But drive on down the road, and you'll hit the surprisingly sophisticated restaurants of Islamorada or the historic charm and raucous nightlife of Key West, where author Ernest Hemingway both imbibed and wrote.

Two things to know about visiting the Keys: (1) Camping is buggy come summer, when it's definitely time to hit a motel; and (2) the beaches are white and soft, but they also tend to be narrow.

Quiet **Long Key State Park** (mile marker 67.5, 305-664-4815, www.floridastateparks.org/longkey, $5 per car) has campsites tucked beneath Australian pines, sea grapes, and palms along the narrow sand; each offers a view of the Atlantic Ocean. Sixty of the sites can be reserved up to 11 months in advance (800-326-3521, www.reserveamerica.com); each has a picnic table, ground grill, water, and electricity, with easy access to shared restroom and shower facilities. Another six sites offer primitive camping and are offered on a first-come, first-served basis. The cost per site is $36.

If you're looking for a bit of activity with your nature, **Bahia Honda State Park** (mile marker 36.8, 305-872-2353, www.floridastateparks.org/bahiahonda, $8 per car) offers a boat ramp, rentals of kayaks and snorkeling gear, and boat trips to the nearby coral reef for snorkeling excursions.

MORE CAMPGROUNDS BY THE SEA

Here are a few campgrounds worth noting:

- **Boston Harbor Islands State Park, Massachusetts.** Less than an hour's ferry ride ($14) from downtown Boston, this state park, tucked with a national recreation area by the same name, offers kayaking, swimming, and nature walks; several of the islands offer rustic camping, usually late May through October, starting at $10 per night. *Boston Harbor Islands State Park, 781-740-1605 ext. 205, www.mass.gov/dcr/parks/metroboston/harbor.htm.*
- **Carolina Beach State Park, North Carolina.** Near the town of Carolina Beach, and home to the Venus flytrap and other exotic plant species, this park offers views of the Cape Fear River, with a short walk to the Atlantic Ocean. Campsites cost $20 per day (no electricity or hookups). *Carolina Beach State Park, 910-458-8206, www.ncparks.gov/Visit/parks/cabe/main.php.*
- **Costanoa, California.** Located an hour south of San Francisco, this eco-adventure resort overlooks the rugged seaside bluffs of California's Highway 1 adjacent to four state parks. While the cabins, lodge, and tented bungalows tend to be pricey, starting at $89, guests can bring their own tents and stay in the KOA campground (650-879-7302, www.koa.com). Bare tent sites from $22.50; sites with electricity also available. *Costanoa, 877-262-7848, www.costanoa.com.*
- **Edisto Beach State Park, South Carolina.** An hour from Charleston, Edisto Beach State Park (one of the settings used in the book and film *Prince of Tides*) features an oceanfront campground on a beach famed for its shells and palmetto trees. Entry to the 1,200-acre park costs $4 for adults; campsites cost $17–$26, depending on facilities; some cabins are also available. *Edisto Beach State Park, 843-869-2756, www.southcarolinaparks.com.*
- **Grayland Beach State Park, Washington.** Thanks to a Pacific beach stretching almost 1.5 miles long, this 412-acre park in southern Washington south of Aberdeen is a hit with kite flyers, saltwater anglers and crabbers, and bird-watchers. Along with primitive sites ($14) and those with hookups ($28), the park offers 16 yurts that sleep five (from $60). *Grayland Beach State Park, 888-226-7688, www.parks.wa.gov.*
- **Mossy's Alaska Seaside Farm, Alaska.** In Homer, Alaska, this location offers cabins (from $55), hostel bunks (from $20), and tent sites (from $10) on a working organic farm with views over Kachemak Bay. *Mossy's Alaska Seaside Farm, 907-235-7850, www.xyz.net/~seaside.*
- **Wild Duck Campground, Maine.** Thanks to its meandering coast, Maine is home to many appealing campgrounds with water views. The Wild Duck Campground in Scarborough, south of Portland, sits on 3,000 acres overlooking a salt marsh. No children are allowed; campsites from $27. *Wild Duck Campground, 207-883-4432, www.wildduckcampground.com.*

The park sits in view of the original railway trestle that brought people to the Florida Keys in the early 1900s, a popular draw today. RV and tent sites cost $36 per night; cabin rentals are offered for $120 in summer, $160 in winter. You can reserve sites 11 months in advance (800-326-3521, www.reserveamerica.com).

Florida Keys Tourism, 800-352-5397, www.fla-keys.com.

St. John, U.S. Virgin Islands. Thanks to philanthropist Laurance Rockefeller, 7,000 acres of the Caribbean island of St. John is a U.S. national park (340-776-6201, www.nps.gov/viis), complete with campsites and permanent tent camps. Reached only by a ferry from St. Thomas or Tortola or by private boat, St. John is one of the trio of U.S. Virgin Islands, a laid-back island of forests, curvy beaches and snorkeling easily reached from shore. Still, the capital Cruz Bay is home to chic shops and restaurants–a beacon for day-trippers and an antidote for city dwellers in need of a shot of retail therapy. From the St. John ferry landing in the cozy town of Cruz Bay, inexpensive open-air group taxis run frequently to the park's beaches and wooded hiking trails.

One of the least expensive camping options is at **Cinnamon Bay** (800-539-9998, www.cinnamonbay.com), which features permanent tents, cottages, and bare campsites–many just feet from the beach. All use shared bathhouses–and all book up quickly. Bare sites are priced from $30, tents from $65, cottages from $77.

Maho Bay Camps (800-392-9004, www.maho.org) runs two eco-camping resorts set against white-sand beaches. The well-known **Maho Bay** has 114 permanent tented huts nestled among the trees; all have cooking facilities and guests use shared bathhouses. The camp is a 30-minute ride from Cruz Bay, so a car is handy, but the resort offers enough activities and facilities that, on a short trip, you can do without. It books up well in advance; prices start at $80 for a double. Maho Bay's second resort, **Estate Concordia Preserve,** is a bit farther from town yet, and without a car you may feel cut off. Permanent eco-tents from $105.

U.S. Virgin Islands Travel and Tourism, 800-732-8784 or 305-442-7200, www.usvitourism.vi.

search for the kirtland's warbler

NORTHERN MICHIGAN

A bird doesn't sing because it has an answer,
it sings because it has a song.

—LOU HOLTZ (B. 1937), COLLEGE FOOTBALL COACH AND COMMENTATOR

36 The world's rarest warbler is a picky customer. It nests on the ground, but only in forests of jack pines, and the trees must be between 5 and 15 years old. Only a few places meet these exacting requirements, most notably sparsely populated northern Michigan.

By all accounts, the Kirtland's warbler, a half-ounce, yellow-breasted songbird, should be extinct. In the 1970s just a few hundred pairs existed. Now the number has reached more than 1,800. And a few pairs have started showing up in Wisconsin and southern Ontario.

"It's a great comeback story," says Jim Enger, chairman of the Kirtland's Warbler Wildlife Festival, which is held every May in Roscommon, Michigan, the center of warblerdom. "There's only going to be one place that you can see this bird. You've got to come to a few counties in northern Michigan. That's it."

Named for the Ohio doctor who discovered the species, the bird is a looker. The male has a bright yellow breast with a few black spots on each side and a gray-blue back. The female isn't quite as flashy, but both sexes have striking white open rings around the eyes. The birds began to die off when settlers came to the Midwest and cleared forests, destroying much of the bird's habitat. Then when humans started to suppress forest fires, the warbler's fate became even more precarious since jack pine cones release seeds after the heat of fire.

But in the mid-1980s, state and federal officials thought the bird could be saved and forged a plan to systematically create the proper habitat. They set aside more than 150,000 acres of national forest to be used for Kirtland's warbler habitat. The Huron-Manistee National Forest and surrounding lands are managed so that at a minimum, 50,000 acres of jack pine are left in conditions perfect for the bird.

In addition, the warbler has to contend with the sneaky cowbird, which moved into the region when fields were cleared. The parasitic bird lays its eggs in warbler nests, leaving unaware foster parent warblers to raise the interlopers' young instead of their own. Scientists have battled this problem by trapping cowbirds in the warbler habitat.

All this effort makes the warblers' renaissance something to celebrate. The one-day, annual Kirtland's Warbler Wildlife Festival (989-275-5000, http://warbler.kirtland.edu) costs $5; attracts about 2,000 visitors; and includes tours, presentations, and demonstrations.

Even if you miss the festivities, a couple different tours are available during nesting season, mid-May through early July. The U.S. Fish and Wildlife Service and the Michigan Audubon Society conduct free trips to the habitat every day at 7 and 11 a.m. from mid-May through July 4; the tours leave from the Ramada Inn in Grayling (2650 I-75S Business Loop, Grayling); see www.fws.gov/midwest/eastlansing/tour.html for more information. The U.S. Forest Service also offers daily tours from May 15 through July 2 at 7 a.m. They cost $10 and leave from the **Mio Ranger District office** (401 Court St., Mio, 989-826-3252, www.fs.fed.us/r9/hmnf/pages/warbindex.htm). Both tours may require you to convoy in your own vehicle to the nesting area.

Guests usually see the tiny bird, and almost inevitably they'll hear it. "When males arrive in early May, they sit atop old dead trees and sing like crazy," says Enger. The song can be heard up to a half mile away. Not bad for a little guy that weighs just a few grams.

There's also a self-guided auto tour starting outside Mio covering more than 40 miles of largely dirt roads through bird habitat, taking in areas that are home to ospreys, eagles, loons, and songbirds. "If you're a birder you can easily spend half a day," says Enger. Information is available from the Mio Ranger District.

Visitors should stop by **Hartwick Pines State Park** (4216 Ranger Rd., Grayling, 989-348-7068, www.michigan.gov/hartwickpines), which has a stand of the state's oldest and tallest red and white pines. The forest is home to a dozen warbler species, which the park's nature center can help you identify. The area is also laced with rivers that are perfect for canoeing, kayaking, and tubing.

Rent canoes and arrange for shuttle services along the Au Sable River from **Hinchman Acres Resort** (702 N. Morenci, Mio, 989-826-3267, www.hinchman.com) or **Rainbow Resort Cabins & Canoes** (731 Camp Ten Rd., Mio, 989-826-3423, www.rainbowresortmio.com). Both also have cabins for rent from as low as $50 per night. At mealtime, try **O'Brien's Dinner Table Restaurant** (320 S. Morenci St., Mio, 989-826-5547) for

SAVING THE CRANE

Tiny warblers aren't the only birds facing challenges. The majestic crane struggles for survival in many areas. The International Crane Foundation in Baraboo, Wisconsin, supports research and conservation efforts to preserve the wetlands and grasslands worldwide that support them. It also offers guided tours—the foundation says it's the only place in the world to see all 15 species of crane, including the rare whooping crane. A visit lasts about two hours and costs $9.50. *International Crane Foundation, 11376 Shady Lane Rd., Baraboo, WI 53913, 608-356-9462, www.savingcranes.org.*

steak and seafood and wonderful homemade breads. Or for something different, head to Roscommon, where **Fred's** (422/430 N. 5th St., 989-275-6565), an eight-lane bowling alley with a restaurant, is a local favorite.

And as you roam the area, take time to consider all the work that has been done on behalf of the warbler. Retired wildlife biologist Jerry Weinrich spent 31 years working in the region with the Michigan Department of Natural Resources; he says some people question whether it's worth the effort to keep a tiny bird alive. He doesn't hesitate with his answer.

"It's a matter of responsibility," Weinrich says. "It was the European influence that got the bird into problems to begin with, and there are things we can do to help. We have a chance to right a wrong even if the wrong was unintentional."

HOW TO GET IN TOUCH

Houghton Lake Area Tourism & Convention Bureau, P.O. Box 1, Houghton Lake, MI 48629, 800-676-5330 or 989-366-8474, www.visithoughtonlake.com.

Roscommon County, www.roscommoncounty.net.

catch a moonbow

CUMBERLAND FALLS STATE RESORT PARK, KENTUCKY

It's something that's not easy to see. You have to be at a certain location at a certain time. And it's not man-made, it's part of the natural world. I would call it mystical.

—STEVE GILBERT, PARK NATURALIST, CUMBERLAND FALLS STATE RESORT PARK

37 There are two places in the world where you can consistently see a rainbow formed by the mist of a waterfall and the light of the full moon. One's in the wilds of Africa. The other's in the hills of Appalachia.

Kentucky's Cumberland Falls might not match the majesty of Zimbabwe's Victoria Falls (the other site), but its moonbow captivates visitors every month. The phenomenon occurs on the five nights centered on the full moon. If the sky's clear, the bow will emerge when the moon is at a 42-degree angle in the sky. Don't worry about calculating the geometry. The park's website lists the dates and times. If the scheduled appearance is over a holiday weekend, thousands of visitors may congregate at the falls for the event; at other times of year, it may just be a hundred or so.

Despite the popularity, you can expect a mellow, family-friendly crowd. People bring lawn chairs and photographers set up tripods trying to capture the remarkable image. "There's an air of

FINGER-LICKIN' MUSEUM

Before Col. Harland Sanders became an internationally recognized fast-food symbol, he was a struggling café and motel owner in rural Kentucky. His original restaurant and kitchen (where he concocted his legendary combination of 11 herbs and spices) is now a free museum attached to a functioning KFC in Corbin, 18 miles from Cumberland Falls State Resort Park.

Along with pressure-cooked fried chicken, Sanders is also known for franchising. He took his successful recipe to the world, eventually making a fortune. It was at this point that he became the man we all recognize, growing a beard and goatee and wearing a white suit and a string tie. And his Colonel title? It's an honorary rank bestowed by a Kentucky governor. Now he's buried several hours away in Louisville's historic Cave Hill Cemetery.

The restaurant includes a life-size statue of Sanders and KFC memorabilia. Visitors see an original cash register and dining room. Most eventually succumb to temptation and order chicken. It's the same meal you can find anywhere else, but somehow it feels more authentic here. *Harland Sanders Café and Museum, 1002 W. Dixie Hwy., Corbin, KY 40701, 606-528-2163.*

excitement," says park naturalist Steve Gilbert. "People see an arc of light. It's kind of ghostly, and on a good night you'll pick up a bit of color."

The Shawnee and Cherokee Indians considered the bow a sign of the Great Spirit, and that carries through to modern visitors as well. A former park superintendent often called the bow spiritual. The falls itself is inspiring, too, tumbling down more than 60 feet.

But the state park isn't just a one-trick destination. It has loads of low-cost activities for those times when a full moon isn't shining. From Memorial Day through Labor Day, the staff offers a full array of activities, from craft classes where families can make leaf-print and tie-dye shirts for a small fee to free evening square, line, and country dances. An instructor will teach the steps, providing an authentic souvenir of the region's mountain culture.

Seventeen miles of hiking trails lace the park. The most popular, the 2-mile round-trip hike to Eagle Falls, features a smaller waterfall with views out to Cumberland Falls. Accommodations couldn't be simpler. There's camping ($12 per night) and rooms in the Dupont Lodge start at around $90. The park's Riverview Restaurant offers simple country-style meals with a stunning view of the falls. Budget motels and restaurants can be found 18 miles away in the town of Corbin.

Other activities take advantage of the park's location. Park staff often lead a caravan for 15 miles to Natural Arch, the state's largest sandstone arch in **Daniel Boone National Forest** (859-745-3100, www.fs.fed.us/r8/boone). Another perfect day trip is to **Big South Fork National River & Recreation Area** (423-569-9778, www.nps.gov/biso), where a 16-mile rail excursion on the **Big South Fork Scenic Railway** (100 Henderson St., Stearns, 800-462-5664, www.bsfsry.com, $18) leads guests to Blue Heron Coal Mining Camp, a National Park Service outdoor museum created from a restored town. The trip leaves from Stearns, Kentucky, and lasts about 3.5 hours.

HOW TO GET IN TOUCH

Cumberland Falls State Resort Park, 7351 Hwy. 90, Corbin, KY 40701, 606-528-4121, http://parks.ky.gov.

swim with the whale sharks

GLADDEN SPIT MARINE RESERVE, BELIZE

It sounds crazy, I know, but when I swim in the sea I talk to it.
I never feel alone when I'm out there.

—GERTRUDE EDERLE, FIRST WOMAN TO SWIM ACROSS THE ENGLISH CHANNEL (1926)

38 Let's get a couple things straight about the whale shark. Neither whale nor shark, the world's largest fish has somehow escaped public attention. At almost 40 feet long and with a tail fin as tall as a man, these gentle giants don't have menacing teeth or personalities. They eat microscopic plankton and fish eggs, and leave humans alone.

Nearby Belize is one of the best places in the world to see—and swim with—the magnificent creatures. But this adventure is best left to certified scuba divers. Although some companies offer trips to snorkel with whale sharks, the waters are usually too rough to make the trip comfortable.

But if you have diving experience, these animals offer a reason to dust off your PADI card. Researchers know the best time to see the animals is at a deepwater nature preserve called **Gladden Spit** in April, May, and June, in the time period running from two days before the full moon to eight days after. That's when huge schools of snapper release eggs and the whale sharks come to dine by swimming through the cloud.

High school principal Tamara Addis says the experience was a dive of a lifetime. She recalls how she and her dive group dropped into the ocean and then formed a large circle about 60 feet underwater. Beneath her, she could see thousands of silver fish—snapper—and then she spied her first whale shark. "It just emerged beneath me, a 35-foot fish." Eventually there were seven

$PLURGE

DIVING INTO BELIZE

Belize's barrier reef is part of the second longest reef system in the world after Australia's Great Barrier Reef. It's a diver's paradise, and not particularly expensive to explore. To make a vacation of it, consider all-inclusive dive resorts like Off the Wall, which occupies its own 13-acre island about an hour's boat trip from Dangriga. A reasonably priced splurge, a basic eight-day dive vacation, including meals, accommodations, and 12 dives, runs $1,695. A day trip to the whale sharks costs $175 extra. *Off the Wall, P.O. Box 195, Dangriga, Belize, www.offthewallbelize.com.*

AQUARIUM ENCOUNTER

You don't have to head to the Caribbean to swim with the magnificent whale shark. In landlocked Atlanta, the Georgia Aquarium has a program to swim with its animals. And no diving or snorkeling experience is required.

The **Journey with Gentle Giants** package provides a full diving suit and an air supply so guests can stay at the surface of the aquarium's Ocean Voyager exhibit. The daily program begins at 4:40 p.m. and lasts 2.5 hours, although the swim portion only lasts 30 minutes. Participants also get a behind-the-scenes tour of the aquarium, one of the world's largest. All guests must be 12 or older, and those under 18 must be accompanied by an adult; the price starts at $225 per person. *Georgia Aquarium, 225 Baker St. NW, Atlanta, GA 30313, 404-581-4000, www.georgiaaquarium.org.*

swimming around the divers, as curious about the humans as they were about the animals. "They were absolutely beautiful and huge," she said. "It was just like a dream."

Access to Gladden Spit Marine Reserve is by permit and only opened to licensed dive boats. Visits are limited to daylight hours to prevent the whale sharks from being harassed or overwhelmed by visitors. Although the dive is considered advanced, Addis said several in her group had minimal experience and did fine.

Many dive boat operators can be found in nearby Placencia. A day trip with **Seahorse Dive Shop** (800-991-1969, www.belizescuba.com), for example, runs $165 and includes two tanks and all diving equipment.

HOW TO GET IN TOUCH

Placencia Tourism Centre, General Delivery, Placencia Village, Belize, 011-501-523-4045, www.placencia.com.

play easy rider

NATIONWIDE

Freedom is something that dies unless it's used.

—GONZO JOURNALIST HUNTER S. THOMPSON,
IN AN INTERVIEW WITH *SALON.COM* MAGAZINE (2003)

39 Whether you're a fast-is-better disciple of the late author Hunter S. Thompson, a counterculture biker like Peter Fonda in *Easy Rider*, or an aging biking Boomer like *Wild Hogs'* John Travolta and Tim Allen, any way you approach it, motorcycles represent freedom—and the open road.

The appeal is more than just youthful fantasy, says Gary McKechnie, author of the best-selling motorcycle guidebook *Great American Motorcycle Tours.* On a bike, "you grab as much coastline as you can, as many back roads as you can. You don't have a schedule . . . you feel the wind in your face, the sun in your face, you smell the trees and the outdoors as you ride. There's more of a sense of exploration."

It's no wonder that organized motorcycle tours are all the rage. Unfortunately, these organized rides aren't always cheap, sometimes costing thousands per week. But if you've got your own bike, have a friend who does, or can afford about $100 a day to rent one, you can easily craft your own voyage of discovery. Companies with nationwide networks include **Eaglerider** (888-900-9901, www.eaglerider.com); **AdMo-Tours** (760-249-1105, www.rental-motorcycle.com); **Street Eagle** (800-717-7970, www.streeteagle.com); and, of course, **Harley-Davidson** (www.hdrentals.com), which maintains a fleet of rental bikes.

Since 2000, McKechnie has mapped out 25 of his favorite back-road rides in each edition of his book. Asked for three of his current favorites, here's what he recommends:

Magical Michigan Tour. Have five days? Rent a bike in Milwaukee, Wisconsin, take the fast ferry to Muskegon, Michigan, and then drive the magnificent Lake Michigan shoreline to Ludington, Leland, Traverse City, Charlevoix, and then on to Mackinaw City before boomeranging back to the ferry in Muskegon.

In **Charlevoix** (800-367-8557, www.charlevoix.org), look for the whimsical hobbit-style homes and lodgings designed by Earl Young in the early 20th century scattered around town.

BIKER FESTS

Even if you're not into the ride itself, dip into biker culture with a visit to a motorcycle festival. Here are three top biker fests:

- **Bikes, Blues & Barbecue.** A mere youngster compared to the Daytona and Sturgis rallies—it began in 2000—this family-friendly Ozarks event has quickly grown in popularity, attracting hundreds of thousands of participants for five days of music, barbecue, and biking in Fayetteville, Arkansas. Most of the festivities are free; the not-for-profit event raises funds for local charities. *Bikes, Blues & Barbecue, 479-527-9993, www.bikesbluesandbbq.org.*
- **Daytona Bike Week.** For a week each February/March, Daytona Beach, Florida, goes hog wild when some 500,000 bikers—from evangelistic preachers to soused partyers—hit town. The action (food, bands, camaraderie, and general insanity) has been going on since 1937 and spans multiple locations, including Bruce Rossmeyer's Destination Daytona, Daytona International Speedway, and Main Street. *Daytona Bike Week, 386-255-0981, www.officialbikeweek.com.*
- **Sturgis Motorcycle Rally.** Since 1938, bikers—now up to 400,000—have glided through South Dakota's dramatic Black Hills each August and taken over the town of Sturgis (pop. 6,500) for this annual celebration, including a mud rally, organized rides, concerts, and motorcycle stunt presentations. *Sturgis Motorcycle Rally, 605-720-0800, www.sturgismotorcyclerally.com.*

Bed-and-breakfast lodgings, including the historic **Aaron's Windy Hill Guest Lodge** (202 Michigan Ave., 231-547-6100, www.aaronswindyhill.com), start at $85. In **Mackinaw City** (800-666-0160, www.mackinawcity.com) don't miss the 1880s **Fort Mackinac** on **Mackinac Island** (906-847-3328, www.mackinacparks.com, $10.50). For a twist, check out the **Icebreaker Museum** (131 S. Huron Ave., 231-436-9825, www.themackinaw.org, $10) aboard a Coast Guard icebreaker. In the summer **Mackinaw Mill Creek Camping** (9730 U.S. 23, 231-436-5584, www.campmackinaw.com) has campsites from $9 and cabins from $30.

Michigan Travel & Tourism, 888-784-7328, www.michigan.org.

Oregon Coast. For a one-day ride, check out the 160-mile stretch of coastal U.S. 101 from Cannon Beach, northwest of Portland, to Florence, west of Eugene. Thanks to a century-old building moratorium, the views are pristine and plentiful. Don't miss the grilled-cheese sandwich at the **Tillamook County Creamery** (4175 U.S. 101N, 503-815-1300) in the town of Tillamook, and the 38-mile Cape Meares loop ride from Tillamook is well worth the extra time—as is the road ahead that will seduce you with views and gentle curves that improve with every mile. Near Tillamook, camp, rent a cabin, or stay in a yurt at **Cape Lookout State Park** (800-551-6949, reservations 800-452-568, www.oregonstateparks.org); tent sites start at $19 and deluxe cabins are $76.

Tillamook Area Chamber of Commerce, 503-842-7525, www.tillamookchamber.org; **Travel Oregon,** 800-547-7842, www.traveloregon.com.

The Plains. Tour the heartland of America by making a 1,144-mile circuit of the plains of northern Kansas and central Nebraska. Start in Omaha, Nebraska, and within 30 miles of heading south of the city, the urban feel starts to dissipate and rural farmland takes over. Travel through small towns like Pawnee City, Nebraska; and Concordia, Beloit, and Oberlin, Kansas; then swing north back into Nebraska to visit Ogallala, Arthur, Thedford, and Broken Bow. The loneliness of the area adds to the haunting appeal of the prairies.

Concordia (785-243-4290, www.concordiakansaschamber.com) offers a few chain lodgings. **Pawnee City** (www.pawneecity.com) offers several bed-and-breakfasts, including **My Blue Heaven B&B** (1041 5th St., 402-852-3131), which has rooms with shared bath from $40. For campsites, check out the **Nebraska National Forest and Grasslands** (308-533-2257, www.fs.fed.us/r2/nebraska) or the **4-H Camp** (308-533-2224) near Halsey, which also has cabin rentals. The larger town of **Valentine** (800-658-4024) has a range of chain and other lodging options.

Kansas Travel & Tourism, 785-296-2009, www.travelks.com; **Nebraska Travel & Tourism,** 888-444-1867, www.visitnebraska.gov.

ENJOY THE RIDE

Gary McKechnie, author of *Great American Motorcycle Tours,* offers these basic tips:

- Be sure your motorcycle is in top condition before you start.
- Get off the blacktop and onto the back roads.
- Ditch your schedule. To leave plenty of time for unexpected discoveries, limit your ride to a maximum of 200 miles per day.
- Dress for the weather; wearing full leathers in a southern summer swelter is no fun.
- Plan to arrive at your evening destination at least an hour before dark.
- Always wear a helmet, even in states that don't require it. Riding otherwise just isn't worth the risk.

stay on a working ranch

AMES, OKLAHOMA

Ain't nuthin' like ridin' a fine horse in new country.

—AUTHOR LARRY MCMURTRY, *LONESOME DOVE* (1985)

40 Of all America's icons, perhaps the cowboy best captures the public's imagination. Independent and resourceful, a wrangler just requires his horse, a rope, and the wide-open range. It's an image well known from movies, and it continues to exist in small pockets across the West. But for travelers, the cowboy experience can be hard to find. Guest or dude ranches let vacationers play at being cowboys, although often the experience is manufactured–and expensive.

You'll find an exception in Ames, Oklahoma, about 100 miles northwest of Oklahoma City. For five generations, the White family has operated a ranch on a 5,000-acre island in the middle of the Cimarron River. They've been in Oklahoma since the land run of 1889, and settled the ranch in 1893. The place looks so authentic that Levi Strauss & Company, Justin Boots, and other makers of Western products have filmed commercials here.

Visitors are welcome to join the Whites at their Island Guest Ranch from April through October. Guests can ride horses every day if they'd like, but they're also invited to join in ranch chores, such as moving the 350 head of Braford, Brahman cross, and longhorn cattle to new pastures, tending the herd of quarter horses, and repairing fences. They can also practice cowboy skills like team penning and roping in a ranch arena. For recreation there's trap shooting, fishing, and swimming in a pool. Guests get three hearty meals a day. Most of the food comes from local sources–expect rib eye and T-bone steaks, fried chicken, locally grown vegetables, homemade bread, cobblers, and apple pie. Another ranch favorite is cowboy stew, a red beans and rice concoction with plenty of vegetables.

This all-inclusive experience runs just $130 a day for adults, less for children–one-half to one-third the cost of most dude ranch vacations, and discounts are available for weeklong visits. Accommodations are in ten air-conditioned cabins, with private bathrooms and queen-size beds.

"You really get the opportunity to experience a Western lifestyle without sacrificing the comforts of modernity," says Jordy White, one of the newest generation to help manage the ranch.

"We try to give people a picture of the West and Oklahoma and what it's like living and working in an idyllic situation where you can just get on your horse and go."

The ranch is home to a variety of wildlife from deer and coyotes to turkey and armadillos. Guests also often see cranes, roadrunners, quail, and scissortail flycatchers.

Horses are carefully matched with riders based on their skill levels and guests who want to can ride several times a day. It's a learning experience for novices though. "You have to remember you're not riding a box or a bicycle, it's a living breathing animal," Jordy says.

In the evening, guests might take a trolley ride pulled by a team of Belgian draft horses. The Whites often invite over a neighbor who sings songs for square or country dancing, or they might host friends who are Cheyenne and Arapaho Indians who will perform a mini powwow for guests. If you're visiting on a Friday or Saturday night, there are usually community rodeos in the region, and the staff can take you even if it's an hour or two away.

Although cowboys are part of the U.S. national heritage, most people checking in to Island Guest Ranch aren't Americans. The property attracts Europeans looking for an authentic slice of the Old West. Perhaps, we're missing something.

In 2011, the ranch plans to start a cowboy school for urban dwellers (that's the politically correct term for "city slickers") who want an in-depth ranch experience. They'll learn how to train and break in horses, cover the basics of working with cattle, and build fences. "They'll really get an understanding of what a cowboy does on a daily basis," Jordy says.

HOW TO GET IN TOUCH

Island Guest Ranch, Ames, OK 73718, 800-928-4574, www.islandguestranch.com.

$PLURGE

FIVE-STAR RANCHING

Montana's Triple Creek Ranch offers amenities that John Wayne would never have recognized. From a wine cellar to in-cabin massages, the ranch, which is a member of the prestigious Relais & Châteaux group of hotels, knows how to take the edge off roughing it. Cabins include stocked wet bars, nightly turndown service, and fresh-baked cookies and trail mix. Although you could spend days visiting nearby art museums or taking a helicopter tour, TC's still a ranch offering a chance to take part in cattle drives, try your hand at fly-fishing, or just hike out into the surrounding Bitterroot National Forest.

None of this comes cheap, of course. Cabins begin at $650 per couple per night, including three meals a day and some activities, such as on-ranch riding, hiking, and fly-casting lessons. The property is located about 65 miles south of Missoula in western Montana. *Triple Creek Ranch, 5551 W. Fork Rd., Darby, MT 59829, 800-654-2943 or 406-821-4600, www.triplecreekranch.com.*

explore underwater

FATHOM FIVE NATIONAL MARINE PARK, CANADA

The sea, once it casts its spell, holds one in its net of wonder forever.

—OCEAN EXPLORER JACQUES COUSTEAU (1910–1997)

41 Diving is usually a tropical pursuit, but to reach one of the best places for underwater adventures, you must go north, not south.

Canada's Fathom Five National Marine Park, located off the tip of Bruce Peninsula on Lake Huron, is home to 27 shipwrecks. The water here is almost turquoise, and when combined with the area's distinctive white dolomite rock formations, it offers a surprising Mediterranean color scheme in the middle of Canada. Furthermore, the water's crystal clear with viz (that's diver talk for visibility) of up to 100 feet. And because it's fresh water, the wrecks are perfectly preserved, looking like ghost ships under the water.

"They're knock-your-socks-off shipwrecks," says Lynn Graham, owner of **Divers Den** (3 Bay St., Tobermory, 519-596-2363, www.diversden.ca). "They look like they can sail away, even 100 feet down."

The national marine park makes exploration simple. Some areas, like the Tugs Site, can be reached from a boardwalk, and some can even be explored by snorkelers, so it's not always necessary to dive the wrecks to enjoy them. Most of the wrecks are clearly marked with buoys, which provide a place to moor your dive boat and lead lines that will take you right to the wreck. The park's visitor center on the outskirts of the nearby town of Tobermory can provide maps and other information.

Don't expect crowds in town or the water. "You're not diving in a site where there are tour boats on top of each other and a hundred of your new best friends out there diving with you," says Scott Parker, a biologist and dive officer with the park. Diving, he notes, is an easily accessible activity. "Technically, it's not hard. You're sucking air underwater. You can take people who can't climb mountains or run around a squash court and they can do it."

One of the most popular wrecks, the schooner *Sweepstakes,* was transporting coal when it went down in 1885, and it still sits 25 feet below the surface. "The hull is intact, and you can stand on the deck," Parker says. Another one, *Wetmore,* has its boiler intact, and divers easily see the anchor, cribbing, and rudder.

Part of the national marine park's appeal is the well-documented history of the shipwrecks. All scuba divers must register at the visitor center for a $4.90 Canadian daily dive tag (or $19.60 for a year), and they receive a booklet with diving and historical information about each of the wrecks. The visitor center also has an auditorium showing a high-definition orientation video, as well as 7,000 square feet of display space about the area's ecology and aboriginal history. As guests learn, although beautiful on a sunny summer day, the Great Lakes can be treacherous during winter storms. The park area is studded with islands, invisible to captains during thick fogs. Most of the wrecks involved vessels running aground, which occurred during the late 1800s, claiming schooners, steamers, and barges.

Even if you're not a diver, there is a lot to do here. The marine preserve is adjacent to **Bruce Peninsula National Park** (519-596-2233, www.pc.gc.ca), which offers hiking and kayaking opportunities–and swimming for the brave, since the water temperature tops out at just 75°F in August. The Fathom Five visitor center also serves as the visitor center for the Bruce Peninsula National Park. Bruce Peninsula separates Lake Huron from the Georgian Bay, and because most of the peninsula is designated parkland, the shore is largely left in its natural state.

From the town of Tobermory, you can take a two-hour glass-bottomed boat tour of the wreck sites with the **Blue Heron Company** (24 Carlton St., 519-596-2999, www.blueheronco.com, $29 Canadian), or hop the ***Chi-Cheemaun* ferry** (8 Eliza St., 800-265-3163, www.ontarioferries.com, $27.50 Canadian) for a scenic four-hour cruise to Manitoulin Island. It's also fun to wander around the pleasantly nautical town.

For a tiny settlement (pop. 500), the town has a sophisticated diving community, with several dive shops and even a hyperbaric chamber in a local hospital. Most divers and snorkelers wear 7-millimeter wet suits even during the summer. **G+S Watersports** (8 Bay St. S, 519-596-2200, www.gswatersports.net) charges $40 Canadian for a single-tank dive. The dive shop also rents snorkeling gear, including wet suits, for $30 Canadian per day; a half-day snorkeling trip runs $40 Canadian.

Tobermory, which sees more traffic than you'd expect because it's a ferry port, has a variety of lodging options. **Bruce Anchor Motel & Cottage Rentals** (7468 Hwy. 6N, 519-596-2555, www.bruceanchor.com) is one of the best bets. Look for rates under $100 Canadian

$PLURGE

ECO-LODGE ON THE BAY

E'Terra proves eco-friendly doesn't mean giving up luxury. The exclusive six-bedroom resort faces the Georgian Bay and is surrounded by forest. It has a spa, organic restaurant, and dreamy four-poster beds. Better yet, you can leave your guilt about carbon footprints at the door. The lodge has unshakable eco-cred, reusing rainwater, using saltwater filtration in its pool, and proudly touting gold-certification by the Canada Green Building Council Leadership in Energy and Environmental Design (LEED). Two-night stays begin at $760. *E'Terra, Bruce St. (Hwy. 6), Tobermory, ON N0H 2R0, Canada, www.eterra.ca.*

before July and in September, when the weather is still wonderful. Or for camping, Bruce Peninsula National Park has sites from $23.50 Canadian a night. While in town, make sure to try the local whitefish. Housed in a former gas station, **Craigie's** (519-596-2575) in Little Tub Harbor serves fish-and-chips for about $12 a plate. Afterward, walk over to the **Sweet Shop** (18 Bay St., 519-596-2705) for fudge or ice cream.

HOW TO GET IN TOUCH

Fathom Five National Marine Park, P.O. Box 189, Tobermory, ON N0H 2R0, Canada, 519-596-2233, www.pc.gc.ca/amnc-nmca/on/fathomfive/index.aspx.

DIVING THE YUCATÁN'S CENOTES

Mexico's Riviera Maya can be little more than a package tourism experience. But leave the hotel compound, and you can explore the world of cenotes, which are natural wells or springs found in the Yucatán jungle. They're a treat for swimming and diving, and they play a large role in Maya history and mythology. Cenotes vary from highly developed to overgrown swimming holes. And some are full-blown tourist attractions. **Hidden Worlds** (www.hiddenworlds.com) tends that way with zip lines, but the setting is certainly authentic. Snorkeling tours include equipment and begin at $20 for adults. **Gran Cenote** (www.grancenote.com), located near Tulum, also offers cave tours for scuba divers.

go wild in utah

MOAB, UTAH

You can't see anything from a car; you've got to get out of the goddamned contraption and walk, better yet crawl, on hands and knees, over the sandstone and through the thornbush and cactus.

—AUTHOR AND ENVIRONMENTALIST EDWARD ABBEY, *DESERT SOLITAIRE* (1967)

42 The Grand Canyon may snag top billing as the nation's most ruggedly picturesque panorama. But the late environmentalist and author Edward Abbey declared the stony red-rock arches of southeast Utah the "most beautiful place on earth," and once you've been there, you'll find it hard to argue the point.

Tim Gearn, an engineer from a small town in Texas, definitely agrees. "People say to me, why do you want to go to the desert? To me, this is the most beautiful country in the world. I think about it almost every day, I absolutely love this part of the world . . . it is so grand, such a magnificent place. And it seems to be unaffected by man."

The rigors of visiting southeastern Utah have been tempered since great portions of this wind-scoured landscape were declared national parklands—you'll find staggering views even from roadways and gentle hiking paths. But there's good reason why outdoors enthusiasts have dubbed the area around Moab the extreme sports capital of the United States. To fully experience this region's vast sweeps of arches, canyons, pinnacles, needles, mountains, and slickrock—more than 900 square miles of public land—get out of the car and onto the trail, on the back of a horse, atop a mountain bike, or ATV; into a Jeep or raft or rock-climbing gear; or even take to the skies in a hot-air balloon.

Spring and early summer are the best time to visit, as the snow will have melted off the La Sal Mountains—which means reasonably warm camping if you're heading on a horse packing trip, wildflowers in the desert parks, and lusty waters in the Colorado and Green Rivers. April and May also bring the UTV rally and classic car show, stargazing events, bird-watching walks, and an art festival. Though temperatures may leap above 100°F in summer, you'll need to come in late August to catch the **Moab Music Festival** (www.moabmusicfest.org).

The area is home to two national parks—Arches and Canyonlands—plus state parks and national forest. That translates

$PLURGE

GO WITH AN OUTFITTER

Outfitter-arranged trips and activities are more expensive but may be a better value in terms of safety and ease if you're looking for a rugged adventure. There are plenty of outfitters to choose from, offering vacations designed for families, singles, women, and other groups. Recommended outfitters include **Adrift Adventures** (800-874-4483, www.adrift.net), **Canyon Voyages Adventure Co.** (800-733-6007, www.canyonvoyages.com), **Moab Adventure Center** (866-904-1163, www.moabadventurecenter.com), **Navtec Expeditions** (800-833-1278, www.navtec.com), and **Western River Adventures** (866-904-1160, www.westernriver.com). The Moab Area Travel Council (www.discovermoab.com) keeps an up-to-date list of which companies offer which types of trips.

One Adrift Adventures excursion includes an overnight ride into the La Sal Mountains plus a two-night white-water ride through the maze of 500-foot-high walls of Cataract Canyon, and down to Lake Powell. The trip is wild enough for a teen, safe enough for urbanites who aren't put off by the inconveniences of toilet-free camping. The cost for this three-day adventure—$950 per adult, $850 ages 10–17—includes experienced guides, gear, and all meals.

into plenty of free and budget-friendly activities including hiking, kayaking, and ranger-led walks and talks. Equipment including bikes and kayaks are often available for rent at reasonable prices. Outfitters abound if you'd rather leave the planning to the experts. But even if you book a trip with an outfitter, allow time to spend three to four days for wandering around the region on your own.

Moab (pop. 5,100) is growing, but it still has a small town allure. Some affordable in-town lodgings have a chain-like feel—but then, this isn't a place you come to sit in a room watching TV. Recommended options include the newly renovated **Apache Motel** (166 S. 400 East, 800-228-6882, www.moab-utah.com/apachemotel/, rooms from $45), once John Wayne's hotel of choice; and the family-owned and remodeled **Bowen Motel** (169 N. Main St., 435-259-7132, www.bowenmotel.com, rooms from $74). Affordable eats include **Moab Brewery** (686 S. Main St., 435-259-6333) for handcrafted ales plus hearty salads and sandwiches, and **Miguel's Baja Grill** (51 N. Main St., 435-259-6546) for yummy fish tacos and margaritas from scratch.

If you're up for a leg-burning hike, make the 3-mile round-trip trek to the Dali-esque Delicate Arch, in **Arches National Park** (435-719-2299, www.nps.gov/arch, $10 per vehicle) located 5 miles north of Moab; go in the afternoon for spectacular photos. If you're interested in one of the ranger-led tours of the Fiery Furnace ($10), reserve well in advance. Campsites at the Devils Garden Campground cost $20; reserve online at www.recreation.gov or call 877-444-6777.

The Green and Colorado Rivers run through the 530 square miles of **Canyonlands National Park** (435-719-2313, www.nps.gov/cany, $10 per vehicle). No roads link the park's three major sections—the Needles, the Maze, and Island in the Sky—and getting from one to another requires several hours of driving. Closest to Moab (32 miles) and easiest to access is Island in the Sky, where the spectacular overlooks show best in the morning light. Campsites are first come, first served ($10 at Island in the Sky, $15 at the Needles).

Near the entrance to Island in the Sky lies **Dead Horse Point State Park** (435-259-2614, www.stateparks.utah.gov, $10), on a mesa overlooking the Colorado River. If you don't have the energy to enjoy one of its hiking and biking loops, at least pay homage to the setting for Thelma and Louise's final celluloid leap. Campsites cost $20; reserve at 800-322-3770.

If you're overnighting on a horse trip or looking for a mountain experience, head for the **La Sal Division of Manti-La Sal National Forest** (435-259-7155, www.fs.fed.us/r4/mantilasal), acres and acres of lovely woods blanketing the La Sal Mountains some 20 miles south of Moab. Interagency Access passes are accepted. (Tip: A lifetime pass for an American 62 and older is $10 and good at all national forests and parks.)

Experienced mountain bikers should head east of Moab to the **Sand Flats Recreation Area,** where the famous Slickrock Bike Trail offers 9.6 miles of rugged adventure riding. Less rigorous trails, including the 3-mile Circle O Trail and the family-friendly 8-mile Bar M Loop, can be found a couple miles north of the entrance to Arches National Park on U.S. 191.

HOW TO GET IN TOUCH

Moab Area Travel Council, 800-635-6622, www.discovermoab.com.

hunt for it

NATIONWIDE

The sport where you are the search engine.

—SLOGAN FOR *GEOCACHING.COM*

43 When engineers designed the first navigation satellites, they perhaps envisioned the devices helping guide drivers to a shopping mall across town. But you can bet they never imagined geocaching. It's hard to believe even now that more than one million caches lie hidden all over the planet for anyone to find—if you have the GPS coordinates and a lot of patience.

Put simple, geocaching is a high-tech treasure hunt combining the power of the Internet and GPS navigation with the craftiness of a spy attempting to leave a clue out in public without anyone seeing it. "I can't believe this," teenager Mackenzie Sexton said the first time he tried the sport at a state park in Alabama. "It's like discovering a secret society that's been hidden all around us."

All you need to geocache is a GPS unit and a free account at geocaching.com, an Internet gaming portal. Type in a zip code and you'll get a list of caches that fellow players have hidden in the area. Enter the latitude and longitude in your GPS unit and off you go. The caches are often plastic containers or surplus army ammunition boxes that might be hidden in bushes, a hollow tree, or anywhere you can (and often can't) imagine. Once you find the cache, you sign a log and take a small prize or gift, and then leave one in return. Prizes are usually trinkets or a gadget from a dollar store. The thrill is the hunt, not the prize.

Caching is addictive, so it's no surprise cachers want to play on vacation. Cities, states, and parks even have created geocaching trails to attract and guide visitors. Many resorts, too.

"Usually people place caches in locations that are historic or places of interest off the beaten path," says Susan Kelley, former president of the Maryland Geocaching Society.

GEOCACHING LINGO

- **FTF:** "First to Find" a cache. A designation of pride, and quite often very competitive.
- **Muggle:** Someone who doesn't know about geocaching.
- **Multi cache:** A cache with several parts. The first cache you find provides the coordinates for the next one.
- **Puzzle cache:** A cache where the coordinates aren't clear, and can only be determined by solving a puzzle.
- **TFTC:** Short for "Thanks for the cache." Often written on cache logs.
- **Travel bug or travel coin:** An object that travels from cache to cache. It has a tracking number so that its progress can be followed online.

Here are a few ideas for a geocaching vacation:

- **Hotel and resort trails.** Many lodgings have created their own geocache programs. Some charge a fee to borrow a GPS device and get lessons; others include it as free activity. A favorite is **Larsmont Cottages** (596 Larsmont Way, Two Harbors, 866-687-5634, www.larsmontcottages.com) on Lake Superior, north of Duluth, Minnesota. The caches are geared toward young visitors. During the summer, rooms begin at $70 on weekdays and $120 on weekends.
- **Mid-Atlantic trails.** The mid-Atlantic seems to be a leader in geotrails. The **Maryland Municipal League** (www.mdmunicipal.org/programs/geocache.cfm) has the nation's biggest, linking 80 cities and jurisdictions in the state from Ocean City on the Atlantic to mountainous Oakland in the west. The **Allegheny GeoTrail** (www.alleghenygeotrail.com) lists caches across ten counties in northwest Pennsylvania. The **Coal Heritage GeoTrail** (www.paintcreekscenictrail.com/geo.html) includes 16 caches in southern West Virginia.
- **Star-Spangled Geotrail.** This trail, developed with Kelley's help, links more than 30 sites connected to the War of 1812 in Maryland, Virginia, and Washington, D.C. Eager cachers can visit Fort McHenry, Maryland, where Francis Scott Key saw "bombs bursting in air," or journey to Tangier Island, Virginia, which can only be reached by ferry. Cachers, who record their geocaching adventures and comments on the Internet, love the trail. "Wow! What a great day!" wrote wolfmansbrother, who was the ninth person to find the cache on Tangier Island. "Loved every minute of the history and crab cakes!" The cache descriptions all outline each site's role in the war, and were reviewed by National Park Service historians. Each site hosting a cache designed and hid it. One was clever enough to conceal it in a fake cannon ball. But we're not going to tell you where. You can find all the sites listed at http://bit.ly/ax67X6.

Once you've geocached a few times, it's simple to find caches anywhere. The challenge is that not all caches are created equal. Some are unimaginative hides in parking lots, while others take you on hikes to gorgeous overviews.

Check the state or city forums for the area you'll be visiting on geocaching.com. When asked for their favorite places to geocache, several members of the staff at Groundspeak, the company that runs the geocaching portal, suggested Red Rock Canyon, near Las Vegas, Nevada, while others mentioned Portland, Oregon, near where geocaching was invented.

HOW TO GET IN TOUCH

Sign up for a free geocaching account, and find caches, at www.geocaching.com.

pack your paddle

NORTHERN MINNESOTA, SOUTHERN ONTARIO

There is nothing, absolutely nothing,
half so much worth doing as simply messing about in boats.

—AUTHOR KENNETH GRAHAME, *WIND IN THE WILLOWS* (1908)

44 Minnesota's called the Land of 10,000 Lakes for a reason. From the air, its one-million-acre **Boundary Waters Canoe Area Wilderness** looks like a Jackson Pollock painting of countless blue spots. Each lake offers the promise of adventure and solitude. You could explore for decades and never see them all. Best of all, an adventure here at the northern edge of the state doesn't require previous experience other than being able to paddle and set up a campsite. "It doesn't take any real skill," says Sheryl Swenson, owner of Canadian Border Outfitters in Ely, Minnesota.

The experience begins as soon as the boat hits the water. "Once you're out there, it's true wilderness," says James Watters, who spent a week in the area on an outfitter-led tour. They covered about 10 miles a day, averaging about 2 to 3 miles an hour. Perhaps the biggest challenge was learning to portage.

Simply put, perhaps several times a day you'll have to pick up your gear, hold your canoe over your head, and walk to the next lake. Portages are measured by the rod, which is 16.5 feet. Some portages can be as short as five rods, while others might be 350 rods long. Outfitters offer Kevlar canoes, which weigh about 45 pounds for a two-person model. They may cost a few dollars more a day than heavier aluminum craft, but if you're doing much portaging, consider it a wise investment.

Outfitters make this trip accessible. For about $100 per person per day—and often less depending on the time of year, trip length, and the number of children—you can be fully equipped for an adventure. "If you have nothing and you want to come, they can supply everything except your clothes," says Sandy Skrien of Superior National Forest, which includes the Boundary Waters area.

A full setup includes canoe, tent, sleeping bag and pad, chair, and food. Usually the victuals are freeze-dried, but you can arrange for fish fixings for the dinner you can quite easily catch. Watters still remembers the northern pike his group had one night.

Along with providing gear and suggesting routes, outfitters secure required permits to enter the wilderness area. A permit limits groups to four boats and nine people. That way you won't encounter flotillas in the middle of your deserted lake. Certain times of year and routes are more popular, so many visitors book their trips in late winter or early spring. That said, there are usually permits available for less popular midweek departures, which are also discounted by outfitters by

BOUNDARY WATERS OUTFITTERS

Here are a few outfitters that operate in the Boundary Waters. Visit the Superior National Forest website (www.fs.fed.us/r9/forests/superior/bwcaw) for a complete list.

- **Boundary Waters Outfitters,** 629 Kawishiwi Trail, Ely, MN 55731, 800-777-7348 or 218-365-4879, www.boundarywatersoutfitters.com.
- **Canadian Border Outfitters,** 14635 Canadian Border Rd., Ely, MN 55731, 800-247-7530, www.canoetrip.com.
- **Canoe Country Outfitters,** 629 E. Sheridan St., Ely, MN 55731, 800-752-2306 or 218-365-4046, http://canoecountryoutfitters.com.
- **Piragis Northwoods Company,** 105 N. Central Ave., Ely, MN 55731, 800-223-6565, www.piragis.com.
- **River Point Outfitting Co.,** P.O. Box 397, 12007 River Point Rd., Ely, MN 55731, 800-456-5580 or 218-365-6604, www.elyoutfitters.com.

5 to 10 percent. A permit gives you the right to enter the wilderness area at a specific place on a specific day. After that, you're free to explore as you desire.

The Boundary Waters abut the similarly lake-filled **Quetico Provincial Park** (807-597-2735, www.ontarioparks.com) in Ontario, Canada. If you're not a Canadian citizen, you must apply for permission to enter the country before starting your trip, pay $30 for a background check, and have a passport to reenter the United States.

High season in the Boundary Waters region lasts from Memorial Day to Labor Day. June is the buggiest month when you're most likely to encounter tics, black flies, and mosquitoes; bug spray is encouraged. July and August are better, and September can be quite nice, although days are shorter and it's a little cooler.

Trips typically last three, five, seven days, or even longer. The lakes fill depressions left by glaciers and can be quite deep, so a life jacket is a must. The islands are home to boreal forest made up of spruce, fir, and red and white pine trees. On a typical trip, you may encounter a menagerie of wildlife from wolves and moose to elk and beaver, and even black bears. Eagles fly overhead and at night you'll hear the mysterious cry of the loon.

"The mystery and the magic and the sheer beauty of the area puts things in perspective," says outfitter Swenson. "It makes you feel very insignificant, but tied into the world in a different way."

HOW TO GET IN TOUCH

Boundary Waters Canoe Area Wilderness, Superior National Forest, 8901 Grand Ave Pl., Duluth, MN 55808, 218-626-4300, www.fs.usda.gov/superior.

hike in a rain forest, swim in a bioluminescent bay

PUERTO RICO

Perhaps the rebuilding of the body and spirit is the greatest service derivable from our forests, for what worth are material things if we lose the character and quality of people that are the soul of America.

—ARTHUR CARHART, FOREST SERVICE LANDSCAPE ARCHITECT (1919)

45 For Americans, a visit to a tropical rain forest usually requires traveling far afield. But in nearby Puerto Rico, you can hike through a rain forest, splash in a waterfall, and dodge "raining" frogs at **El Yunque National Forest,** all on a reasonable, wallet-friendly budget.

The 28,000-acre forest sits in the volcanic Luquillo Mountains, rising to more than 3,500 feet. Thanks to the altitude, the rain forest maintains an average temperature of 73°F year-round, which means it's rarely steamy, though at the higher elevations often wet or cloudy. Of course, heavy rainfall means you'll see La Coca Falls at its full 85-foot glory. Park trails wind through ferns, red ginger, banana plants, and blooms of hibiscus; some paths are gentle enough for younger children, others are for the hale and hearty.

For those who would like to explore in the company of a guide, one-hour Forest Adventure Tours ($5) are offered several times daily from the national forest's Palo Colorado Interpretive Site. And for those who really don't want to walk, the national forest visitor center at El Portal offers a film for $3 per person. Entry to the forest is free. (Hint: Bring sunscreen, a hat, and bug repellent; this is the tropics!)

The forest is open only during the day; the only way to stay within it is by camping, which requires a free permit. Most visitors opt to stay 25 miles to the west in San Juan and come for the day; many hotels offer tours that include transportation. Lodgings closer to the park cost $100-plus, but a few rustic cabins are available. At the nearby **Phillips Fruit Farm** (787-874-2138

RAINING FROGS

In seemingly a scene from the artsy film *Magnolia,* frogs sometimes drop out of the sky in Puerto Rico. When the humidity gets high, coqui frogs climb high in the forest canopy for relief; however, to escape any predators that lie in wait for them, the frogs often fling themselves through the forest rather than climb down. The tiny frogs are nearly weightless and typically don't get hurt.

or 787-414-9596, www.rainforestfruitfarm.com), the cost is $40. **Glorias' Casa Linda del Este** (787-461-6666, www.elyunque.com/glorias.htm) also offers an apartment for $75 per night. Both are south of the national forest, far from the entrance at El Portal. On the north and closer to the entrance are **Sue's Place** (787-889-1243 or 787-435-1760, www.rainforestrental.com), with a loft apartment starting at $95 per night, and the **Rainforest Inn B&B** (800-672-4992, www.rainforestinn.com) with villas from $145. You can find a wealth of information on other places to stay around the national forest on the Internet at www.elyunque.com.

About 10 miles east of El Yunque lies the town of **Fajardo,** known for its snorkeling and diving. One of its chief attractions is its bioluminescent bay, **Laguna Grande.** Visit on a dark night and run your hand through the water to see your arm light up with glowing plankton, single-celled organisms called dinoflagellates—the underwater equivalent of fireflies. Several local companies offer tours by kayak, including **Kayaking Puerto Rico** (787-435-1665, www.kayakingpuertorico.com), which runs excursions starting at $45 per person.

There's also a bioluminescent bay on the island of **Vieques** east of Puerto Rico's main island. The island can be reached by ferry from Fajardo; the 1.5-hour ride costs $2.25 and goes several times per day, but seats are limited and boats are sometimes canceled. If you go, be sure to stay over a night—or two; **Mosquito Bay** is on the opposite side of the island from the ferry terminal, and since the bio bay tours are only held at night, you won't have a choice. You'll find plenty to enjoy; although once perhaps best known as a former U.S. Navy bombing site, Vieques is now a seductively tranquil place. Grab a book and a beer, and head for the beach. If you're lucky, you might be the only one there.

HOW TO GET IN TOUCH

El Yunque National Forest, 787-888-1880, www.fs.fed.us/r8/Caribbean.

Puerto Rico Tourism, 800-866-7827, www.gotopuertorico.com.

camp at the ymca

NATIONWIDE

It's fun to stay at the Y-M-C-A.

—VILLAGE PEOPLE, "Y.M.C.A." (1978)

46 Remember summer camp? A typical day might include swimming, hiking, and making crafts. Evenings were reserved for campfires and long conversations. You can relive those idyllic days at a YMCA family camp. At several sites, the service organization purposely re-creates the experience for vacationers, with the goal of bringing families closer together.

But at these camps, you don't have to sleep in a bunk with strangers. Instead you'll find basic motel- and lodge-style rooms, or cabins. Activities such as guided hikes and nature programs aim to get visitors to slow down and appreciate the simple things. But don't expect TVs, telephones, or video games. Families spend their evenings playing miniature golf or board games. Or there might be a movie night, campfire, or other evening program. Within hours of arriving, you can feel the stress disappearing.

"I call it heaven on earth for kids, and it's the same thing for adults," says Lynn Ketelsen, long-time visitor to the YMCA of the Rockies, some 65 miles north of Denver. Most camps have a meal plan. Food is basic—think meatloaf, spaghetti, or baked chicken, plus a vegetarian option—but tasty. Others have snack bars and more formal restaurants, too. Consider staying for a while at one of the following YMCAs:

Frost Valley YMCA. This camp in New York's Catskill Mountains has a split personality. During the summer it's a traditional Y camp for children, but from late August through spring, it welcomes families every weekend. Winter visitors can hit 15.5 miles of cross-country ski trails, with free instruction and equipment rental. There's also snowshoeing, ice fishing, and ice-skating. A favorite activity comes every March when guests are welcomed to the Maple Sugar House to learn about (and taste) maple syrup, which is made from the camp's sugar maples. There are many other traditional camp activities, and several special ones like naked-eye astronomy, and yoga and wellness classes. The camps run from Friday night to Sunday afternoon and include accommodations, meals, and programs. Prices can be as low as $100 per person, but are generally $143 in a cabin with bunk beds.

Frost Valley YMCA, 2000 Frost Valley Rd., Claryville, NY 12725, 845-985-2291, www.frostvalley.org.

Silver Bay YMCA of the Adirondacks. For more than a century, this retreat on the western shore of Lake George, New York, has welcomed families with a full offering of camp activities, from archery to boating to tennis lessons. There are also beach games, a Slip 'n' Slide, campfires, and evening movies. For additional fees, you can take watercolor or craft classes. Rates begin at about $100 per person per night for food and basic accommodations, with prices lower during spring and fall. Guests must also pay for membership, which runs about $55 a day for families, with discounts for longer stays.

Silver Bay YMCA of the Adirondacks, 87 Silver Bay Rd., Silver Bay, NY 12874, 518-543-8833, www.silverbay.org.

YMCA of the Ozarks. This camp is set on a mountain lake, about 75 miles south of St. Louis. Along with traditional camp activities like archery, riflery, swimming, and bicycling, there's lake swimming, a rope swing, kayaking, and four zip lines. Most visitors stay in 79-room Trout Lodge, which overlooks the 360-acre spring-fed lake. Spring rates, which include a lodge room, three meals a day, and most activities, begin at $99 for the first adult, $69 for additional adults, and up to three children 17 and under are free. During summer the base rate rises to $149 for the first adult.

YMCA of the Ozarks, 13528 State Hwy. AA, Potosi, MO 63664, 573-438-2154, www.ymcaoftheozarks.org.

YMCA of the Rockies. This YMCA, with two camps, has developed a stellar reputation with families. Its 860-acre **Estes Park Center** is nestled in Rocky Mountain National Park, where summer activities center on hiking, and in the winter, snowshoeing and snowboarding. But that just scratches the surface. Ketelsen, who has come with his family for more than 20 years, says first-time visitors can't believe the crafts studio. "It's a wonder. There are literally hundreds and hundreds of different projects to do and people to show you how." There's also everything from skateboarding to a ropes course with climbing wall. You'll find Frisbee golf and even a prayer labyrinth.

The second camp, **Snow Mountain Ranch,** is in Winter Park, west of Denver. While popular for winter activities, there's ample summer programming, too—everything from canoeing to scavenger hunts to magic lessons. In the evenings, activities might include a dance or a movie screening.

Rooms at both locations begin at $79 during parts of winter and spring. At the height of summer, a five-bedroom vacation home at Snow Mountain runs $449 a night, but it sleeps up to 12 people. Reservations are taken months early, so plan ahead. You don't have to be a YMCA member to stay, but the $200 annual fee does offer some discounted rates.

YMCA of the Rockies, Estes Park Center, 2515 Tunnel Rd., Estes Park, CO 80511 or Snow Mountain Ranch, 1101 County Rd. 53, Granby, CO 80446, 800-777-9622, www.ymcarockies.org.

ride with wild horses

SIERRA NEVADA, CALIFORNIA

A lovely horse is always an experience . . . It is an emotional experience of the kind that is spoiled by words.

—BERYL MARKHAM, AFRICAN PILOT AND RACEHORSE TRAINER (1902–1986)

47 Wild horses live large in the American psyche. For many of us, they symbolize the Wild West, the majesty of nature, and the freedom of open country. Although it seems the stuff of old Hollywood Westerns, you may be surprised to learn that even in these days of interstates and exurban shopping malls, untamed herds of mustangs still roam pockets of the nation.

One of the best ways to see these beautiful creatures is on a pack trip in the Sierra Nevada mountains. Perhaps fittingly, you'll travel on horseback through John Wayne–inspired country on a three-day camping outing to reach them.

"When you get out and see horses living as a field animal, living with nature, living on the land, it's a dream come true," says Craig London, owner of Rock Creek Pack Station tour company, based in Bishop, California.

There's debate on the horses' origins. Some believe the herd first formed when animals escaped from prospectors that came to the region in the mid-1800s searching for gold. Others think they go back even further and are descendants of stock brought to California by the earliest Spanish explorers. But what is known is that unlike other wild horse herds, actively managed by the federal government, this population is kept in check by natural predators. Mountain lions feed on foals and cull the herd's older and weaker members. What visitors see is a balance maintained by nature.

It's something guests learn to appreciate. "It's not just a sightseeing trip, it's really an educational venture," says Ann Driscoll, who has twice traveled

$PLURGE

GO ON AN AUTHENTIC PACK RIDE

If seeing horses in the wild whets your appetite for Old West adventure, why not take part in a real horse drive? Twice a year **Rock Creek Pack Station** invites guest to join them on a four-day 100-mile adventure, moving their pack stock, 120 horses and mules, from Owens Valley up into the Sierra Nevada mountains in June, or back down again to the winter range in late September.

"There are very few places in the world where you can do this," London says. "You're starting in the deepest valley and you end up at 10,000 feet." Riders should expect to be in the saddle for long stretches. The cost: $925, plus $92.50 in fees.

from her home in New Hampshire to camp with London and gaze on the wild mustangs. "It's an extraordinarily beautiful open space that goes on and on and on and on. The sky and land changes throughout the day."

You don't have to be a cowboy to undertake this adventure, although guests must be in reasonable shape. Before the trip starts, guides split the group by riding ability. Those with little previous time in a saddle might ride for four or five hours a day. More seasoned guests could be out on the range for six hours or more. And the experience doesn't cost a bundle. A basic four-day adventure starts at $495. For a bit of comfort, you can spend the first night at the historic **Old House B&B** at Benton Hot Springs for $100 more per person.

When the groups return to the base camp, everyone usually is wearing a smile. And it only gets better. Although accommodations are rustic (it's mountain camping at 7,000 feet elevation, after all), it's still camping in comfort. The outdoor kitchen has a generator and a propane-run water heater feeding a shower tucked back in the willows for privacy. Guests need to bring a sleeping bag, but other than that, guides provide and look after everything else, from cowboy coffee in the morning to educational lectures at night.

CHINCOTEAGUE'S WILD HORSES

The West can't lay sole claim to wild horses. Several herds still live along the mid-Atlantic, most famously in Chincoteague, Virginia, where the wild horses live on nearby Assateague Island. Once a year, the Chincoteague Volunteer Fire Department rounds up the animals to thin the herd. Foals are sold at auction and some are domesticated, as was famously recounted in the children's book *Misty of Chincoteague.*

Watching the roundup and swim, which occurs on the last Wednesday and Thursday of July, is an unforgettable experience. The horses swim across the island channel at slack tide and are run through town, where they are penned. If you don't mind getting your feet wet, head to the end of Pony Swim Lane and wade out into the marsh for a great view of the swim.

Motels and campgrounds in Chincoteague fill up, so reservations are essential and often made a year in advance. **Snug Harbor Marina and Cottages** (757-336-6176, http://chincoteagueaccommodations.com) charges about $1,500 to rent a two-bedroom cottage for the week of Pony Penning. The cheapest accommodations are at **Tom's Cove Campground** (Chincoteague, 757-336-6498, www.tomscovepark.com), which charges $31.50 a night for tent camping, with a three-day minimum during the Pony Penning. Another place to camp is at Maryland's **Assateague Island National Seashore** (410-641-3030, www.nps.gov/asis), which fronts the Atlantic Ocean. If your stay doesn't overlap with the swim, you may have horses wandering through your camp, nonchalantly nibbling on vegetation. The **Chincoteague Chamber of Commerce** (6733 Maddox Blvd., Chincoteague Island, VA 23336, 757-336-6161, www.chincoteaguechamber.com) can provide more information on accommodations.

Andrew Riha of Los Angeles says he and a few friends first signed up for the trip eager to experience California's wild spaces. He was astounded the first night when the guides hooked up a computer projector to the generator and used the side of a canvas tent as a screen. What followed was a detailed presentation about the mustangs everyone had seen that day, covering their history, habits, anatomy, and physiology.

Even a few years later, Riha clearly remembers one of his first encounters with the animals. "We spotted some over a ridge. They couldn't see us, but we could watch them." Then Riha stood up for a better view. He was wearing a white shirt and when the mustangs saw him, they galloped away in a plume of dust. But one of the horses turned around and came back, stopping within 100 feet of the group. "It was definitely an immersive experience," Riha says. "It was spectacular."

HOW TO GET IN TOUCH

Rock Creek Pack Station, P.O. Box 248, Bishop, CA 93515, 760-872-8331, www.rockcreekpack station.com.

take a scenic drive along an ice field

ALBERTA, CANADA

Everybody needs beauty as well as bread,
places to play in and pray in, where nature may heal
and give strength to body and soul alike.

—NATURALIST JOHN MUIR (1838–1914)

48 Alberta, Canada's **Icefields Parkway** has long been called one of North America's most beautiful drives, offering spectacular views as the route winds through some 70 peaks of the Canadian Rockies on a Depression-era tarmac from Jasper to Lake Louise.

"The peaks along this route are quite dramatic," says Roger Hostin, who supervises the region's Parks Canada national park visitor centers. Even after 30 years in the area, the landscape that changes with every turn of the road still amazes him. "Around every corner there's something new and amazing to look at. There are amazing vistas—lakes, glaciers, canyons, waterfalls, wildlife . . . it's a constant barrage of wonder."

But to catch the full glory of this mountain parkway, you will want to get there sooner than later. Because of global warming, glaciers around the world are fading fast. Some experts predict that in the United States, Montana's Glacier National Park will be entirely glacierless by 2020. And while Alberta's ice fields sit farther north than the alpine glaciers of Glacier, even the ice here is expected to retreat noticeably in the coming years.

In fact, Hostin has already seen some changes in the past decade or so along the 143-mile-long Icefields Parkway. Nevertheless, the drive still offers one wow after the next, leading past waterfalls, rocky pinnacles, turquoise lakes, and its namesake ice. On a clear day, you may catch glimpses of as many as a hundred glaciers. At its highest point, Bow Summit, the road reaches almost 6,800 feet in elevation—more than 1.25 miles above sea level.

BANFF & JASPER NATIONAL PARKS INFORMATION CENTERS

- **Banff,** 224 Banff Ave., 403-762-1550.
- **Jasper,** 500 Connaught Dr., 780-852-6176.
- **Lake Louise,** Samson Mall, Village of Lake Louise, 403-522-3833.
- **Icefield Centre,** Hwy. 93 (Icefields Parkway, 64 miles S of Jasper), 780-852-6288.

FAMOUS GLACIERS WORLDWIDE

- **Franz Josef,** New Zealand
- **Hubbard Glacier,** Alaska
- **Jakobshavn,** Greenland
- **Lambert Glacier,** Antarctica
- **Perito Moreno,** Argentina

The leisurely drive takes about three hours round-trip—providing you don't leave your car too often. But don't count on that. It's likely that even urban dwellers will be tempted by the wide selection of hikes—short or multiday—leading to frothy cascades, mountain overlooks, wildflower-strewn meadows, and unpopulated landscapes where you're more likely to spot grizzlies, bighorn sheep, moose, and elk. Among the most popular day hikes are Five Lakes, about 6 miles south of Jasper; Wilcox Pass and Parker Ridge, both near the Athabasca Glacier; and walks in the Bow Summit area, 15 miles north of Lake Louise, to Bow Glacier Falls and Peyto Lake.

For many visitors to the Canadian Rockies, the centerpiece of an Icefields Parkway excursion is the namesake Columbia Icefield. Even a short 30-minute hike from the Icefield Centre (open April–mid-Oct.) will bring you to the leading edge of the Athabasca Glacier, one of the Columbia's main "toes." [$PLURGE: If you feel like splurging, partake in the **Columbia Icefield Glacier Experience** (877-423-7433, www.explorerockies.com), an 80-minute ride on the ice field in a specially fitted bus for about $49 Canadian (ages 16 and up); alternatively, you could book a two-hour ice-field walk for $38. Both the walk and bus tours are offered spring through early fall and depart from the Icefield Centre.]

The Icefields Parkway runs through two Canadian national parks, Jasper and Banff; entry costs about $10 Canadian per adult and covers both parks, while a family/group ticket covering the entire car costs about $20. There are many levels of accommodations to be found within the parks. The most budget-friendly option is to camp. Park campground fees run $15 Canadian and up, depending on the facilities offered. For information on the various campgrounds and reservations, check online at www.pccamping.ca/parkscanada or call 877-737-3783.

Rooms at **Glacier View Inn** (877-442-2623, www.nationalparkreservations.com/jasper.htm), located near the Icefield Centre, start at $115 Canadian in spring and fall and $260 mid-June through mid-September; the inn is open mid-April through mid-October. Numerous hostels and bed-and-breakfasts are available at either end of the parkway—in Jasper, at the parkway's north end, and in the towns of Banff and Lake Louise, to the south. [$PLURGE: For a real splurge on accommodations, consider staying at one of the region's historic railway hotels, each one sited to take full advantage of the stunning views: **Banff Springs Hotel, Chateau Lake Louise,** and **Jasper Park Lodge,** now run by the upscale Fairmont Hotels group (800-257-7544, www.fairmont.com).

Even if you stay elsewhere, be sure to wander through these amazing lodgings. The first two were built in the late 19th century, while the third dates from the 1920s.]

If you crave adventure, check out the parkway in winter, when the vagaries of the weather create drama and force the odd road closure. Embrace the cold. Troop through the snow counting elk foraging for food, then warm up at the **Banff Upper Hot Springs** (403-762-1515, www.hotsprings.ca, $7.30 Canadian). If you forget your bathing suit, don't worry: You can rent one—and towels—for a few dollars. As the snow flurries around you, you won't have a care in the world.

HOW TO GET IN TOUCH

Alberta Tourism, 800-252-3782, www.travelalberta.com.

Banff/Lake Louise Tourism, 403-762-8421, www.banfflakelouise.com.

Jasper Tourism, 800-473-8135 or 780-852-3858, www.jaspercanadianrockies.com.

Parks Canada, www.pc.gc.ca.

sleep in a tree house

TAKILMA, OREGON

Treehouses lift the spirits. They inspire dreams. They represent freedom: from adults or adulthood, from duties and responsibilities, from an earthbound perspective. If we can't fly with the birds, at least we can nest with them.

—AUTHOR PETER NELSON, *TREEHOUSES: THE ART AND CRAFT OF LIVING OUT ON A LIMB* (1994)

49 Talk about staying in a high-rise. At the Out 'n' About Treesort in Takilma, Oregon, guests can bunk down in one of 13 different tree houses. All have electricity, and some even have indoor plumbing. As the pun-loving staff at this family-run property put it: The experience is treemendous.

The Treesort began in 1990 when Michael Garnier decided a fledgling bed-and-breakfast business might get more attention if he put the beds up in a tree. Guests loved it, but the local building inspectors didn't, and Garnier found himself ensnared in a multiyear battle to win the right to rent out tree houses. In 1998 the officials finally backed down and agreed to the alternative building plans. Garnier, who had developed special equipment to support the houses and prevent damage to the host tree, now runs workshops to teach the fundamentals of building tree houses.

ALL ALONG THE WATCHTOWER

The U.S. Forest Service rents out several dozen fire towers, simple perches in some of the country's most beautiful settings. The towers are concentrated in the West, primarily in Montana and Oregon, although you'll find some in Idaho, California, Washington, Wyoming, and South Dakota.

Rentals are a relative bargain at about $50 a night, plus a $9 reservation fee, but this isn't posh penthouse living. Instead, consider the experience glorified camping. Although most towers are equipped with pots and pans and a stove, you'll have to supply sleeping bags, and often potable water. Your restroom will likely be a nearby outhouse. Bring binoculars because what these towers lack in amenities they more than make up in views!

The list of towers available to rent is constantly changing, but a good place on the Internet to check is the Forest Fire Lookout Association rentals page at www.firelookout.org/lookout-rentals.htm. Make reservations by calling 877-444-6777 or visiting www.recreation.gov.

TWO OTHER TREE HOUSES

- **Carolina Heritage Outfitters.** Top off a day of canoeing South Carolina's Edisto River with a night in a tree house. Carolina Heritage Outfitters rents its two tree houses to guests taking a two-day, 20-mile canoe trip. The homes come equipped with a kitchen, outdoor grill, and dining deck. They're screened, with a bathroom a short walk away. The homes rent for $125 per person, but that includes two-day canoe rental and shuttle service to drop-off and pickup points. *Carolina Heritage Outfitters, Hwy. 15, Canadys, SC 29433, 843-563-5051, www.canoesc.com.*
- **Spirit of the Suwannee Music Park & Campground.** At this campground in northern Florida, about 85 miles west of Jacksonville, a tree house offers a literal bird's-eye view of a music festival stage. The house, which sleeps six and is built around a live oak tree, runs $179 a night when there's not a concert or festival. (It's considerably more during performances.) It's equipped with a microwave, a coffeemaker, and a bathroom with a clawfoot bathtub. Guests can hike on the 800-acre property. For an extra fee, there's golf nearby and canoe trips available. The property's also home to the world's largest bat house, and the nightly emergence of hundreds of thousands of the insect eaters is astonishing. Don Miller has stayed in the house several times. "Your senses soar from the feeling of being up in a tree," he says. *Spirit of the Suwannee Music Park, 3076 95th Dr., Live Oak, FL 32060, 386-364-1683, www.musicliveshere.com.*

None of this matters, though, when you open your eyes in the morning and the first thing you see is a tree trunk in the middle of your room. It's fun and a little unbelievable, says Scott Miller, who has twice brought his family from Pasadena, California, to the resort. Both times he reserved the tree house named Pleasantree, which is built in a Douglas-fir—and more importantly has a bathroom. His wife, Miller says, wasn't interested in climbing down a tree in the middle of the night if nature called. The house, which can sleep five, is reached by winding stairs and rope bridges. Miller says his family first came to the resort after he and his son built a tree house in their backyard. But after visiting, they realized they hadn't planned big enough, and expanded the size of their retreat as soon as they returned home.

Guests are advised not to bring suitcases, but duffle bags work fine with a customized luggage pulley system. Houses are equipped with a refrigerator, have windows, and are heated. Although each tree house has the comforts of a cozy inn, on a breezy night you can still tell you're not in a Motel 6. "When the wind blows, there's kind of a swaying motion," Miller says.

Rates for the smallest house begin at $110 per night in the off-season. It's $10 more during high season, which runs from mid-June through October, and when multiple-night stays are required. But don't worry; the Treesort offers much more than the novelty of sleeping off the ground. With 36 acres adjacent to the **Rogue River–Siskiyou National Forest** (www.fs.fed.us/r6/rogue-siskiyou), there's nearby hiking and exploring. Many families are drawn to the Treesort's zip lines, which cost $45. But you can try out your Tarzan moves at no charge on a rope swing, which is accessed from a three-foot platform. There's also swimming and horseback riding, which cost $35, and craft activities, $20. Some visitors take day trips to nearby **Oregon Caves National Monument** (www.nps.gov/orca), which offers tours ($8.50) from late March through November, and **Redwood National Park** (www.nps.gov/redw). Wine lovers will want to tour an area winery, such as **Bridgeview Vineyard & Winery** (4210 Holland Loop Rd., Cave Junction, 877-273-4843, www.bridgeviewwine.com) or **Foris Winery & Vineyards** (654 Kendall Rd., Cave Junction, 800-843-6747, www.foriswine.com).

The Treesort considers itself a branch-and-breakfast, providing a complimentary full spread for guests every morning. For other meals, guests have access to an outdoor cooking area, or they may choose to eat in nearby Cave Junction. **Wild River Brewing & Pizza Company** (249 N. Redwood Hwy., 541-592-3556) and **Nacho Mamas Taqueria** (131 N. Redwood Hwy., 541-592-2200) are particularly popular and offer entrées for less than $10 a piece. But make sure to get back home in time for the nightly campfire and a chance to tell stories, make s'mores, and meet your fellow tree dwellers.

HOW TO GET IN TOUCH

Out 'n' About Treehouse Treesort, 300 Page Creek Rd., Cave Junction, OR 97523, 541-592-2208, www.treehouses.com.

cycle the natchez trace

TENNESSEE TO MISSISSIPPI

It is by riding a bicycle that you learn the contours of a country best, since you have to sweat up them and coast down them.

—AUTHOR ERNEST HEMINGWAY (1899–1961)

50 America's earliest superhighway cut across mountains, rivers, and swamps. Initially, it provided a path for wildlife, Native Americans, and pioneer traders. Now, the Natchez Trace is favored by vacation drivers and bicyclists.

The 444-mile route leads from Nashville, Tennessee, to Natchez, Mississippi. The top speed limit is 50 miles an hour and commercial vehicles and billboards are barred. Simply put, it's a pretty country ride that can last for days.

Native Americans used the trace, which was actually a series of paths, for centuries to track game and travel through the region. As white settlers pushed into the area, they also began using the primitive Indian trails, with the heaviest traffic occurring in the 1800s, when the trace was developed as a path for boatmen who would take loads down the Mississippi River, sell everything, and then walk home. Famous Americans who traveled the "Old Natchez Trace" range from Abraham Lincoln's father to Andrew Jackson to John James Audubon.

But the trace fell into disuse with the rise of the steamboat and train. Its resurrection started in 1937, when it was developed as a linear parkway that roughly paralleled the original trace, although construction wasn't completed until 2005. The route makes a memorable bike trip, but beware: There are no shoulders and cyclists must share the road with auto traffic. "It's not like Mom and Dad and the kids are going to go out for a bike ride here," says Amy Genke, a National Park Service interpretive ranger.

But with a little preparation, you can have a wonderful experience. "It's scenic. It's beautiful," she says. "It has a relaxed pace and an off-the-beaten-track appeal."

Although cyclists often take a week or more to cover the entire length, it's easy to carve out a few day trips. Some visitors favor the northern end near Nashville,

$PLURGE

VBT'S GUIDED BIKE TOURS

If you'd love to bike the trace but not worry about logistics (or flat tires), you can take a seven-day guided tour. VBT, a decades-old tour company offering trips around the world, will provide a bike, accommodations at historic inns, most meals, and full van support. But you still have to do the pedaling. Trips from $1,795. *VBT, 614 Monkton Rd., Bristol, VT 05443, 800-245-3868, www.vbt.com.*

which features rolling mountainous terrain that's beautiful in the fall. Charles Cather has taken groups of Boy Scouts biking on the trace for years. He says the worst hill is at the start, and he advises his troop to walk up the incline. After that, it is rolling terrain for 60 miles to the Meriwether Lewis Campground.

"You might grind it out going up hills, but you really enjoy it coming down," he says. Tip: **Loveless Café** (8400 Hwy. 100, Nashville, 615-646-9700), near the start of the trace in Nashville, is famous for its biscuits, perfect for carbo-loading before the trip.

Other sections have different appeal. Perhaps the easiest part is a 100-mile section south of Kosciusko, Mississippi, Oprah Winfrey's hometown, where non-campers can stay in the **Maple Terrace Inn B&B** (300 N. Huntington St., Kosciusko, 662-289-5353, www.mapleterraceinn.com, rates from $95). The trace passes by a cypress swamp draped in Spanish moss, and it adjoins a lake for about 15 miles. Then it leads through Jackson, Mississippi, although it's so wooded you might never realize you're passing through a busy capital city. Along the trace, cyclists find drinking-water stops about every 15 miles. There are three general campgrounds along the route and five bicycle-only facilities. Although you can find bed-and-breakfasts, motels, and private campgrounds near the route, they may be several miles from the trace, which will feel much farther after a long day of biking, so it's best to make reservations.

As you navigate the trace, you'll soon become an expert in mileposts. The park is numbered from south to north. Must-stops include the four visitor centers: Mount Locust, at mile marker 15.5, is home to the only "stand," or historic inn, remaining on the trace, preserved as a museum; Ridgeland, just north of Jackson, is at mile marker 102.4; the Parkway Headquarters in Tupelo, at mile marker 266; and Colbert Ferry, at mile marker 327.3, offers fishing, boating, and birding.

Of course, you can always drive the trace and bike for short sections, too. About a dozen shops along the way rent bikes, and some will even let you ship your bicycle to them and they'll assemble it for you. Find a list at www.scenictrace.com.

HOW TO GET IN TOUCH

Natchez Trace Parkway, 2680 Natchez Trace Pkwy., Tupelo, MS 38804, 800-305-7417, www.nps.gov/natr.

zip through the canopy

HOCKING HILLS, OHIO

Aerodynamically, the bumblebee shouldn't be able to fly,
but the bumblebee doesn't know it so it goes on flying anyway.

—MARY KAY ASH, FOUNDER OF MARY KAY COSMETICS (1918–2001)

51 Blame it on bumblebees, Superman, Tarzan, or Peter Pan—when it comes to childhood fantasies, nothing quite measures up to the idea of flying.

Unfortunately, the laws of physics still rule. For human mortals, zip lines are the compromise, allowing you to literally fly at dozens of miles per hour—but with the protections of sturdy steel cables, harness, and helmet. Until a few years ago, though, most zip-line operations were located in the rain forests of the Caribbean and Latin America. Now you can find them in Alaska, aboard cruise ships, and in the continental United States.

All those safety measures add up—which means zip lining is never cheap. But if you choose a cost-conscious location where you can limit your other expenses, it can be part of a budget-friendly vacation. And Ohio's Hocking Hills region, about 40 minutes south of Columbus, is just such a place.

If you're into hiking, waterfalls, bird-watching, beaver-watching, kayaking, crafts, archery, star-gazing, prowling for night owls, feeding hummingbirds by hand—yes, you read that right—you'll find it in the Hocking Hills region, home to nine state parks and forests. Entry to all is free. At **Hocking Hills State Park** (19852 Rte. 664S, 740-385-6842) at Logan, don't miss the sandstone caves and the hikes leading to them; Ash Cave, Cedar Falls, and Old Man's Cave are the most popular. Rock climbing and rappelling are allowed at **Hocking State Forest** (19275 Rte. 374, Rockbridge, 740-385-4402). Hummingbird feedings take place at **Lake Hope State Park** (27331 Rte. 278, McArthur, 740-596-5253) from mid-June through Labor Day on Wednesdays, Fridays, Saturdays,

MORE PLACES TO RIDE A ZIP LINE

- **Forever Florida.** Near St. Cloud, Florida, 866-854-3837, www.floridaecosafaris.com.
- **Royal Caribbean's *Oasis of the Seas* and *Allure of the Seas*.** Included in the price of the cruise, www.royalcaribbean.com.
- **Scream Time Zipline.** Boone, North Carolina, 828-898-5404, www.screamtimezipline.com.
- **WildPlay.** Nanaimo and Whistler, British Columbia, Canada, 888-668-7874, www.wildplay.com.

and Sundays. Free naturalist-led stargazing programs are held during peak star showers in August and November at **Conkle's Hollow** (24858 Big Pine Rd., Rockbridge, 740-385-6842). .

Other cost-friendly pastimes include **Etta's Lunchbox Café & Museum** (35960 Rte. 56, New Plymouth, 740-380-0736), where you can eat for less than $10 and wander around for free; **Paul Johnson's Pencil Sharpener Museum** (740-753-4634, call for appt. & info) in Carbon Hill; factory tours at the **Columbus Washboard Factory** (14 Gallagher Ave., 740-380-3828, www.columbuswashboard.com) in Logan, which stages the annual Washboard Festival over Father's Day weekend; the outlet store **Rocky Boots** (45 E. Canal St., Nelsonville, 740-753-3130, www.rockyboots.com/OutletStores/), where you can pick up gear as well as order a bison burger or ham loaf in the diner; taking a **glass workshop with artist Marco Jerman** (740-385-1384, http://jermanartglass.com, from $25); and excursions ranging from moonlight paddling trips to qigong clinics (about $25 each) from **Touch the Earth Adventures** (740-591-9094, www.hockinghills.com/earthtouch/).

Hocking Hills lodging ranges from state park campsites and cottages (nonelectric sites start at $18, cottages start at $65) to the wooden "gypsy" wagons and medieval cottages of **Ravenwood Castle** (800-477-1541, www.ravenwoodcastle.com, from $50 per night) to privately owned rustic cabins in the woods. Of the latter, **Getaway Cabins** (888-587-0659, www.getaway-cabins.com) and **Deerwatch Cabins** (740-385-7132, www.deerwatch.com) are good bets; rates start from around $95.

After all that, you won't cringe to find out that canopy tours by zip line start at $80 per person at **Hocking Hills Canopy Tours** (10714 Jackson St., Rockbridge, 740-385-9477, www.hockinghillscanopytours.com). On a 2.5-hour tour, you'll traverse five sky bridges and ten zip lines (one stretches 572 feet) linking platforms high in the trees. If that's not high, fast, or wild enough, add on a super zip experience that will send you speeding up to 50 miles an hour along a quarter-mile-long line.

HOW TO GET IN TOUCH

Hocking Hills Tourism Association, 800-462-5464, www.1800hocking.com.
Ohio State Parks, www.dnr.state.oh.us/parks.

collect waterfalls

TUMBLER RIDGE, BRITISH COLUMBIA, CANADA

From the waterfall he named her, Minnehaha, Laughing Water.

—POET HENRY WADSWORTH LONGFELLOW, *HIAWATHA* (1855)

52 : Researchers still debate the reason, but it's a proven fact that we feel better around negative ions. You'll find these charged air particles near water. Moving water is even better, and waterfalls are unbeatable. So there's no doubt you'll feel like a million bucks near Tumbler Ridge, Canada, at the foot of the Rockies in northeastern British Columbia. It's home to literally dozens of falls.

For the subculture of people that collect waterfalls the way kids amass baseball cards, this place is legendary. For the rest of us, Tumbler Ridge, a mining town of 2,400, makes a worthwhile detour from the Alaska Highway, or a surprising North Country destination. It's about a 2.5-hour drive from Fort St. John, which is served by Air Canada through Vancouver. You'll come for the waterfalls and stay for the away-from-it-all atmosphere. The area is laced with hiking trails leading to mountains, lakes, and, of course, cascades. Thirteen trails lead to a total of 22 waterfalls.

The can't-miss site is **Kinuseo Falls** in **Monkman Provincial Park** (www.env.gov.bc.ca/bcparks/explore/parkpgs/monkman). At 197 feet, it's higher than Niagara Falls, and perhaps because it's set in the wilderness, looks even grander. By road, it's a 40-mile drive south from Tumbler Ridge on bumpy gravel roads. The route offers a chance to catch two other falls, warm-ups for the big show. The first stop, **Barbour Falls,** about 21.75 miles south of Tumbler, is reached by an easy 1.2-mile hike. Another half mile farther down the road, you'll find the trailhead for **Nesbitt's Knee,** reached on a 2-mile round-trip hike.

[SPLURGE: For a splurge, skip the driving and approach Kinuseo by jetboat via the Murray River. The aluminum boat stops on a sandy island and a trail leads to a gasp-worthy view of the falls from the base. The trip lasts about four hours and is smooth but noisy. Bring a sandwich and water to have on the way. The river level is at ideal height for excursions from mid-June through early September, and reservations are recommended; contact the Tumbler Ridge visitor center (250-242-3123). Trips run $125 Canadian per person, with a minimum of four participants.]

If you love a hike, you'll want to catch **Bergeron Falls,** an astounding plunge over a sandstone lip into a horseshoe-shaped bowl 328 feet below. It's the highest accessible waterfall in the region, reached by a circular hiking trail that opened in 2010. Get there by driving north of Tumbler for 3 miles, and then turning 5 miles down a gravel road, which ends at the trailhead. The moderate

TEN FALLS IN A DAY

Oregon's **Silver Falls State Park** is said to be home to the largest concentration of waterfalls in North America. The highest, South Falls, clocks in at 176 feet, which you'll see on the park's Trail of Ten Falls, a 8.7-mile circuit that links four of the park's trails. Four other falls drop into an amphitheater-like setting, allowing you to walk behind the cascades. The trail cuts through old-growth Douglas-fir, cedar, and hemlock trees as it makes its way along the north and south forks of Silver Creek. The 8,800-acre park, Oregon's largest, is located about 25 miles east of Salem in the Cascade Range. *Silver Falls State Park, 20024 Silver Falls Hwy. SE, Sublimity, OR 97385, 503-873-8681, www.oregonstateparks.org/park_211.php.*

hike takes half a day and is 6.2 miles round-trip. Side trails offer views of four other falls.

After that adventure, you deserve a laid-back cascade. Reach **Flatbed Falls** from a trailhead off Highway 29 near town. It's an easy hike through a spruce, aspen, and pine forest. A marsh area created by beaver dams attracts mallards and Canada geese. The falls themselves are a mere 13 feet, but they're surrounded by rocks that are popular for sunbathing, and a pool at the bottom of the falls is perfect for swimming.

Adventurous travelers will be tempted by the **Cascades Trail,** a multiday 26-mile round-trip experience. Plan on three days of hiking or mountain biking to take in eight thundering falls separated by placid pools. Rent gear from **Monkman Expeditions** (780-518-9115, www.monkmanexpeditions.com).

Tumbler Ridge has another claim to fame. It's dinosaur country. In 2000, two boys discovered footprints they were sure came from the distant past. Although their parents were skeptical, their find was confirmed and now the area has several documented trackways and bone beds, which can be seen by visitors. The **Dinosaur Discovery Gallery & Trackway Tours** (255 Murray Dr., Tumbler Ridge, 250-242-3466, www.trmf.ca) has Canada's largest collection of dino footprints, all recent finds. The gallery also leads tours to see footprints in the wild. An evening lantern tour is not only atmospheric but also instructive as the shadows accentuate the rock depressions.

Lodging and dining is limited in Tumbler Ridge. The **Wilderness Lodge Tumbler Ridge** (360 Northgate Dr., 877-242-5405 or 250-242-5405, www.wildernesslodgetumblerridge.com) has rooms beginning at $129 Canadian. **Sheila's Place** (340 Front St., 250-242-0090) is the place for soup and sandwiches, while the best bet for dinner is the **Tumbler Ridge Golf & Country Club** (103 Golf Course Rd., 250-242-3533).

HOW TO GET IN TOUCH

Tumbler Ridge Visitor Centre, 270 Southgate, Tumbler Ridge, BC V0C 2W0, Canada, 250-242-3123, www.tumblerridge.ca/DiscoverTumblerRidge/VisitorInformation/tabid/92/Default.aspx.

check out "unknown" parks

NATIONWIDE

National parks are the best idea we ever had. Absolutely American, absolutely democratic, they reflect us at our best rather than our worst.

—AUTHOR WALLACE STEGNER, IN A 1983 ESSAY

53 Yellowstone and Yosemite. Everyone has heard of these blockbuster national parks. Visitors are drawn by wonders of nature, but they also get to see . . . other visitors.

Not all national parks come with crowds, though. In a National Park System of nearly 400 sites, a few national parks undeservedly get little notice . . . and that's where you should consider going.

Great Basin National Park. A wonder on the Utah-Nevada border, Great Basin has 5,000-year-old bristlecone pines and a mountain peak topping 13,000 feet, but attracts few people. The park's isolation might be a factor, but that isolation also means that the night skies are stunning: On clear, new-moon nights, you can see up to five planets, meteors, satellites, and the Milky Way, all with the naked eye. The park offers stargazing programs throughout the summer. You'll find hiking options galore, from short nature strolls to longer loops leading to natural arches over mountain ridges and through forests. You can also see wonders by driving the 12-mile **Wheeler Peak Scenic Drive,** a winding road that climbs to the heavens with grades as steep as 8 percent. The park appeals to all senses–and in the fall, that includes your taste buds. Visitors are allowed to gather nuts from the park's piñon pine forests for personal use–up to 25 pounds per household. Winter visitors can enjoy snowshoeing and skiing; the weather and roads are generally clear late June to October.

Camping options abound within and near the park, but nearby Baker, Nevada, has a few lodging options. Try the **Border Inn** (U.S. 6/50, 775-234-7300) for basic motel rooms, friendly service, and a restaurant with homemade soups and chicken-fried steaks.

Great Basin National Park, 100 Great Basin National Park, Baker, NV 89311, 775-234-7331, www.nps.gov/grba.

Isle Royale National Park. If Great Basin is often overlooked, Isle Royale isn't even on the radar. Only about 25,000 people visit the park annually, which is how many visitors some parks can get in an afternoon. The secret is location. Isle Royale lies in Lake Superior and is accessible only by boat and seaplane. From fall through spring, ferries run regularly from Houghton and Copper Harbor, Michigan, and Grand Portage, Minnesota. But don't try coming during winter. The weather's so tough that Isle Royale is one of the few national parks that closes completely for the season, from November 1 through mid-April.

Visitors to Isle Royale are drawn by the boating and hiking. Nearly 150 miles of trails lace the park, including the Greenstone Ridge Trail, which stretches 40 miles across the island. There are also canoe trails, complete with portages connecting island lakes. The park also has 36 campgrounds for hikers, backpackers, and boaters. [$PLURGE: **If you want a comfy bed, you'll have to splurge on Rock Harbor Lodge (summer 906-337-4993, winter 866-644-2003, www.rockharborlodge.com). Cabins start at $216 for two adults during low season, and include an unexpected amenity: use of a canoe.**]

The cheapest way to reach the island is on the Park Service's *Ranger III*. The 128-passenger ferry leaves from Houghton, Michigan, and the trip takes six hours. Bring camping equipment or make lodge reservations because even during high season, the ferry doesn't return until the next day, and doesn't run at all on Sunday, Monday, or Wednesday. Fares are $60 per adult during high season, but are discounted 15 to 25 percent if you buy a package with lodging at Rock Harbor Lodge.

Isle Royale National Park, 800 E. Lakeshore Dr., Houghton, MI 49931, 906-482-0984, www.nps.gov/isro.

North Cascades National Park Service Complex. It's possible to hike into North Cascades National Park Complex in Washington State, but like Isle Royale, most visitors arrive by boat or floatplane. The park contains three sections: North Cascades, Ross Lake, and most notably Lake Chelan National Recreation Area, which is reached via a memorable ride up a glacier-carved lake taking at least 2.5 hours. The boat docks in the tiny town of Stehekin, which is surrounded by the park. You'll find all the Pacific Northwest necessities here: bakery, massage service, and bike rental. But you'll want to get out into the wilderness, among the most rugged in the lower 48 states. Here you'll find old-growth forests, alpine meadows, and gleaming glaciers.

Stay a few days. **Stehekin Landing Resort** (800-536-0745 or 509-682-4494, www.stehekinlanding.com) has rooms from $112, and camping is free. Many visitors base in Stehekin and take day hikes.

North Cascades National Park Service Complex, 810 Rte. 20, Sedro-Woolley, WA 98284, 360-854-7200, www.nps.gov/noca.

$PLURGE

DISCOVERY BIKES BREAKFAST RIDE

For a fun morning splurge, sign up for the Discovery Bikes Breakfast Ride (www.stehekindiscoverybikes.com), which starts at 8 a.m. with a 9-mile van ride up the Stehekin Valley, where you'll be served a hearty breakfast. Afterward you're free to explore the area, and eventually bike back to town by early afternoon. The fee is $30 per person.

head for the hills

CRESTED BUTTE, COLORADO

Most people come for the winters, but all of us stay for the summers.

—SHERI COVEY, LONGTIME RESIDENT OF CRESTED BUTTE

54 A ski resort town in winter can be intimidating. Men, women, and children, bundled in colorful high-tech jackets, swoosh past the rest of us who are delicately trying to extricate ourselves out of a snowbank where we just crashed. But come summer, it's a different story. Those slick slopes now welcome hikers. Jagged peaks are softened by fields of wildflowers. And outdoor concerts give a reason to stay out and soak in the alpine glow.

Truth is that winter mountain resorts are just as lovely—some would say even more appealing—during the summer. Plus, without the cost of expensive ski equipment and lift passes, a ski resort town can be a bargain. Top-end resorts can be pricey all year-round. So look for ones a little off the beaten path.

Crested Butte, Colorado, is a favorite. And under a cloudless deep-blue sky, with an evergreen-scented breeze blowing down the mountain, you'll understand why.

Any summer weekend is a perfect time to visit this west-central Colorado town, but Fourth of July is particularly memorable. The action starts at 7 a.m. with the Crested Butte Fire & EMS Department Pancake Breakfast, a hearty $7 meal that supports a good cause. By late morning, half the town of 1,500 seems to be waving American flags along Elk Avenue, or perched atop storefronts awaiting the start of the parade. The other half is marching. This is the town's chance to finally shake off winter, so expect wacky costumes and floats, including one equipped with a waterslide. Watch out for the mayor, though. He's been known to toss water balloons at the crowd. At night, there's a choice of fireworks displays, including one over Mount Crested Butte.

But you don't have to come on a holiday. The town calls itself the wildflower capital of Colorado, and mid-July's **Crested Butte Wildlife Flower Festival** (970-349-2571, www.crestedbuttewildflowerfestival.com) shows why. You can sign up for guided hikes, 4x4 adventures, and even yoga in an alpine meadow. Most events carry a charge.

The **Crested Butte Music Festival** (970-349-0619, www.crestedbuttemusicfestival.com) schedules concerts throughout July. Take your pick of jazz, symphonies, chamber music, dance, opera, or bluegrass. Although a few performances can be pricey, there are nearly a dozen free concerts and several pay-what-you-can performances. Families particularly like the free concerts on Saturday mornings.

A variety of other summer concerts also fill the calendar. Crested Butte Mountain Resort offers free concerts (970-349-4769, www.livefrommtcb.com), featuring everything from swing to country to world music, on Wednesday evenings in July and August. And all of CB, as it's called, comes out for the free Monday night Alpine Glow Concerts in the town park. Bring lawn chairs, watch the local characters, and don't worry about the odd rainstorm. Tradition is that the weather will always clear in time for the concert.

OTHER NOTABLE SUMMER SKI RESORTS

- **Saddleback, Maine.** Big on fun, not flash, this family-style resort and the surrounding Rangeley Lakes region make for a perfect summer destination. The 111 Rangeley Lakes (and ponds) are famous for fishing (especially fly-fishing), boating, and hiking along the Appalachian Trail. There's free swimming at Rangeley's Lakeside Park. Or take a free evening moose tour offered twice a week by Saddleback on the "pickle"—an old school bus painted John Deere green. You'll find a handful of locally owned stores, but no fast-food restaurants and chain motels. Instead there are cabins and condos at the mountain. Accommodations begin at around $85 for bed-and-breakfast inns, and $100 for motels. At the Saddleback ski resort, one-bedroom condos begin at $175 a night. *Saddleback Maine, P.O. Box 490, 976 Saddleback Rd., Rangeley, ME 04970, 866-918-2225, www.saddlebackmaine.com or Rangeley Lakes Maine Chamber of Commerce, 6 Park Rd., Rangeley, ME 04970, 800-685-2537, www.rangeleymaine.com.*
- **Taos Ski Valley and Angel Fire, New Mexico.** In the mountains north of Santa Fe, you'll find two lovely ski resorts—and summer destinations. Taos Ski Valley and Angel Fire are about an hour's drive apart, so you can stay at one and make a day trip to the other.

  At Taos Ski Valley, you'll find free opera and chamber music concerts from Memorial Day through the middle of August thanks to the resident Taos Opera Institute and the Taos School of Music. Come during a full moon and join the mayor on a night hike to Williams Lake, timed to arrive just as the moon rises. The average summer motel price is about $75. *Taos Ski Valley Chamber of Commerce, P.O. Box 91, Taos Ski Valley, NM 87525, 800-517-9816, www.taosskivalley.com.*

  At Angel Fire, guests come for golf, fishing, and mountain biking. The ski lift ($10 for one trip, $20 for a day pass) might sound pricey, but it's a scenic wonder on one of the country's longest lifts. At the top, you can picnic, play disc golf, and hike. Or bring a bike and you can coast all the way down. Once a week, there's a free movie under the stars and complimentary popcorn. And on most Saturday nights, the new country club offers free dance lessons and music. Make sure to schedule a stop at the state's moving **Vietnam Veteran's Memorial** (575-377-6900, www.angelfirememorial.com), one of the first in the country. Area lodging begins at $65. *Angel Fire, P.O. Box 130, 10 Miller Ln., Angel Fire, NM 87710, 800-633-7463, www.angelfireresort.com.*

You'll have a chance to soak in the arts, too. The **Crested Butte Arts Festival** (970-349-1184, www.crestedbutteartsfestival.com) brings out hundreds of craftspeople in one of the country's top-rated fine art shows. It offers music, a hands-on kids area, and even culinary arts demonstrations—that's art you can eat!

But of course, it wouldn't be Colorado without enjoying the incredible outdoors. You'll find miles of hiking and biking trails. Crested Butte shares the honor of being the birthplace of mountain biking with Marin County, California, as you'll learn at the town's **Mountain Bike Hall of Fame** (970-349-6817, www.mtnbikehalloffame.com). And even if you're not interested in flying down a mountain on two wheels, no one can resist renting a townie (one-speed bike) and tooling around downtown. You'll see these bikes everywhere, and since it's such a small town, no one bothers to lock up. And even if you're not interested in working your muscles, you can grab a free Mountain Express shuttle bus 3 miles to Mount Crested Butte and take the chairlift to the summit for a peak picnic experience.

Cheap eats are found all over town. Try the early bird special at the **Timberline Restaurant** (201 Elk Ave., 970-349-9831) from 5:30 to 6 p.m. every night. For $15, you get a three-course meal; grab a seat on the front patio for outdoor dining. Other favorites include pizza, beer, and people-watching from the deck of the **Brick Oven Pizzeria** (223 Elk Ave., 970-349-5044) and **Donita's Cantina** (330 Elk Ave., 970-349-6674), which offers big baskets of chips and fresh salsa.

Lodging doesn't have to be a budget breaker. The cheapest sleeps are at **Crested Butte International Lodge & Hostel** (615 Teocalli Ave., 888-389-0588, www.crestedbuttehostel.com), which has bunks, individual rooms, and apartments—a private room for four runs about $100. Or try locally owned **Old Town Inn** (708 6th St., 888-349-6184, www.oldtowninn.net), where summer rates begin at $119, including breakfast. Also look for deals at **Crested Butte Mountain Resort** (800-810-7669, www.skicb.com).

HOW TO GET IN TOUCH

Gunnison-Crested Butte Tourism Association, 202 E. Georgia, Ste. B, Gunnison, CO 81230, 800-814-7988, www.gunnisoncrestedbutte.com.

roughing it in comfort in a state park

NATIONWIDE

In a cottage, there may be more happiness than a king or his favorites enjoy.

—ROMAN POET HORACE (65 B.C.–8 B.C.)

55 There's one problem about getting back to nature. Bedtime. Luckily, there are ways to commune with the wild, and still sleep in comfort. Many state parks offer a cost-effective way to stay in the great outdoors without camping: cabins. Several park-owned cabins have historic touches and in recent years, some parks have opened new, or radically refurbished, structures. If you're picturing a cinder block square out in the woods, think again. Here are a few state parks that offer cabins with character to spare:

Cama Beach State Park, Washington. Cama Beach State Park, located on Camano Island, took its inspiration from the past, refurbishing a 1930s-era Puget Sound fishing resort listed on the National Register of Historic Places and reopening it as a new 443-acre park. The waterfront cedar cabins and bungalows are basic (only some have private baths) but they're cute and offer easy access to the area's stunning scenery. Inside, you'll find beds covered with handmade quilts, a small refrigerator/freezer, and a microwave, all just steps from a mile-long beach.

Once you're here, there's no reason to leave. Among other things, the park offers beach walks, kids' crafts, and boatbuilding classes. You can go crabbing, play horseshoes, or just relax. Rates range from $45–$129 per night during the summer. Camano Island is about a 1.5-hour drive from Seattle and is connected to the mainland by a bridge.

Cama Beach State Park, 1880 S. West Camano Dr., Camano Island, WA 98282, 360-387-1550, www.parks.wa.gov/camabeach.

Crystal Cove State Park, California. You can find a bit of Hollywood glamour at Crystal Cove State Park, near Newport Beach in southern California. Although movie stars once flocked to this 3.5-mile stretch of sand, it is now known as an affordable beach vacation close to Los Angeles but far removed from the frenzy. The park's cottages are now preserved as a historic district with beachfront bungalows, originally built between the 1920s and '40s. More than a dozen have been restored and outfitted with vintage furniture. They rent from as little as $60 per night, for dorm-style accommodations, although the average rate is $180 in a private cottage.

Crystal Cove State Park, 35 Crystal Cove, Newport Coast, CA 92657, 800-444-7275, www.crystalcovebeachcottages.com.

David Crockett State Park, Tennessee. After a day of exploring David Crockett State Park in Lawrenceburg, Tennessee, you'll feel good about spending the night in new environmentally friendly cabins. The seven accommodations have cork flooring and native plant landscaping and are silver-certified by the U.S. Green Building Council Leadership in Energy and Environmental Design (LEED) project. The two-bedroom, two-bath cabins overlook Lindsey Lake, about 80 miles southwest of Nashville. Come for hiking, fishing, swimming, and boating. Cabins run $135 a night and rentals have a six-day minimum from Labor Day to Memorial Day and a two-day minimum other times of year.

David Crockett State Park, P.O. Box 398, 1400 W. Gaines, Lawrenceburg, TN 38464, 877-804-2681 or 931-762-9408, www.tennessee.gov/environment/parks/DavidCrockettSP.

Gulf State Park, Alabama. With furnishings from Pottery Barn and satellite televisions with DVD/VCR players, you can't say you're roughing it at Alabama's Gulf State Park. Its 11 three-bed, three-bath cottages each have equipped kitchens, screened porches, and lakefront decks. But there are plenty of reasons to go outside. The park faces a fishing lake and is just a few miles from the beach and a 1,544-foot fishing pier, the longest on the Gulf of Mexico. Cottages range from $188–$210 per night.

Alabama's Gulf State Park, 20155 State Hwy. 135, Gulf Shores, AL 36542, 251-948-7275, www.alapark.com/gulfstate/cottages.

Kiptopke State Park, Virginia. Virginia's Eastern Shore has never been short on scenery and natural attractions. Kiptopke State Park sits along a major flyway, providing a chance to see migratory birds. The park is an important bird population studies site, and visitors can see researchers band birds of prey September through November. There's also swimming in the Chesapeake Bay, hiking and biking trails, and beach bonfires.

For a unique sleeping experience, try Virginia's only state park yurt, which runs $98 per night. For big groups, the park has five family lodges, each sleeping as many as 16. They have covered porches, gas logs, heating and air-conditioning. A rental runs $371 a night, with at least a two-night minimum, for out-of-state visitors (less for Virginians). Fill it up for a family reunion, and it comes out to less than $20 per person per day.

Kiptopke State Park, 3540 Kiptopke Dr., Cape Charles, VA 23310, 757-331-2267, www.dcr.virginia.gov/state_parks/kip.shtml.

Table Rock State Park, South Carolina. A South Carolina jewel set in the Appalachian Mountains and dotted with lakes and waterfalls, Table Rock State Park covers more than 3,000 acres and is about a half-hour drive west of Greenville. Built in the 1930s by the Civilian Conservation Corps, the property preserves the era's careful stonework and architecture, with many of the buildings on the National Register of Historic Places. A giant granite outcropping lords above, adding grandeur to the setting. Come here for swimming, boating, and an array of hiking options. Cabins have heating and air-conditioning. Ask for cabins 5, 6, 7, or 8, which are right on Pinnacle Lake. Prices range from $75–$120 per night.

Table Rock State Park, 158 E. Ellison Lane, Pickens, SC 29671, 864-878-9813, www.southcarolinaparks.com.

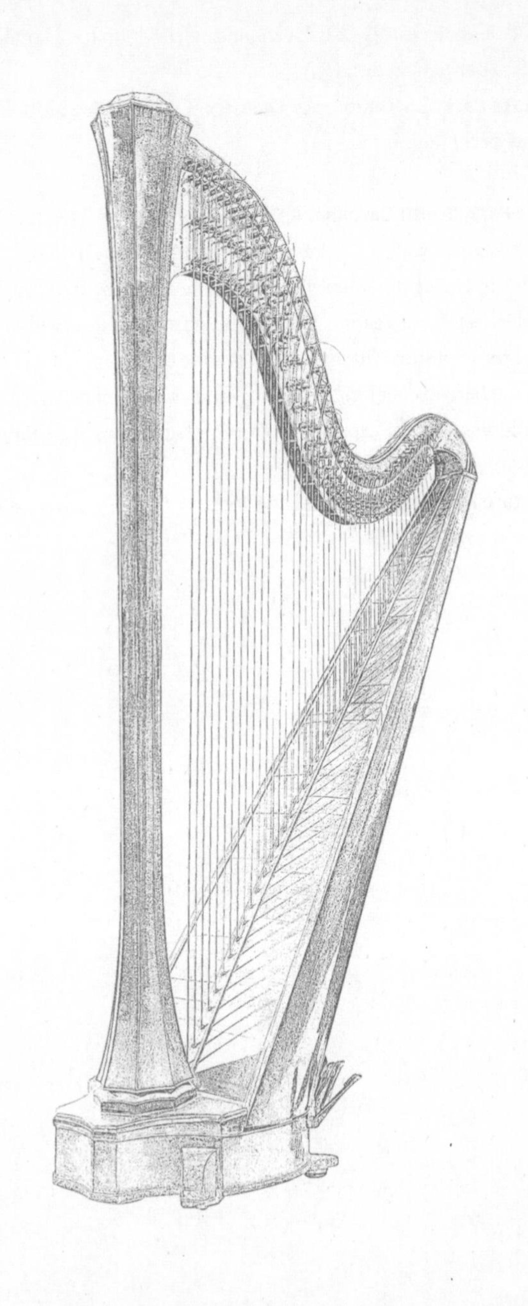

CHAPTER 3

quest for knowledge

What did you bring back from your last vacation? A tan, a T-shirt, and a pile of postcards? That's fine, of course, but most of us want something more. Time we know is precious. Lounging around has its moments, but recreation can really be that: re-creation.

The wonderful thing about a vacation is that you can learn new skills, indulge a creative streak, and maybe find inspiration to do something completely different with your life—all at low cost and with minimal time commitment.

Some are organized programs. For more than a century, the Chautauqua Institution has brought travelers together in what can really only be called an adult theme park for the mind that allows you to explore issues of the day and questions of the ages with some of the best minds on the planet. You can go to a university and explore the great books, or sign up for a learning tour and literally travel to the places where history was made and contemporary culture is changing.

And that's just the traditional pursuits. How about taking a class in comedy improv, sushi-making, or forming a rock band? You'll discover programs that can take you down roads you might have dreamed about but never knew how to pursue.

And don't forget the vacations that nurture your inner artist. For less than you'd spend on a week at the beach, you can learn to paint, draw, or make music. You can come back literally dancing from a ballroom weekend. Go to a writer's conference and you'll find fellow travelers eager to offer support as you spread your literary wings. Whether your passion is wooden boats or tying flies for fishing, a learning vacation can help you pursue your desires.

When you come back home, you won't be the same. And you'll have much more than memories to share with friends and family.

see the birthplace of skyscrapers

CHICAGO, ILLINOIS

Architecture, of all the arts, is the one which acts the most slowly, but the most surely, on the soul.

—ERNEST DIMNET, FRENCH PRIEST AND WRITER (1866–1954)

56 If you want to see movie stars, you go to Hollywood. For politicians, D.C.'s your destination. But if architecture is what interests you, book a ticket for Chicago.

The City of Big Shoulders invented the skyscraper in the late 19th century, and it hasn't looked back. It offers visitors a gallery of the architectural trends of the past century, from prairie style to modernism, and everything in between. It's home to the two tallest buildings in the country, the Willis Tower (formerly named the Sears Tower, 1974) and the Trump International Hotel and Tower (2009).

An easy (and inexpensive) way to take in the scope of the city is to follow the lead of commuters: Buy a ticket for the El, the Chicago Transit Authority's elevated train (888-968-7282, www.transitchicago.com, $5.75 for an all-day pass). "It's a viewing platform for the city," says Jason Neises of the Chicago Architecture Foundation. "I know of no other place in the world that offers something like this. You can literally see it all on the El."

The Brown Line loops through downtown, weaving through the skyscraper district, and then meanders through neighborhoods. The Green Line heads west to Oak Park, home to the Frank Lloyd Wright Foundation. On the way, it literally passes through the Illinois Institute of Technology campus, the largest concentration of Ludwig Mies van der Rohe buildings in the world, and home to the innovative McCormick-Tribune Campus Center by Rem Koolhaas.

Exploring on your own is the most frugal way to sightsee, but if you want some guidance, sign up for one of the **Chicago Architecture Foundation**'s many tours. It offers tours by foot, bus, bike, Segway, and boat, focusing on entire schools of design, individual architects, and even specific buildings. Tip: If you plan to take a few tours, buy a membership. It entitles you to free walking tours (usually $15 each), and provides a two-for-one pass for the "Architecture River Cruise," which costs $32. If you live more than a hundred miles from Chicago, an individual can join for just $40.

With more than 70 tours on offer, it's hard to know where to start. Neises suggests the foundation's "Historic Downtown (south): Rise of the Skyscraper" walking tour. As he explains it,

Chicago was a boomtown during the late 1800s, after the great fire had literally burned it to the ground, growing faster than any other city had up to that point in history. Since the downtown was hemmed in by rivers and lakes, builders had nowhere to go but up. As the city was developing, so were new technologies: steel framing, electricity, plumbing, telephone and telegraph, and the ability to make plate glass. "They came all together at just the right time for Chicago to invent the skyscraper," he says.

The walking tour takes in some of the earliest incarnations, including the 1888 Rookery building designed by Daniel Burnham and John Root, with a restored interior by Frank Lloyd Wright, and the 1889 Auditorium Building by Dankmar Adler and Louis Sullivan.

With planning, visitors can take in a second tour in a day. Most popular is the 90-minute "Architecture River Cruise," which runs May through November. Passengers see and learn about 60 buildings. "It's wildly popular," Neises says. The trip is narrated by docents passionate about architecture and the city.

On another day, a visitor might take the "Frank Lloyd Wright by Bus" tour to Oak Park, once home to Frank Lloyd Wright. It includes a visit to his studio, a walking tour of the historic district, and a visit to Wright's famed Unity Temple.

Or sign up for the daylong "Farnsworth House Plus By Bus." This modernism tour visits the Illinois Institute of Technology and then heads about 55 miles west of the city to the famed Farnsworth

MUST-SEE CHICAGO BUILDINGS

It's impossible to limit Chicago's architecture to just a handful of buildings. Every list will be different, but here are a few you'll want to see:

- **Chicago Board of Trade Building,** 141 W. Jackson Blvd.
- **Crown Hall,** 3360 S. State St.
- **Glessner House,** 1800 S. Prairie Ave.
- **James R. Thompson Center** (formerly State of Illinois Center), 100 W. Randolph St.
- **John Hancock Center,** 875 N. Michigan Ave.
- **Marina City,** 300 N. State St.
- **Monadnock Building,** 53 W. Jackson Blvd.
- **Robie House,** 5757 S. Woodlawn St.
- **Rookery Building,** 209 S. LaSalle St.
- **Unity Temple,** 875 Lake St., Oak Park
- **Willis Tower** (formerly Sears Tower), 233 S. Wacker Dr.

House, a glass building designed by Ludwig Mies van der Rohe, that attracts visitors from around the world. The tour includes lunch and runs $58 for members, $70 for nonmembers.

Chicago dining and lodging don't have to break your budget. The Windy City's famed deep-dish pizza can be had at classics like **Gino's East** (www.ginoseast.com), with several area locations. For lodging, the **Chicago Gateway Hostel** (616 W. Arlington Pl., 773-929-5380, www.getawayhostel.com) offers private rooms from $57. The city's hotels often run weekend specials. [$PLURGE: **For a splurge, stay in a boutique hotel named for a famed Chicago architect: Hotel Burnham (1 W. Washington St., 312-782-1111, www.burnhamhotel.com), a national historic landmark, offers rooms from $159 on weekends.**]

HOW TO GET IN TOUCH

Chicago Architecture Foundation, 224 S. Michigan Ave., Chicago, IL 60604, 312-922-3432, http://caf.architecture.org.

spend a night at the museum

NATIONWIDE

Museums, I love museums.

—ACTOR TONY RANDALL (1920–2004)

57 What really happens at a museum when the lights go out? Even if dinosaurs don't come to life as in the *Night at the Museum* movies, there's still plenty of action after dark at some museums offering special overnight programs.

Although geared toward local residents, an overnight stay is a great way for visitors to expand their minds after hours. You'll save on a night's hotel cost and get a chance to experience special programs, like IMAX movie viewings, scavenger hunts, science experiments, games, and even dances. Usually snacks and breakfast are supplied, sometimes dinner, too. But when it comes time for bed, you're often literally sleeping on the floor. Check with the museum; most suggest bringing a sleeping bag, pad, and pillow.

For kids, it's an unforgettable experience. Even several years later, 13-year-old Grant Wideman remembers spending the night at the McWane Center, a hands-on science museum in Birmingham, Alabama. "It was great. We had the whole museum to ourselves!"

It's the same story in New York. Gregory Cox has accompanied his grandson five times on sleepovers at Manhattan's American Museum of Natural History. He says children quickly form a bond with the famed institution. "They leave feeling like they own part of the museum," Cox says. It's also a shared adventure for a family. "You're making a memory and you know it right away. I know long after I'm gone, he's going to remember spending the night at the museum with Grandpa."

Most sleepover programs are geared for school, church, or scout groups, but many sites have family nights throughout the year, and a few even have adult programs. Usually children need to be at least age five. As with most sleepovers, there's not always much sleeping, and there's usually no way to go to bed before official lights-out, usually 11 p.m. or midnight.

Here are some museums to consider, as well as science centers, zoos, and aquariums that also offer overnight adventures:

- **American Museum of Natural History, New York, New York.** Don't expect Ben Stiller as your night guard, but you'll still have an unforgettable experience prowling around this museum, the setting for the first *Night at the Museum* film. Guests watch an IMAX movie and can participate in activities such as origami, totem pole construction, and making moon crater rubbings on a bronze lunar model. There's usually a live exhibit of snakes, raptors, or butterflies, but the highlight is exploring the famed dinosaur halls by flashlight on a scavenger hunt. Guests can bed down there on provided cots or under the museum's massive blue whale. The $129 per-person fee includes a snack, breakfast, and museum admission the following day. Still sounds pricey? Consider it a unique Manhattan hotel and it will seem like a bargain. *American Museum of Natural History, Central Park West at 79th St., New York, NY 10024, 212-769-5100, www.amnh.org.*

- **COSI (Center of Science and Industry), Columbus, Ohio.** The first museum "camp-in" was held here in 1972, and in 2009 the top-rated museum welcomed its one-millionth sleepover guest. COSI's program is still one of the best, and cheapest, at $32 per camper, an incredible bargain since it includes a two-day admission to the hands-on museum and a big-screen movie (the two of which alone can cost $20), plus breakfast and a souvenir patch. An optional dinner runs $8 per person. *COSI, 333 W. Broad St., Columbus, OH 43215, 888-819-2674, www.cosi.org.*
- **Monterey Bay Aquarium, Monterey, California.** Literally sleeping with the fishes, you'll have this usually crowded attraction almost to yourself, providing a chance to marvel at the sardines without worrying about the crowd behind you. For an otherworldly slumber, set up camp in front of the jellyfish exhibit. It's like going to sleep in the middle of a giant lava lamp. The Family Seashore Sleepover runs $75 a person and includes a movie, breakfast, and a behind-the-scenes tour of one of the world's top aquariums. *Monterey Bay Aquarium, 886 Cannery Row, Monterey, CA 93940, 831-648-4888, www.montereybayaquarium.org.*
- **Toronto Zoo, Toronto, Canada.** A camp-in can really be a camp out. Here families sleep on cots in safari-style tents at the Serengeti Bush Camp, the zoo's African-themed area in the suburbs of Toronto. You'll check in on rhinos, elephants, and hippos before dinner, and then explore the savanna at night by flashlight. A campfire follows and then a comfy bed—with flush toilets nearby. The next morning, you're awakened by African drums for breakfast and a morning hike that provides a chance to see zoo animals when they're most active. It costs $70 Canadian for children 6 to 11, $90 over 12, and includes a buffet dinner and breakfast. *Toronto Zoo, 361A Old Finch Ave., Toronto, ON M1B 5K7, Canada, 416-392-5929, www.torontozoo.com.*

- **Ship stays.** For a unique night's sleep, climb into a sailor's bunk during an encampment aboard the **Battleship *New Jersey*** (62 Battleship Place, Camden, NJ 08103, 856-966-1652, www.battleshipnewjersey.org), permanently anchored in Camden, New Jersey, across from Philadelphia. The World War II vessel invites families to sleep over as long as one member is between 6 and 17. As a temporary crew member, you can explore the nooks and crannies of the country's most decorated battleship, which stretches nearly 300 yards long and stands 11 stories tall. Kids love to climb up to the 16-inch guns turret, which could hit targets up to 23 miles away. Dinner in the ship's mess hall is included. The cost is $51 per person.

  The Wisconsin Maritime Museum in Manitowoc hosts several family overnights each year aboard the **U.S.S. *Cobia* submarine** (75 Maritime Dr., Manitowoc, WI 54220, 866-724-2356, www.wisconsinmaritime.org). The price is $39 per person. And the **U.S.S. *Hornet* aircraft carrier** (707 W. Hornet Ave., Alameda, CA 94501, 510-521-8448, www.uss-hornet.org) berthed in Alameda, California, near Oakland, also welcomes family sleepovers. The $60 per person price includes dinner and breakfast.

$PLURGE

SAN DIEGO ZOO

The San Diego Zoo offers several overnight options just for adults and women. They include a dinner buffet and drinks, and a wake-up mimosa delivered to your tent. Prices begin at $139 per person. *San Diego Zoo, 2920 Zoo Dr., San Diego, CA 92101, 800-407-9534, www.sandiegozoo.org.*

learn to build a wooden boat

WASHINGTON STATE & MAINE

We are tied to the ocean. And when we go back to the sea, whether it is to sail or to watch—we are going back from whence we came.

—PRESIDENT JOHN F. KENNEDY,
ADDRESS DURING THE AMERICA'S CUP RACES, NEWPORT, RHODE ISLAND (1962)

58 From Homer to Hemingway, writers have reflected man's fascination with the mystery, the mercurial nature, and the sheer vastness of the sea. Images of Phoenician sailors, the settlers of Easter Island, Christopher Columbus, and Captain Ahab lure us into the deep. Or, in the case of some modern mariners, into courses on building wooden boats.

Andrew Washburn, who runs the Center for Wooden Boats at Cama Beach State Park outside Seattle, Washington, explains the appeal: "There's this kind of truth and beauty of wooden boats. A well-made wooden boat is a beautiful thing in the way a well-made fiberglass boat is not. The process of it is beautiful. You're using hand tools. There's the feel and smell of the wood."

For Bob Welbon, a longtime Florida sailor and self-described "gadget guy" who grew up sailing wooden prams, a boatbuilding vacation combines love of the water with his love for woodworking. "It gets me into a different environment. I can hone up on skills I have and learn different skills. It gets me into some techniques that I'm afraid are being lost over time."

And perhaps as importantly, it's a return to youth. "As I boy, I spent my summers at summer camp. This is Big Boy Camp." Doesn't that just say it all?

Wooden boatbuilding courses are dotted around the country at various waterfront locations; some are for at-risk high school students, some for those interested in a career, and some for hobbyists like Welbon who want to spend a vacation honing an affection for seagoing traditions. Here are two schools that are perfect for the hobbyist:

Center for Wooden Boats, Cama Beach State Park, Washington. About 90 minutes north of Seattle lies a 1930s-era family resort on Puget Sound that became Cama Beach State Park in the 1990s. Facilities include the original boathouse and some 40 wooden boats—providing a perfect tie-in with Seattle's Center for Wooden Boats, which offers woodworking, boatbuilding, and maritime photography classes in the city and at Cama Beach. Some are specially designed for women and families.

One of the most popular courses at Cama Beach teaches participants to build a Norwegian pram. The course runs Saturday to Friday on select dates and costs $1,000. Participants typically stay in cozy 1950s-era cabins (from $65 per night during the summer/fall months) on the rocky shore, where they cook their own meals or grill with the neighbors. The 400-acre park offers hiking, wildlife-watching, fishing, and boat rentals—plenty to occupy family and friends who aren't into working with their hands.

Center for Wooden Boats, 360-387-9361, www.cwb.org.

WoodenBoat School, Brooklin, Maine. The most popular course of the many taught at this school overlooking Eggemoggin Reach south of Bar Harbor is "Fundamentals of Boatbuilding." In this two-week class students work on three different boats in various stages of construction—beginning a boat, planking, and finishing—at both blackboard and bench, learning about techniques and tools. Classes typically run from 8 a.m. to 5 p.m., with free time on Saturday afternoon and evenings for rowing, sailing, and visiting local boatyards.

The course costs $1,150 per person and is open to anyone, though it helps to have some familiarity with both woodworking and boating. Room and board in simple shared rooms with shared bath costs $450 per person per week; campsites cost $100 per week. Nonparticipating family members can also stay on the premises.

The WoodenBoat School offers a host of other classes, including boat repair and canoe construction. Some courses allow you to build your own kayak, dory, or dinghy—even carve a wooden duck decoy.

WoodenBoat School, 207-359-4651, www.thewoodenboatschool.com.

MORE BOATBUILDING SCHOOLS IN NORTH AMERICA

- **Arques School of Traditional Boatbuilding,** Sausalito, California, 415-331-7262, www.arqueschl.org.
- **Chesapeake Light Craft,** Annapolis, Maryland, 410-267-0137, www.clcboats.com.
- **Chesapeake Bay Maritime Museum,** St. Michaels, Maryland, 410-745-2916, www.cbmm.org.
- **Great Lakes Boat Building School,** Cedarville, Michigan, 906-484-1081, www.greatlakesboatbuilding.org.
- **Northwest School of Wooden Boat Building,** Port Haddock, Washington, on the Olympic Peninsula, 360-385-4948, www.nwboatschool.org.
- **Silva Bay Shipyard School,** Gabriola Island, British Columbia, Canada, 250-247-8809, www.boatschool.com.

get into the kitchen

NATIONWIDE

Cooking is like love. It should be entered into with abandon or not at all.

—HARRIET VAN HORNE, SYNDICATED NEWSPAPER COLUMNIST (1920–1998)

59 Postcards and paintings might make appealing souvenirs, but they fade over time. However a cooking class can last a lifetime. It's a souvenir that lets you literally bring the flavor of your journey home—that you, your friends, and family can all enjoy.

In recent years, cooking schools have gone mainstream. Demonstration classes let you watch a chef make dishes and allow time for nibbling. Think of it as a fancy meal with an educational component, and it's really quite a bargain. Participation classes are a bit more expensive, but they provide a hands-on experience preparing the food. Nearly every city has them, and all welcome visitors.

The classes listed below are all located in popular travel destinations that have a distinct culinary tradition. Some programs include enough activities that you can build a whole trip around. Others make a great way to spend part of a day. You'll have a chance to meet and cook beside locals, giving you a better understanding of your destination. Plus you'll eat well, too.

Chinese Southern Belle, Atlanta, Georgia. Atlanta's culinary scene has evolved well beyond Southern staples likes grits and barbecue. The city attracts immigrants from around the world, and most of them seem to shop on Buford Highway. A mother-daughter company, Chinese Southern Belle, offers bargain-priced classes at the **Buford Highway Farmers Market** (5600 Buford Hwy. NW, Doraville, 770-455-0770, www.aofwc.com), which isn't really a market, but a sprawling international grocery store. Two-hour demonstration classes cover topics like Asian dumplings, spring rolls, and sushi. The classes promise "hands-on demo, eating, kitchen/cooking/shopping tips, and entertaining Buddha-to-Bubba family stories." Classes run $25, but you get a goodie box and a $10 store gift card. Plus if first-time students mention the secret code—"*Ni Hao*, Y'All"—when registering, the class is only $10.

Chinese Southern Belle, 404-494-0088, www.chinesesouthernbelle.com.

Crescent City Cooks!, New Orleans, Louisiana. As any visitor to New Orleans knows, food is as much a part of the city as jazz and Mardi Gras. What better way to remember your trip than a cooking class? Crescent City Cooks! covers all the Cajun and Creole standards, for a moderate $30 a class, and those who take two in a week get 20 percent off supplies and souvenirs in their shop.

Classes are offered on a rotating schedule: Monday, Red Beans & Rice and More; Tuesday, Chicken & Andouille Gumbo; Wednesday, Jambalaya; Thursday, Shrimp Étouffée; Friday, Seafood Gumbo; Saturday, Jambalaya; and Sunday, Crawfish Étouffée.

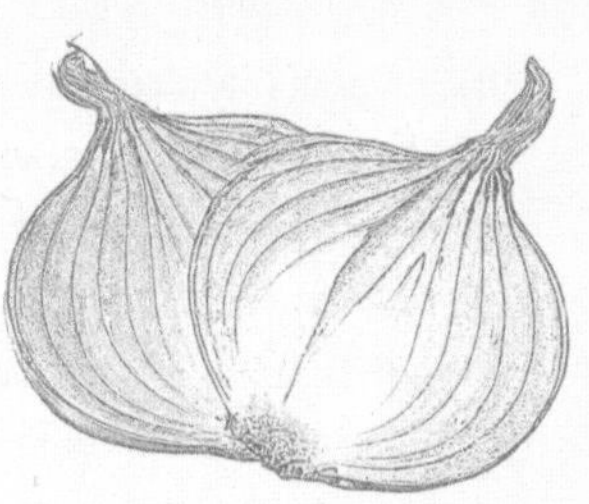

Crescent City Cooks! 1 Poydras St., New Orleans, LA 70130, 504-529-1600, www.crescentcitycooks.com.

Fresh & Wyld Farmhouse Inn, Paonia, Colorado. About two hours from Aspen, you can build a trip around a culinary experience. The Fresh & Wyld Farmhouse Inn has its own vegetable gardens, chickens, goats, berry patch, and heirloom apple trees to feed its guests. Cooking classes run $40 for four hours and include lunch. For a foodie getaway, arrive by noon on Wednesday for a S.O.U.L. (sustainable, organic, unprocessed, local) class, which covers topics as varied as Brunchy Things, Chicken in the Pot, or Date-Night Dinners. Spend Thursday and Friday visiting the area's acclaimed wineries or hiking in **Black Canyon of the Gunnison National Park** (102 Elk Creek, Gunnison, CO 81230, 970-641-2337, www.nps.gov/blca), but be sure to make it back for Friday Feasts, communal-style home-cooked dinners that run just $15. If you're visiting May through October, then spend Saturday morning in a farm-skill class to learn about tomato canning, applesauce-making, game sausage preparation, or apple picking and pressing. But what makes it an even better deal is that cooking class participants get 25 percent off room rates, which start at $95 and include a gourmet, farm-style organic breakfast.

Fresh & Wyld Farmhouse Inn, 1978 Harding Rd., Paonia, CO 81428, 970-527-4374, http://freshandwyldinn.com.

Silver Dollar City, Branson, Missouri. Who'd think you could learn something from a theme park? Branson's Silver Dollar City will let you expand your cooking skills while others in your party fling themselves around on thrill rides and take in musical performances and craft demonstrations.

$PLURGE

NEW YORK'S CULINARY INSTITUTE

With some of the nation's top international restaurants, New York City is a dining capital. Visitors can tap into that expertise at Manhattan's comprehensive Institute of Culinary Education. Recreational classes cover everything from Italian cooking to American comfort foods. It even offers grazing tours that wander the city to sample treats like dim sum or French macaroons. Classes run about $115, while tours are about $85. *Institute of Culinary Education, 50 W. 23rd St., New York, NY 10010, 800-522-4610, http://rec.iceculinary.com.*

Silver Dollar City's culinary classes not only cover home-style cooking and regional specialties, like Savory Skillet Dinners and Ozark succotash, but the park also offers classes tailored to special events and seasons, such as international specialties during the park's World-Fest; barbecue tips and side dishes during its Bluegrass & BBQ festival; and hearty stews, soups, and pies during the fall and Christmas season. Classes cost $12, on top of park admission, which runs $56.96 for adults, although local discounts are often available.

Silver Dollar City, 399 Silver Dollar City Pkwy., Branson, MO 65616, 800-475-9370, www.silverdollarcity.com.

Whole Foods Market, Austin, Texas. Whole Foods Market has helped raise the eating standards of the nation, bringing organic and gourmet foods to the masses. And although their prices aren't exactly discount (some folks call the store Whole Paycheck), you can find some bargains at their cooking classes. The chain's flagship store in Austin, Texas, has a dedicated culinary center. Midday Lunch Express demonstration classes run $18 and might include cooking with greens, steakhouse techniques, or southern Italian dishes. The hour-long sessions include a filling lunch. [$PLURGE: **For a splurge, consider hands-on classes like those devoted to vegetarian tapas or seafood grilling for $65 and up.**] Even if you're not interested in a class, the store offers a variety of entertainment from beer tastings to free movies on the rooftop plaza. About 30 other store locations around the country offer classes too, and theirs usually cost much less–some are even free. Find schedules through www.wholefoodsmarket.com/stores/.

Whole Foods Market, 525 N. Lamar Blvd., Austin, TX 78703, 512-476-1206, www.wholefoodsmarket.com/storesbeta/lamar.

delve beneath the headlines

CHAUTAUQUA, NEW YORK

When you step through Chautauqua's gates, you enter another world. It is one rooted in the past, but focusing very much on the present and future.

—FORMER SUPREME COURT JUSTICE SANDRA DAY O'CONNOR, IN *NATIONAL GEOGRAPHIC TRAVELER*

60 How would you like to spend your vacation with U.S. senators, Pulitzer Prize winners, filmmakers, and research scientists? It sounds like one of those annual gatherings reserved for world leaders, but this one is open to the public—and it's a bargain to boot.

For more than 135 years, the tiny upstate town of Chautauqua, New York, has been a summer gathering place for enlightened and enlightening discussion. The eponymous institution—first created to teach Methodist Sunday school teachers—was founded on the principles of art, education, religion, and education. For a visitor, that means you might catch a presentation by documentary filmmaker Ken Burns in the morning, and golf on a championship course in the afternoon. Your day can include a nondenominational service led by best-selling author and former Episcopal bishop John Shelby Spong or a class on Benjamin Franklin's worldview or the intricacies of genealogy.

Chautauqua's heyday was in the 1920s, when it traveled from city to city on a lecture circuit, reaching an estimated 40 million people. Now it's happily settled in its home base. During summers, the town of 1,500 reaches the density of Manhattan—without the traffic jams. In Chautauqua's 250-acre gated campus, you'll find few cars but scores of pedestrians. A free shuttle service means you can park your vehicle and forget about it. Most visitors stay Saturday to Saturday. A weeklong $362 gate pass allows entrance to most events.

Although Chautauquans would hate the expression, the town is really a theme park for thinking adults. Put simply, your pass gives you access to some of the brightest minds of our era. Although many of the issues discussed may be contentious—from same-sex marriage to genetic engineering—the emphasis is on exploring issues, not making points. "We're a kind of place that people can come and discuss a controversial topic in a very civil way," says Mike Sullivan, Chautauqua's director of institutional relations. "There's no place exactly like this."

Despite the heady atmosphere, Chautauqua is a family place, where doors are left unlocked and a bike is the preferred transportation. While parents are hearing the latest lecture on sustainable

OTHER CHAUTAUQUAS

At the height of the movement during the 1920s, towns across the nation hosted Chautauqua lectures. Although nowhere near the scale of the New York institution, a few locations keep the tradition alive with their own institutions, complete with lodgings.

- **Boulder, Colorado.** This Chautauqua campus dates from 1898 and is now a national historic landmark. With a wealth of educational resources at the nearby University of Colorado, the programming focuses on recreation and entertainment, including the six-week summer **Colorado Music Festival** (303-665-0599, www.coloradomusicfest.org), which offers four concerts a week. There's usually a silent movie shown once a week, and often kids' educational programs are scheduled. The bungalow-style cottages and lodges are situated below the distinctive Flatiron rock formations, providing easy access to thousands of acres of hiking. The Chautauqua is open year-round; although programming might be limited at certain times of year, the staff has listings of nearby lectures and activities. Cabins and rooms don't have phones or televisions. Summer pricing begins at $70 a night for an efficiency apartment in the Columbine Lodge. *Colorado Chautauqua Association, 900 Baseline Rd., Boulder, CO 80302, 303-442-3282, www.chautauqua.com.*
- **Lakeside, Ohio.** This Chautauqua opened in 1873 and every summer since has hosted leading scholars, authors, and chaplains at its idyllic campus on Lake Erie halfway between Cleveland and Toledo. About 5,000 guests attend during a typical week. Weekly topics might range from medical ethics to race in America to financial planning.

  There are also concerts, fitness classes, swimming, and many other recreational activities. Nightly entertainment ranges from comedians to musicians or acrobats. Adult gate passes run $17.50 per day or $122.50 per week; the last week of summer, rates are reduced. You can camp or stay at the historic Hotel Lakeside from $69 a night. Many of Lakeside's private cottages are available for weekly rental beginning at about $850 a week. *The Lakeside Association, 236 Walnut Ave., Lakeside, OH 43440, 866-952-5374, http://lakesideohio.com.*

energy technologies, kids can have a ball at preschool classes ($175 a week) or day camp ($170 a week). But everyone will want to come out for evening performances by notables like comedian Bob Newhart and country star Gretchen Wilson.

It's literally impossible to do everything, and for a first-time Chautauquan, a weeklong visit can be overwhelming. Sullivan suggests that visitors take a $5 campus tour on Saturday to get the lay of the land, and make sure to catch the orientation lecture Sunday night.

You'll definitely need a plan. Some guests sign up for Special Studies classes, an array of about 50 options from book discussions to sailing instruction. These carry an additional charge of about $50. But it's quite easy to fill your week without them.

The summer program is built on nine theme weeks stretching from the last week of June to the week before Labor Day. One topic might be the Ethics of Leadership featuring *New York Times* columnist David Brooks. A popular repeat topic has been Roger Rosenblatt and Friends, featuring the prize-winning author and folks like PBS journalist Jim Lehrer and playwright Marsha Norman, author of *Night Mother.* Each morning at 10:30, one of these speakers will take the stage at the 5,000-seat, covered amphitheater for a morning lecture.

Accommodations run the gamut from boardinghouses with shared bathrooms (about $75 a night) to rental houses, which can run thousands a week. [$PLURGE: **A room in the historic Athenaeum Hotel** (4 S. Lake Dr., 800-821-1881, http://athenaeum-hotel.com), on the grounds of the institution, begins at about $300 a night, including three meals a day for two people. Options are detailed on the institution's website.] Despite the notable names, for some the best part of Chautauqua is meeting other guests. Every summer evening for more than a century now, visitors have ended their day congregating on the front porch of their home or boardinghouse to discuss the day's lectures, entertainment, and insights with neighbors and new friends.

HOW TO GET IN TOUCH

Chautauqua Institution, P.O. Box 28, 1 Ames Ave., Chautauqua, NY 14722, 800-836-2787, www.ciweb.org.

find out how cranberries *really* grow

MASSACHUSETTS & WISCONSIN

It has been an unchallengeable American doctrine that cranberry sauce, a pink goo with overtones of sugared tomatoes, is a delectable necessity of the Thanksgiving board and that turkey is uneatable without it.

—ALISTAIR COOKE, BRITISH JOURNALIST AND COMMENTATOR (1908–2004)

61 If you think of cranberries as a Pilgrim thing, you're partly right. Yes, we eat cranberry sauce with Thanksgiving turkey, and yes, that's partly because cranberries—one of America's few indigenous fruits—grow on Cape Cod, Massachusetts, where the Pilgrims set up shop in the early 17th century. But these days, the world's largest producing cranberry state is Wisconsin—which means those curious about cranberries have two places to find out how they *really* grow.

Whether you're heading to the East or the Midwest, prime time for cranberry visits is the fall harvest season, when there's plenty to see in the bogs and cranberries galore to enjoy eating.

Cape Cod, Massachusetts. In Massachusetts, the Columbus Day weekend is the peak time to visit. That's when the Cape Cod Cranberry Growers' Association and the A.D. Makepeace Company—the world's largest cranberry grower—join forces to sponsor the annual Cranberry Harvest Celebration held at **Makepeace's Tihonet Village** (158 Tihonet Rd., 508-295-1000, www.cranberryharvest.org, $2) in Wareham, with crafts, music, cranberry cooking demos, pony and wagon rides, and visits to a cranberry bog. At other times of year, you can check out the **Tihonet Village Market** (508-295-5437, www.tihonetvillagemarket.com, closed Sun.) for fresh fruits, vegetables, and specialty items, including fresh cranberries in season.

Come any time in October and stay at **On Cranberry Pond B&B** (508-946-0768, www.oncranberrypond.com, double room with breakfast from $120) in Middleboro,

COOL CRANBERRY FACTOIDS

- 10.8 billion cranberries are consumed each holiday season.
- More than 94 percent of all Thanksgiving dinners include cranberry sauce.
- Americans consume more than 5 million gallons of jellied cranberry sauce each year during the holidays.

Source: Ocean Spray agricultural cooperative

and owner Jeannine LaBossiere-Krushas says she'll fix you up with a private bog visit. Come at another time of year and you can still gobble up her cranberry-and-apple pancakes, cranberry-banana-chocolate muffins, or other cranberry-flavored breakfasts.

Both On Cranberry Pond and A.D. Makepeace are an easy jaunt from the historic whaling center of New Bedford and historic Plymouth, where the Pilgrims landed. Neither is technically on Cape Cod, which has its own bogs as well. Some Cape Cod bogs offer tours (508-432-0790, www.cranberrybogtour.com, $15). **An English Garden B&B** (888-788-1908, www.anenglishgardenbb.com) in Dennisport has rooms from $100 in the fall. Tip: When in Falmouth, don't miss **Betsy's Diner** (457 Main St., 508-540-0060) for regional comfort food from quahogs to homemade pies in a classic diner.

Cape Cod Chamber of Commerce, 888-332-2732 or 508-362-3225, www.capecodchamber.org; **Southeastern Massachusetts Convention & Visitors Bureau,** 800 288-6263 or 508-997-1250, www.bristol-county.org; **Massachusetts Office of Travel & Tourism,** 800-227-6277, www.massvacation.com.

Wisconsin Rapids, Wisconsin. In Wisconsin, cranberry growers and tourism types have set up a Cranberry Highway via the Wisconsin Rapids Area Convention & Visitors Bureau (715-422-4650, www.visitwisrapids.com). In June, the region hosts a **Cranberry Blossom Festival** (800-554-4484, www.blossomfest.com), with a parade, music, and, of course, cranberry-flavored goodies. During the fall harvest season—usually late September through early November—cranberry aficionados can find vacation packages starting at $200 that include two nights' lodging for two people, tickets to local cranberry attractions, and a cranberry trail map; they are available through the visitors bureau's website.

If the packages are all booked, try hotels directly. **Hotel Mead** (800-843-6323, www.hotelmead.com) is most often recommended; the area also boasts several chain motels.

During the harvest season, you can bike or drive yourself on a self-guided trip or take a tour of the marshes of the 6,000-acre **Glacial Lake Cranberries farm** (715-887-4161, www.cranberrylink.com/glacial.html, tour $10) or visit several marshes with the **Future Farmers of America from Pittsfield High School** (715-884-6412).

If you snag a Glacial Lake Cranberries tour during harvest season, blossom season, or another time of year, you might catch up with Mary Brazeau Brown, owner of this farm that has been producing cranberries since 1873. She explains how cranberries *really* grow: not in the water like those guys you see in the Ocean Spray commercial, but on a perennial vine in sandy acidic land. Though the berries do require a lot of water, the bogs typically are flooded only for harvest, she says.

CRANBERRIES IN NEW YORK CITY

If you just can't get to Massachusetts or Wisconsin, head to **New York's Rockefeller Plaza** in those three days just before Thanksgiving. For several days, the cranberry growers' cooperative you know as Ocean Spray sets up a 1,500-square-foot bog, complete with a cranberry grower who can answer your questions.

The ripe berries float to the surface of the water after they are knocked off the vine, making for easy picking.

As for the best way to eat cranberries, she recommends taking raw berries, poking them with a toothpick topped by an American flag, and dipping them in hot caramel, like an apple. "People just go nuts," she says. Yum.

Whether you visit during fall or another time, check out the **Wisconsin Cranberry Discovery Center** in Warrens (204 Main St., 608-378-4878, www.discovercranberries.com, $4, call for hours), featuring historic displays, a bakery (think cranberry pies and scones), and an ice-cream parlor serving—what else?—cranberry ice cream.

Wisconsin Department of Tourism, 800-432-8747 or 608-266-2161, www.travelwisconsin.com.

journeys of discovery

NATIONWIDE

Live as if you were to die tomorrow. Learn as if you were to live forever.

—MAHATMA GANDHI, INDIAN PHILOSOPHER
AND SPIRITUAL AND POLITICAL LEADER (1869–1948)

62 Some trips seem out of a budget traveler's means. Sure we'd like to stay in an exclusive retreat built for gilded age millionaires. Or pass days touring Los Angeles' top museums with a private guide. But who has the money for that?

With Road Scholar, either experience could be yours for less than $600, including all accommodations, tours, and most meals. Until recently Road Scholar was called Elderhostel and its programs were largely reserved for folks over the age of 50. But the organization's new name is meant to appeal to visitors of all ages, who are welcome to choose from literally thousands of trips. But be warned: These are not laze-by-the-pool-and-work-on-your-tan vacations. As the Road Scholar motto promises, they are "Adventures in Lifelong Learning."

Tours are led by experts and hosted by local sponsors, usually colleges, universities, or other education centers. That means you'll get some classroom time before seeing the sights, resulting in a deeper, more meaningful vacation. "There's always a local host, so you know you're getting the real deal," says Teresa Wilkin, a longtime Road Scholar customer.

Take for instance the gilded age adventure set in New York's Adirondacks region. It's called the Vanderbilt Great Camp and the Great Outdoors and it includes lodging in Great Camp Sagamore, the national historic landmark camp that belonged to the Vanderbilts. Another trip focusing on

ROAD SCHOLAR TRIPS FOR LESS THAN $600

- **Adventures on Water.** Cape May, New Jersey, three nights, four days, $565.
- **Art and Literature of the American West.** Poteau, Oklahoma, five nights, six days, $528.
- **Avenues of History—From Colonial America to Camp David.** Sharpsburg, Maryland, five nights, six days, $573.
- **Drawing and Watercolor for Nature Journaling.** St. Joseph, Minnesota, five nights, six days, $563.
- **Outdoor Discovery Camp.** Canoeing, kayaking, caving, rock climbing; Carbondale, Illinois, four nights, five days, $499.

Find more trips online at www.roadscholar.org/programs/bargains.asp.

MAKE EVERY TRIP A LEARNING VACATION

Special tours are nice, but here are a few ideas to enrich any journey:

- Check with local museums for programs or day trips.
- Scan the local paper for lectures and special events. Weekly alternative papers usually have extensive listings.
- If you're passing by a college or university, take a few minutes to read the bulletin boards at the student center. You'll often discover a visiting scholar is speaking or a performance is scheduled.
- Ask questions. People will be glad to tell you about local history or demonstrate how a local product is made.
- Check with a friend, or a friend of a friend, who lives in or has knowledge of the area. They're sure to have suggestions.

a great residence is the Los Angeles tour, which is a three-night excursion that centers around the Getty mansion in Malibu.

The programs were first designed to give older Americans access to the type of trips that younger travelers enjoy while tramping around Europe and staying in inexpensive youth hostels. Originally most accommodations were in college or university dormitories and most meals were from a cafeteria. Since then Road Scholar has grown up. While their trips aren't luxurious, most guests stay in motel-style rooms. And meals are memorable too.

Wilkin recently completed a tour of Savannah and St. Simons Island, Georgia. Although the topic was the early colonial settlers, the trip included dinner at Food Network personality Paula Deen's famous restaurant, The Lady & Sons.

Fellow participants are another bonus. "It's just a great way to travel with like-minded people," says Wilkin, "people who are curious and interested in the world."

The traditional Road Scholar tour includes local bus transportation and group meals, lectures, and tours. Prices can range from a few hundred dollars to several thousand. But it's usually much less than you'd pay for a typical vacation. Some travelers might bristle at being slowed down by a tour group, particularly one that despite the name change tends toward seniors, but you're always free to venture out on your own. Or you might consider Independent City Discoveries, which are more active and limited to smaller groups. A few specialized tours let you take part in service programs, rebuilding historic cabins in Montana or helping endangered terns in Maine, for example. Other programs include Adventure Afloat, which are based on cruise ships, women-only outings, and intergenerational trips for grandparents and grandchildren. Plus there's a phone-book-size catalog of international trips.

For Wilkin, who usually takes two trips a year, Road Scholar keeps travel affordable and invigorating. On one trip she stayed at a research center in Bermuda for two weeks at a fraction of the cost she would have had to pay for a hotel on the pricey island. On other adventures she has explored West Texas and Maritime Canada, where many British Loyalists fled after the Revolutionary War. Wilkin, who is single, always agrees to have a roommate. More often than not, though, there's no one to match her with, so she gets private accommodations without having to pay a singles supplement.

HOW TO GET IN TOUCH

Road Scholar, 11 Avenue de Lafayette, Boston, MA 02111, 800-454-5768, www.roadscholar.org.

play sherlock holmes

CAPE MAY, NEW JERSEY

When you have eliminated the impossible, whatever remains, however improbable, must be the truth.

—AUTHOR SIR ARTHUR CONAN DOYLE, IN THE GUISE OF SHERLOCK HOLMES, *THE SIGN OF THE FOUR* (1890)

63 High ratings for the shows of the *CSI* franchise prove what authors P. D. James, Agatha Christie, and Sir Arthur Conan Doyle have long understood: We love to puzzle through murder mysteries.

Did Colonel Mustard commit murder with a candlestick in the library, or was it Miss Scarlett in the conservatory with the rope? Such classic who-done-its are the realm of purists, who sign up for murder dinners and weekends at bed-and-breakfasts around the country, mystery train rides, and the twice-yearly Sherlock Holmes weekends at the Mid-Atlantic Center for the Arts.

For more than two decades, this center in Cape May, New Jersey, has hosted Holmes weekends drawing dozens of participants for each mystery. "Some are really into the search for clues, some are dyed-in-the-wool Sherlock Holmes fans," explains Mary Stewart, who has been involved with the weekends since their inception. "Some people just seem to be fascinated with the idea of participation; I don't think they care if they figure it out."

Part of the lure is the gingerbread-village ambience of Cape May, a designated historic landmark city dating from the late 1800s and home to some 600 Victorian homes. The Holmes and other mystery dinners and events hosted by the center are part of a long-standing effort to preserve the town, in part by bringing tourists to the area during the slow season. (That's why the mystery weekends are scheduled for November and May.)

The weekend starts with the Friday night coffee-and-dessert event, when as many as 150 guests—many in Victorian dress—meet for the first time to watch the first act of the mystery drama that will play out both on stage and off throughout the weekend. Characters (all with motive and opportunity) are introduced; a crime is committed; a sheet of clues is handed out. Saturday morning is time for leisure, but come Saturday afternoon, mystery hounds embark on a two-hour self-guided Search for Clues Tour through local bed-and-breakfasts, hunting for links between the crime, the clues (often historic artifacts like maps or birth certificates), and those sneaky characters. The "detectives" then submit their clue sheets filled in with potential plots, twists, and solutions—unfortunately before

MORE MYSTERIES TO SOLVE

- **The Citadel, Phoenix.** Book at least a month in advance for a chance to battle the Citadel, a spy network at the heart of a live-action, role-playing game complete with high-tech flourishes and live actors who perform at changing locations throughout the city. Don't come alone; the game requires a team of four, paying $125 per person. And don't be in a rush; a typical game runs six hours or more. *The Citadel, 40 N. Central Ave., Ste. 1400, Phoenix, AZ, 602-795-0300, www.citadelphoenix.com.*
- **"CSI: The Experience," Las Vegas.** If you just want to play CSI for a bit, you can roll it into a Las Vegas weekend at "CSI: The Experience," an interactive exhibit at the MGM-Grand hotel featuring three murder cases complete with "crime scenes," "labs" for analysis, and an "office" where you can work out your case. Most visitors stay 60 to 90 minutes. Tickets cost $30 for ages 12 and up (younger participants are allowed, but the experience isn't recommended for those under 12). *"CSI: The Experience," MGM-Grand, 3799 Las Vegas Blvd., Las Vegas, NV, 877-660-0660, www.csiexhibit.com.*
- **Road Scholar, various locations.** If you're interested in incorporating CSI science into your weekend, the group Road Scholar—formerly known as Elderhostel and oriented to travelers over 50—offers several five-night CSI-style learning vacations. Among them are a program in Riverside, California, featuring area crime lab directors and medical examiners (about $913); a program in Deland, Florida, that includes a visit to the Florida Department of Law Enforcement Crime Lab ($575); and a program for teens and grandparents at Buena Park, California (about $865). Prices are all per person and include all meals, lodging, and instruction. *Road Scholar, 11 Avenue de Lafayette, Boston, MA, 800-454-5768, www.roadscholar.org.*

a second act of the play fills in more of the gaps. On Sunday, all is revealed in a third act of the play. The detective whose clue sheet has produced the most correct answers wins $250; one earnest but misguided snoop is dubbed the "Clueless Wonder" and gets a gift certificate for a return visit.

Weekends are set up with plenty of leisure time for wandering the town and checking out local restaurants. But for diehards, a local theater company offers a Saturday night performance of—what else?—a murder mystery.

Weekend packages cost $95 per person without accommodations, or $270 per person with the mystery, two-nights lodging, and some meals. If that's too steep, you could just snag the $15 ticket for the Search of Clues Tour. You probably won't have enough details to solve the mystery, but unless you've got a Holmes twist of mind, having all the other clues might not help, either.

HOW TO GET IN TOUCH

Chamber of Commerce of Greater Cape May, 609-884-5508, www.capemaychamber.com.
Mid-Atlantic Center for the Arts & Humanities, 609-884-5404, www.capemaymac.org.

see television being made

LOS ANGELES, CALIFORNIA

The damned thing works!

—INVENTOR PHILO FARNSWORTH, IN A TELEGRAM ANNOUNCING THE FIRST SUCCESSFUL TELEVISION BROADCAST (1927)

64 Like it or not, TV governs our lives. From infancy to old age, we tune in for entertainment, news, and even company. But how much do you know about what's involved in putting together the programs and broadcasts that we encounter every day?

Truth is, making television isn't easy. It takes teamwork, cooperation, and patience. And often it's an art form that's created in public, free for interested viewers. In fact, some productions even give you refreshments while you watch them work.

Any visitor to Los Angeles should catch at least one television taping—it's fun to see celebrities, of course, and it lets you see inside a production studio—however, television enthusiasts can easily build a vacation around the medium. A major clearinghouse for tickets is **Audiences Unlimited** (www.tvtickets.com). Simply go to their website and see what's available in the next 30 days. If there's a show you're particularly interested in seeing, check back at 9 a.m. Pacific time every morning, when the site is updated. And return often, as productions are often added at the last moment. The websites **On Camera Audiences** (www.ocatv.com) and Hollywoodtickets.com also distribute tickets.

In addition, some shows give out their own tickets—for example, ***The Tonight Show*** (www.nbc.com/the-tonight-show/tickets/)—and you can request tickets from their websites.

While it may be hard to get a ticket to see popular shows, such as *Two and a Half Men,* perhaps the best introduction to the world of television comes from watching the taping of television pilots. From February through April, production studios are busy creating new shows they hope will be accepted for the coming fall television season. Not only will you have a chance to see a potential future hit in its infancy, but you also can see how producers, actors, and writers change the show based on the audience's reaction. Yes, you can shape a work in progress.

"They really count on the audience," says Lynda Latronico, group coordinating manager for Audiences Unlimited. "If something's not funny and the audience's not laughing, and they're supposed to be laughing, they may rewrite it on the spot."

Another busy time is August through November, when network studios tape shows for the current TV season. April through July is perhaps the slowest time for tapings.

Although most shows—including situation comedies and game shows—last just 30 minutes with commercials when they air on TV, the time it takes to tape them is another story altogether. Expect to be seated for about three hours. Usually a stand-up comic will entertain you as the crew and actors prepare, but for the most part you'll be watching professionals at work, sometimes shooting a scene again and again. "Watch the director, and sound booth behind you. They're the ones doing the actual taping," Latronico says.

If you haven't been able to secure a ticket, you'll often find people giving them away at popular tourist spots, like **Grauman's Chinese Theatre** (6925 Hollywood Blvd., 323-464-8111) in Hollywood and Universal Studios, north of Hollywood. In addition, **visitor information centers in downtown Los Angeles** (685 S. Figueroa St., 213-689-8822) and **Hollywood** (6801 Hollywood Blvd., 323-467-6412) sometimes have tickets, too.

Other things to know:

- Most shows have minimum ages, and even those seeking young audience members ask that someone over 18 accompany the minor.
- Eat before you go. Tapings may continue for hours. Often the production company will provide pizza or bottled water, but usually it's just a snack, not a meal.
- Leave backpacks, large bags, and cell phones in the car. Even if cell phones are turned off, some studios don't want them in the production area for technical and/or security reasons.

TUNE IN TO THIS L.A. MUSEUM

Want to watch *My Favorite Martian,* or relive news footage of the moon landing? You can catch these and 140,000 other television and radio shows and news broadcasts from the past century at the ambitious **Paley Center for Media.** The center (formerly the Museum of Television and Radio) takes the lowly TV program to new heights in a sleek contemporary L.A. building. Simply type your selection into a computer catalog, and head to a semiprivate booth to take it in. Fortunately commercials are included, because they're often just as entertaining as the programs. Suggested donation: $10.

An active public lecture series features big names from the entertainment world discussing their craft and, often, the societal impact of it. Programs might range from Hollywood's take on the immigrant experience to a discussion on the influence of the music show *Soul Train.* There are often panels with screenwriters, directors, and actors about new and classic shows. Admission ranges in price from free to $15 or more for special events. *Paley Center for Media, 465 N. Beverly Dr., Beverly Hills, CA 90210, 310-786-1000, www.paleycenter.org. Open Wed.–Sun. 12 p.m.–5 p.m., & Thurs. until 8 p.m.*

- Most studios are in Burbank, Hollywood, and Culver City. Get directions, and allow plenty of time to get there.
- A ticket doesn't always guarantee admission. Visitors are seated on a first-come, first-served basis, but those who aren't seated are usually offered tickets for another taping that night.
- Dress nicely and arrive early to up your chances of getting a seat or perhaps sitting up front. You might even get a cameo.
- Wear layers. With all the lighting, the stages can get warm, and studios often compensate by cranking up the air-conditioning.

HOW TO GET IN TOUCH

LA Inc., 333 S. Hope St., 18th Fl., Los Angeles, CA 90071, 800-228-2452 or 213-624-7300, www.discoverlosangeles.com.

learn to survive in the wild

ARIZONA & TENNESSEE

To survive it is often necessary to fight and to fight you have to dirty yourself.

—AUTHOR GEORGE ORWELL, *LOOKING BACK ON THE SPANISH WAR* (1943)

65 On a sun-stroked afternoon, the outdoors can seem like a haven. But nature isn't necessarily kind—or even benign—especially when the weather turns vicious or you sprain an ankle. Getting caught in the wild without the appropriate knowledge, skills, or gear can be downright dangerous, as unfortunate hikers learn every year. Courses such as the two noted here can help you prepare, both physically and mentally. And even if you limit your nature encounters to gazing through a picture window, you'll enjoy them more if you understand the forces lurking outside the glass.

Ancient Pathways' Desert Survival Course, Colorado Plateau. If you're seriously into *Man vs. Wild* and *Survivorman,* this course could be for you. Participants head out into the Arizona desert to study firsthand how to deal with heat-related injuries, build improvised shelters, locate water, build a fire, and dodge desert monsters like snakes and scorpions.

For three days guests practice skills like making mud huts and discerning edible plants from the poisonous ones. Most important, perhaps, they learn how to get their minds into survivor mode. The $350 course includes group camping, instruction, and two meals daily.

If that's not quite rugged enough, check out Ancient Pathways' five-day hunting and trapping course in Utah, where you'll kill, skin, and cook your dinner. The cost is $495.

Ancient Pathways, 928-526-2552, www.apathways.com.

BE PREPARED

Don't leave home without telling others where you're planning to go and when you expect to return. Be sure to take the proper gear, including the following:

- Sufficient water (probably more than you think you need)
- A hat appropriate for the weather
- Sturdy hiking boots
- Trail snacks and necessary food
- Pocket knife
- Extra socks
- Matches
- Flashlight
- Rain gear (depending on the terrain)
- Gloves (in winter)
- Cell phone for emergencies (they do sometimes work in surprising places)

Wilderness Wildlife Week, Pigeon Forge, Tennessee. This festival is proof that you don't have to become Daniel Boone to enjoy the outdoors in winter. Twenty years ago, this started out as a one-day event—partly as a way for Gatlinburg photographer Ken Jenkins to share his love of the Great Smoky Mountains, and partly to draw tourists in January. Now the event spans a week and draws more than 24,000 visitors for hikes in the Great Smoky Mountains National Park and nearby forests (one of the most popular: a nighttime "owl prowl"), photography classes, sing-alongs, lectures about raptors, and seminars on how to use a compass and recognize the signs of changing weather.

"Visitors come once, and then they're Wilderness Wildlife Week junkies," says Leon Downey, executive director of Pigeon Forge Department of Tourism. Jenkins still participates. And true to his vision, the classes and events and festivities remain free.

Chain motels and cabin rentals start at less than $100 per night. One option to consider: **Affordable Cabins in the Smokies** (3536 Parkway, 866-456-3781, www.affordablecabinsinthesmokies.com).

Wilderness Wildlife Week, 800-251-9100, www.mypigeonforge.com/events_winterfest_wilderness.aspx.

go back to school

INDIANA & MAINE

Be a student so long as you still have something to learn, and this will mean all your life.

—HENRY L. DOHERTY, FOUNDER OF CITGO (1870–1939)

66 If youth is wasted on the young, there's no better example than college. Students trudge off to classes, not realizing that in a few years they'll pine for the days of exploring new ideas, meeting with professors, and soaking up the intellectual atmosphere of a campus.

Well, there is such a thing as a second chance. Every summer, colleges, facing the challenge of utilizing a largely empty campus, have opened their doors for short-term noncredit programs. Problem is that like college in general, these classes aren't always cheap. But two schools manage to buck the trend: Indiana University and Colby College.

Indiana University, Bloomington, Indiana. For perhaps the biggest bargain, head to Indiana University. Every summer since 1972, the school has hosted a weeklong Mini University, which is open to all—even alumni from Big 10 rivals, like the University of Wisconsin, where Walt and Mary Prouty met and went to school. But for ten years now, the couple has been heading to IU every June. "We've told our family, the week after Father's Day is our week, and they shouldn't plan anything then. And that includes weddings, baptisms, and family reunions," Mary says.

Why the Hoosier loyalty? The couple loves the variety of the hundred-plus classes on offer. Most classes meet for just one session, meaning there's no homework or term papers to foul up the experience. In recent years, Walt, a retired biochemist, has been drawn to the liberal arts. He gravitates toward lectures from political scientists, economists, and historians, who explore contemporary issues like whether the national debt is really a concern. He also has taken in physiology lectures about the effect of aging on sleep and appetite patterns, and a class on bioethics. Mary gravitates to sessions on performing arts. Indiana is known for its music school, and some classes feature dance and classical lectures and performances. "The biggest frustration is that you can't be in three places at the same time," she says.

The Proutys suggest asking other Mini U students for recommendations—everyone, it seems, has a favorite professor.

The program itself is a bargain, costing $295 per person. Registration opens in March and usually sells out quickly. Many attendees choose to stay on campus at the school's **Biddle Hotel**

$PLURGE

THE OXFORD EXPERIENCE

If you're heading back to college, why not go to one of the world's most famous? England's Oxford University welcomes summer students in its noncredit Oxford Experience program. The weeklong sessions start at 1,050 British pounds, and include room, board, and, most important, a chance to study in Christ College. Classes range from "Jane Austen's Heroines" to "Scientific Breakthroughs of the Twentieth Century." You'll even have a chance to dine in Tudor Hall, which will be recognizable to some people as the inspiration for Hogwarts in the Harry Potter films. Register quickly, though. Applications are usually available by February and classes do sell out. *The Oxford Experience, OUDCE, 1 Wellington Square, Oxford OX1 2JA, UK, www.conted.ox.ac.uk/courses/details.php?id=134.*

(900 E. 7th St., 800-209-8145 or 812-856-6381, www.imu.indiana.edu/hotel/), which is located in the Indiana Memorial Union, the massive student center where most classes are held. Rooms run from $89 to $229 per day and include free parking. You can stay off campus for less and buy a parking pass good for the week for $25. The union has a food court, and registration includes several free events, such as a faculty reception at the university president's house. But make sure to leave some time to sample Bloomington's restaurants. The Midwest city is home to the Dalai Lama's brother, and thus some surprising Tibetan eateries. Try **Anyetsang's Little Tibet** (415 E. 4th St., 812-331-0122), where you can choose from more than a dozen specialties with soup and salad for less than $10. The **Runcible Spoon** (412 E. 6th St., 812-334-3997) is another campus favorite, a café and coffee roaster that also offers imaginative dinner entrees like phyllo-wrapped chicken and vegetables for less than $10.

As tempting as it is to explore, don't forget to socialize with your fellow students. You might win recognition. Friday brings a mini-commencement ceremony, and the awarding of the Green Beanie honoring the most enthusiastic "freshman."

Mini University, IU Alumni Association, 1000 E. 17th St., Bloomington, IN 47408, 800-824-3044 or 812-855-4822, http://alumni.indiana.edu/events/miniu/.

Colby College, Waterville, Maine. For many of us, reading and vacation go together. It's the only time during the year when you can retreat from the daily grind and responsibilities and think about ideas and literature. That's the idea behind the Wachs Great Books Summer Institute at Colby College, which began in 1956. Attendees all read the same books before coming to campus, and then spend a week discussing them. In recent years, it has focused on Nobel Prize winners or classic volumes like *War and Peace*. Think of it as a book club on steroids.

Attendees gather in groups of 10 to 12 every morning and tackle the books' weighty topics. Some sessions are led by a volunteer, while other sessions are purposely leaderless. But in all cases, the college gives the groups general guidelines and a few ground rules. Number one: No discussing the book if you haven't read it. And keep the discussion to the book itself—no fair bringing in outside sources. As you can imagine, the gatherings lead to spirited conversations.

The sessions have proved so popular that the college has added a Junior Great Books program for the children or grandchildren of attendees, who read classic children's literature like Newbery Award winners.

But one thing's beyond debate. The program is an incredible bargain. The $525 per person fee covers room, board, and all your books. The junior program requires children to stay with an adult and costs $340 for ages 10 to 16, $300 for 5 to 9. The schedule leaves afternoons open to explore the campus, which has a noteworthy art museum, lake, hiking paths, tennis courts, pool, sauna, pitch and putt golf course, and croquet. One afternoon features an optional trip to the Maine shore for $25, and most evenings include social activities, including a Friday night lobster bake with drinks.

Wachs Great Books Summer Institute at Colby, 824 Thomas Rd., Lafayette Hill, PA 19444, 215-836-2380, www.greatbooksdiscussionprograms.org/.

tune up your garage band

NATIONWIDE

Rock & Roll is not an age,
it's an attitude.

—MUSICIAN DAVE MASON (B. 1946)

67 When New York media executive Rik Kirkland was a teen, his rocker days were cut short by his parents, who thought his burgeoning band was a bad influence. When he hit his 40s, "rather than getting a red Porsche for my midlife crisis, I started playing a guitar again," he says.

Another friend had a saxophone. "Then sure enough the boyfriend of someone was a bass player and came and joined us, then someone else's brother played drums." Eventually the friends became The Prowlers, and some 15 years later, the eight musicians—guitarists, singers, a saxophonist, harmonica player, and mandolin player—are still playing together. A few times a year, they're even booked for gigs. Free gigs, but gigs nonetheless.

For those people who don't have a ready-made group of musical buddies—or who always wanted to play but never quite smoothed out their chords—several music programs around the country are designed to take you beyond *Guitar Hero.*

The flashier programs involve name rockers and come with the splurge price tag you'd expect. So for an option that won't knock the leather off your wallet, check out Rock Boot Camps, weekend-long immersion instruction for ages 13 and up that is offered in various locations around the country. The schedule varies year to year; past cities hosting the camps have included Phoenix, Arizona; Salt Lake City, Utah; Cleveland, Ohio; and

$PLURGE

ROCK 'N' ROLL FANTASY CAMP

Created by concert producer David Fishof (who reunited the Monkees and worked with Ringo Starr to put together the All Starr Band), Rock 'n' Roll Fantasy Camp lets you live the dream of jamming, writing songs, and performing on a major concert stage (think Liverpool, England's Cavern Club; Philadelphia's Trocadero; San Francisco's Fillmore) with name rockers (Todd Rundgren, Jeff Beck, Dickey Betts, and Mark Hudson have all made appearances at the fantasy camp). Weekend packages start at $2,000; hotel is extra. A youth program is also offered. *Rock 'n' Roll Fantasy Camp, 888-762-2263, www.rockcamp.com.*

WEEKEND WARRIORS

If a less expensive "mental vacation" fits your needs, various high-end music shops around the country sponsor Boomer-oriented Weekend Warrior programs that bring musicians and would-be rockers together. These programs typically last a few hours per weekend on subsequent weeks or over a period of a month—providing a break from the grind of a workday week, and a jump start on putting together your own band.

Now a nationwide program, Weekend Warriors got its start in the 1990s when Skip Maggiora of Sacramento, California, a former rocker turned music store owner, saw contemporaries and former band members disappear—and then turn up in his store, **Skip's Music** (2740 Auburn Blvd., Sacramento, CA 95821, 916-484-7575, www.skipsmusic.com). "I figured out if I made it easy for them," he says. "If it didn't take up much of their time, and they didn't have to worry about not having a place to play or friends to play with—it would give them a way to get music back in their lives."

At Skip's, rehearsals take place for four consecutive weeks, two hours at a time; the fifth week the band plays a concert for family and friends, who then get hooked. "The first year I had a band that had a rice farmer and a lawyer in it. The next time, I had a band called A Rice Farm and Four Lawyers." At Skip's the four-week program costs $100.

Weekend Warriors has now spread across the country, thanks to the **National Association of Music Merchants** (760-438-8001, www.namm.org). Other stores offering the program include Iowa-based **West Music** (800-373-2000, www.westmusic.com), Wisconsin-based **White House of Music** (262-798-9700, www.whitehouseofmusic.com), and **Mom's Music** (502-897-3304, www.momsmusic.com) in Louisville, Kentucky.

Greensboro, North Carolina. The price is $299, and you're on your own for accommodations. Participants typically bring their own instruments.

Aspiring musicians can range from beginner to intermediate guitar and bass players, and from drummers to singers, says program organizer Grant Ferguson. The musical weekend kicks off Friday night with an open jam session; participants are then evaluated and grouped into bands based on experience. (Adults are often grouped together.) Each band then chooses a name and a song to perform at the end-of-camp final concert; the rest of the weekend is filled with rehearsals, individual instruction, and informative seminars on the music industry, audio recording, and touring. A digital arts track runs simultaneous for people who do not want to play music but are interested in learning to build a band image through posters, social networking media, and video. At the end of the rock-and-roll weekend experience, both groups come together for the final concert.

Kevin Melmud of Phoenix—a drummer who, like Kirkland, rejoined a band in his early 40s—signed up with his teenage son, Max. "It was mostly for him and me just to do something where we have the common interest," Melmud says. And though most of the other campers were teens at that camp, Melmud wasn't the only adult. "It's very intense. The kids have a blast, and they develop good relationships."

Mom Perri Worthey had a similar experience. Her teen son Sterling likes the camp so much he's attended five times. "He has stepped out of his shell so much," she says. "I never thought I'd see him get up on stage. It's really helped his sense of timing to play with other musicians."

HOW TO GET IN TOUCH

Rock Boot Camps, 866-448-3007, www.rockbootcamps.com.

pen your memoir

ERIE, PENNSYLVANIA

If there's a book you really want to read, but it hasn't been written yet, then you must write it.

—TONI MORRISON (B. 1931), 20TH-CENTURY AMERICAN AUTHOR

68 Writing is a solitary pursuit. Ultimately, it's just you and a blank screen or sheet of paper.

But that doesn't mean writers have to struggle on their own. Conferences and workshops are a proven and popular way to jump-start your writing and develop new techniques. Just as important, it offers a chance to learn from other scribes. You'll discover even best-selling novelists have bouts of frustration and self-doubt—just like you. The experience is educational and ultimately inspirational. You'll leave a writers conference recharged and eager to jump into your manuscript.

The challenge is that the most popular writer workshops can be expensive and selective. Some limit attendance to established and published writers, which shuts the beginner out. Others last two weeks or longer, a hefty commitment for someone just starting out or with a day job. But a few gatherings are particularly well suited for novices.

One of the best, the Pennwriters Conference, purposely keeps its doors open to everyone. For one intense, packed long weekend in May, writers and writer wannabees are thrown together with editors, instructors, book agents, and published authors. "Everybody there is to be supportive

KEEP A TRAVEL JOURNAL

A journal is one of the most precious souvenirs you can bring back from a trip. Here are a few tips for creating one you'll treasure for years:

- A journal should be more than just a list of your day's activities. Write about people you meet, memorable moments, or striking scenes.
- Use all your senses. Write about the smells, tastes, and sounds as well as the sights.
- Bring a glue stick to keep tickets, brochures, postcards. Or get a journal with pockets or transparent display pages.
- Have colored pencils to capture a scene. Or invite a child to draw one for you.
- Write down the wording on signs, ads, or graffiti that captures your attention.
- Go digital: Blog your thoughts and pictures. If you don't have a blog, you can get a free one at Internet sites like www.travelpod.com.

of one another," said Lisa Kastner, who attended her first Pennwriters Conference in 2003, and became the group's president within just a few years. "At my first conference, I was amazed how welcoming the people were. I could walk up to anyone and they would help me."

The group started as an organization limited to Pennsylvania writers. Although it still holds its annual conference in the Keystone State, attendees now come from as far away as England, Puerto Rico, and Alaska. The meetings alternate every year between Pittsburgh and Lancaster. The organizers note that each location offers enough nearby attractions that some attendees bring their families, who spend the time exploring while one family member remains at the conference. Then they can meet up at the end of the day back at the hotel.

Unlike other similar events, Pennwriters doesn't limit its focus to one type of writing. You'll find more than 30 workshops, covering everything from memoirs to science fiction, poetry to thrillers. "Every genre can learn from another," Kastner says. "Although someone might not be a fantasy writer, they'll find value in attending

FIND A WORKSHOP

You'll find writing events across the country. One of the best sources is ShawGuides (www.shawguides.com), which lists nearly a thousand writing conferences and workshops. Here are three that are both low cost and novice-writer friendly:

- **Grub Street's Muse and the Marketplace.** This Boston-based conference helps writers understand the publishing world, and offers plenty of opportunities for networking with editors and agents. The weekend gathering includes six workshops covering writing topics like how to use images in writing and crafting characters from real people, plus two seminars and a luncheon. Cost: $345 for nonmembers, or $235 for one day. *Grub Street's Muse and the Marketplace, 160 Boylston St., 4th Fl., Boston, MA 02116, 617-695-0075, www.museandthemarketplace.com.*
- **Iowa Summer Writing Festival.** More than 1,500 people attend this festival every June and July. You need only be older than 21 and have a desire to write. The weekend and weeklong sessions cover 130 different workshop options across all writing genres. The price is $560 per week and $280 per weekend. Nearby accommodations begin at $74 per night. *Iowa Summer Writing Festival, University of Iowa, C215 Seashore Hall, Iowa City, IA 52242, 319-335-4160, www.continuetolearn.uiowa.edu/iswfest/.*
- **Split Rock Art Program.** This program offers three- and five-day workshops at the University of Minnesota's 3,400-acre Cloquet Forestry Center in northern Minnesota. Topics range from screenwriting and memoirs to writing about grief. Cost: $370–$555, plus $55 registration. Housing runs $485 for six nights. *Split Rock Arts Program, University of Minnesota, 360 Coffey Hall, 1420 Eckles Ave., St. Paul, MN 55108, 612-625-1976, www.cce.umn.edu/Split-Rock-Arts-Program.*

a worldbuilding course because all fiction writers are creating imaginary worlds." In a typical year, sessions may cover writing a memoir, graphic novels, or horror. Others will be devoted to topics that often bedevil writers, such as crafting dialogue, creating characters, and working with conflict.

The conference runs Friday morning through lunch on Sunday. The group does its best to keep costs low—another way to attract and support beginners. Pricing options allow you to attend for one day ($114) or for the full three days ($225). The registration includes several meals, including a lunch with a keynote speaker. An evening banquet (in 2010 it was with best-selling thriller writer James Rollins) carries an extra charge. The group also keeps expenses down by holding the conference in locations like an airport hotel instead of a fancy resort.

The conference usually attracts around 250 registrants, plus a few dozen instructors and special guests. Former participants say they find talking to other attendees is as valuable as the workshops. "Experienced writers are willing to reach down the ladder to help those just on the first step," said Annette Dashofy, a published nonfiction and short-story writer, who is trying to become a mystery novelist. She offers a simple tip to meet anyone at the conference. "Ask someone what they're writing. You'll always get an answer and you'll have a conversation."

She warns against overscheduling yourself, though: Your brain will be fried. "Spend some time in the hospitality suite and at the bar." That's where many Pennwriters have struck up conversations with agents and editors, who eventually ended up publishing their work.

HOW TO GET IN TOUCH

Pennwriters, 823 Oregon Ave., Erie, PA 16505, 814-838-6870, www.pennwriters.org.

get your hands dirty at a farm stay

NATIONWIDE

Farming looks mighty easy when your plow is a pencil and you're a thousand miles from the cornfield.

—PRESIDENT DWIGHT D. EISENHOWER, SPEECH IN PEORIA, ILLINOIS (1956)

69 For urbanites, agriculture can be a conceptual art. Farm stays let you see where your veggies and sheep's wool really come from—and what "organic" really means.

"Nobody has any grandparents to go to a family farm at Thanksgiving or in the summer anymore," says Scottie Jones, who started offering farm stays at her **Leaping Lamb Farm** (877-820-6132, www.leapinglambfarm.com) near Portland, Oregon, about five years ago. Many of her guests are families who come to get into nature, reconnect—her farm's rental cottage doesn't have a television—and teach their children that "eggs don't just come from a carton in Safeway."

"People may understand their food comes out of the ground, but they haven't understood what work is involved in doing it," Jones says. At Leaping Lamb, guests pay $125 for two people ($25 per person more up to six people total) for lodging in a cabin and the fixings to make their own breakfast. They can collect their own eggs in the morning, pet the donkey, and forage in the farm's gardens for apples, raspberries, blueberries, potatoes, corn, and lettuce.

Jones and her husband, Greg, started offering farm stays to supplement her family's income and she is trying to help other small farmers do the same through **Farm Stay U.S.** (www.farmstayus.com). **Sleep in the Hay** (www.sleepinthehay.com) has a similar mission. Founder Kari Brayman teaches elementary and middle school students in the North Carolina mountains about growing food. "So many times kids ask, 'Where does milk come from?' They think it comes from the store, not a cow," she says.

Both websites will lead you to a variety of working farms, comfy bed-and-breakfasts, hostels, and camps that offer a visitor-friendly experience with a cabin or room for lodging. Here are a few of the options available:

- **Casa de la Pradera.** At this bed-and-breakfast near Sacramento, California, guests pay $80 per night to stay on an organic farm, where they stroll among the gardens and learn about organic practices before heading off to visit gold rush towns and the nearby wineries of Amador County. *Casa de la Pradera, 209-245-6042, www.fiddletownfarms.com.*

- **Farm Sanctuary.** This organization has two shelters that take in animals rescued from slaughterhouses and factory farms, one in northern California near Orland (530-865-4617) and the other in upstate New York near Watkins Glen (607-583-2225). Both offer tours for a minimal fee. Stay overnight at either farm for $95 double occupancy, breakfast and tour included. Out of respect for the animals, only vegan food is allowed on premises. *Farm Sanctuary, www.farmsanctuary.org.*
- **Mango Sunset.** Located on Hawaii's Big Island, this bed-and-breakfast with ocean views and four guest rooms is set on an 8-acre certified organic Kona coffee farm; rooms from $100. Guests who ask in advance can get an estate tour and learn how the organic beans are grown and roasted. *Mango Sunset, 808-325-0909, www.mangosunset.com.*
- **Maple Hill Manor.** At this Springfield, Kentucky, establishment, guests stay in an award-winning antebellum bed-and-breakfast on a working alpaca and llama farm; rooms start at $119. Even if you're not staying at the inn, you can take a free tour to learn about alpacas and buy sweaters, finger puppets, and jewelry made from alpaca fibers. *Maple Hill Manor, 859-336-3075, www.maplehillmanor.com.*
- **Turquoise Barn.** Located in New York's Catskill Mountains, Turquoise Barn offers guests the chance to help in the intimate organic vegetable garden, chat with the artists turned farmers who live there, eat a vegan or vegetarian meal, and join fellow guests by the bonfire. A bed in a hostel room costs $35. *Turquoise Barn, 607-538-1235, www.turquoisebarn.com.*

WILL WORK FOR FOOD

Some farm visits allow you to learn about rural life and volunteer at the same time.

- **Farm Rescue.** Through this Jamestown, North Dakota–based organization, volunteers can help family farmers hit with illness, injury, or some other disaster by working in fields or helping with website design, accounting, and other needs for the farm or for the nonprofit organization. Volunteers pay their own transportation to the place they are volunteering; Farm Rescue provides lodging and some meals on the ground. *Farm Rescue, 701-252-2017, www.farmrescue.org.*
- **Virgin Islands Sustainable Farm Institute.** In St. Croix in the U.S. Virgin Islands, the Virgin Islands Sustainable Farm Institute focuses on ecological organic farming and education, including work-study farming programs and Slow Food internships. Regular nonworking guests also are welcome; room and board starts at $35 per night. *Virgin Islands Sustainable Farm Institute, www.visfi.org, e-mail: info@visfi.org.*

For more locations where you can trade work for food and accommodations, search online at www.wwoof.org, www.growfood.org, and http://helpx.net/.

sip your way through wine country

EL DORADO COUNTY, CALIFORNIA

You have only so many bottles in your life, never drink a bad one.

—LEN EVANS, AUSTRALIAN WINE WRITER (1930–2006)

70 Beer may try to pass itself off as America's beverage, but wine can just as easily make that claim. It's made everywhere these days from Maine to Florida, North Dakota to Alaska. And although some vintages feel a bit like novelties (Hawaiian passion fruit wine, anyone?), others are quietly building a reputation for quality.

A wine vacation doesn't have to involve tasting fees, crowds, and hype. Hundreds of winemakers are eager to share their vintages and wisdom with visitors. And with the money you save, you can pick up a bottle or two to enjoy with friends at home, who will undoubtedly be impressed by your new wine knowledge.

California's El Dorado County offers everything that its more famous Golden State brethren do—only in a more relaxed atmosphere. Its winemakers, clustered around Placerville, also make a point of offering free tastings, something you'll rarely find in Napa or Sonoma.

"It's a more casual environment," says Jenna Palacio, who lives in nearby Lake Tahoe and has visited many of the county's 60 vineyards. "I don't feel like I need to dress up to go wine-tasting. If I spill something on myself it's OK."

The county's oldest winery, **Boeger** (1709 Carson Rd., Placerville, 800-655-2634 or 530-622-8094, www.boegerwinery.com), is a great picnic spot and grows surprising grapes like Tempranillo, usually associated with Spain. "They do some really cool blends," Palacio says. During summers it hosts free Friday night Summer Sippin' concerts. Pick up a picnic at **Dedrick's Cheese** (312 Main St., Placerville, 530-344-8282) and get a bottle on site. As a plus, Boeger is located in the Apple Hill area, with 50 different orchards. If you're in the area in season (early Sept.–early Dec.), make sure to try an apple doughnut at **Rainbow Orchards** (2569 Larsen Dr., Camino, 530-644-1594, www.rainboworchards.info).

If you can come during the annual Bring Out the Barrel wine tasting event, held the last weekend in January, you'll get a winemaker's view on the craft, allowing you to sample wines at different stages of maturity, straight from the barrel.

WINE, WINE EVERYWHERE

Almost anywhere you visit, you'll fine wineries. These two regions get rave reviews:

- **Missouri River Region, Missouri.** Some of the West's oldest wineries are found along the Missouri River, not far from St. Louis. Several are concentrated between Augusta and Hermann, a quaint town with German heritage. Try **Stone Hill Winery** (Hermann, 800-909-9463, www.stonehillwinery.com), where wine made from the Norton grape (Missouri's official state grape) has won numerous awards. *Wine & Grape Board, 1616 Missouri Blvd., P.O. Box 630, Jefferson City, MO 65102, 800-392-9463, www.missouriwine.org.*
- **North Fork of Long Island, New York.** Long Island's southeast end with its bounty of beaches has long attracted Manhattanites, but the island's northeast end has been steadily gaining ground due to its growing wine and food scene. The region's oldest winery, **Castello di Borghese** (Cutchogue, 631-734-5111, www.castellodiborghese.com), has won honors for its Pinot Noir, Sauvignon Blanc, Meritage, and Chardonnay. *Long Island Wine Council, 5120 Sound Ave., P.O. Box 600, Riverhead, NY 11901, 631-369-5887, www.longislandwinecouncil.com.*

Unaged wine, you'll learn, may taste like dirty socks, but over time it becomes something to savor. Nearly two dozen wineries participate, and although visitors pay about $20 for the special event, they can save a bundle on wine since many wineries are trying to clear their cellars in preparation for newer vintages.

But anytime is good for a visit. **Jodar Vineyards & Winery** (3405 Carson Ct., Placerville, 530-644-3474, www.jodarwinery.com) is known for a variety of red wines including Black Bear Port, which got its name because the winemaker struggles to get the grapes before the area's black bears. Family-owned **Lava Cap Winery** (2221 Fruitridge Rd., Placerville, 800-475-0175 or 530-621-0175, www.lavacap.com) is one of the county's biggest producers, bottling around 20,000 cases per year. In the county's Pleasant Valley area, stop by **Miraflores Winery** (2120 Four Springs Trail, Placerville, 530-647-8505, www.mirafloreswinery.com), one of four area vineyards known for grape varieties associated with France's Rhône Valley. The winery recently opened a stunning new tasting room built with recycled antiquities, including timbers from the Port of San Francisco and stone floors salvaged from Cyprus. And try to sneak in a visit to **Sierra Vista Vineyards & Winery** (4560 Cabernet Way, Placerville, 800-945-3916 or 530-622-7221, www.sierravistawinery.com), which has views of the Sierra Nevada and a friendly tasting room staff.

As one might expect, all the fine wine has attracted good food. In the Fair Play area, make it a point to catch happy hour at the **Gold Vine Grill** (6028 Grizzly Flat Rd., Somerset, 530-626-4042), where you can sample several local wines and an appetizer for $15 per person. Interestingly, two wineries in Fair Play feature pizza on most Friday nights May through September: Charles B. Mitchell and Fitzpatrick. **Charles B. Mitchell** (8221 Stoney Creek Rd., 530-620-3467, www.charlesbmitchell.com) makes gourmet pizza in an Italian oak-barrel-fired oven and pairs them with Italian-style wines. Between sipping, try the bocce courts; unlimited pizza and salad runs $15 per person. At **Fitzpatrick Winery** (7740 Fair Play Rd., 800-245-9166, www.fitzpatrickwinery.com), there's often live music to accompany your meal.

You won't have to break your budget at bedtime. Bunk down in Placerville at newly renovated **Gold Trail Motor Lodge** (1970 Broadway, Placerville, 530-622-2906), where rooms have all the expected amenities and run just $50. Or consider the historic **Cary House** (300 Main St., Placerville, 530-622-4271, www.caryhouse.com), which plays up the area's gold rush roots; rooms from $89. [$PLURGE: But if you'd like to splurge, retreat to **Eden Vale Inn** (1780 Springvale Rd., Placerville, 530-621-0901, www.edenvaleinn.com). This luxury bed-and-breakfast, hewn out of an old hay barn, offers five unique and very private rooms, with deep soaking spa tubs. Rooms from $149, but ask about midweek specials.]

HOW TO GET IN TOUCH

El Dorado County Visitors Authority, c/o Chamber of Commerce, 542 Main St., Placerville, CA 95667, 800-457-6279 or 530-621-5885, www.visit-eldorado.com.

El Dorado Winery Association, P.O. Box 1614, Placerville, CA 95667, 800-306-3956, www.eldoradowines.org.

learn to make jewelry—and more

NORTH CAROLINA

Crafts make us feel rooted,
give us a sense of belonging and connect us with our history.

—PHYLLIS GEORGE, FORMER MISS AMERICA AND AUTHOR OF SEVERAL CRAFTS BOOKS

71 Whether it's a gift or pure self-indulgence, jewelry is a winner with Americans, who spend some $30 billion annually on the bling. But if your interest is more about filling your creative well than your armoire, head to the Blue Ridge of western North Carolina for a jewelry-making class at the John C. Campbell Folk School.

Born in Indiana in 1867, John C. Campbell studied education and theology in New England. In the early 1900s Campbell and his young wife went to study conditions in the then impoverished mountains of Appalachia and dreamed of creating a folk school that would preserve the region's culture and improve education. After Campbell died in 1919, his wife, Olive, and her friend Marguerite Butler traveled to Scandinavia to study folk schools there and returned to found the John C. Campbell school in 1925.

Students range from young mothers to retirees, says Barbara Joiner, who runs the school's jewelry programs. "Some are looking for a new skill, some are looking to improve skills. Other people come because their husband or wife is taking a class, and they just pick something."

That "something" might be a weekend class in metal wire weaving or making paper beads, a five-day class in cloisonné enameling, or a six-day class in stone setting. Courses teach students to set up a loom for weaving a bead bracelet or launch them into silversmithing. In recent years, classes that mix clay with metals and stones to make jewelry have become increasingly popular. In a weekend, students typically can make a ring, a pair of earrings, and a bracelet to take home.

But the real takeaway may be a sense of curiosity whetted. If jewelry isn't your thing, try one of the school's other 850 short classes. There's wood turning, blacksmithing, needlework, painting, photography, broommaking, quilting, dance, cheesemaking, glass-bead making, marbling, storytelling, spinning, pottery, gardening—even kaleidoscope making. Classes typically are small, from a handful to as many as a dozen students; all last a week or less.

Costs vary by class, but as a general rule, tuition costs less than $100 per day and includes all supplies. Lodging is extra and starts at $18 per day for a tent site (meals extra); $79 for dorm space (including three meals daily); and $108 per person for a shared room with bath (including meals).

The setting is part of the attraction: 300 acres of farmlike land and woods in the Blue Ridge near Brasstown, North Carolina, with simple but comfortable accommodations, hearty food, and a comfortable, noncompetitive environment. Brasstown, located in Clay County, is southeast of Murphy, North Carolina, and just north of the Georgia border.

Even if they don't leave as a burgeoning Louis Comfort Tiffany or Louis Cartier, students go home with a sense of self. "When they're here, they feel like they're part of a community of people working together, having fun, being active and intelligent. And in a lot of cases, inspired," says school director Jan Davidson. No wonder most students come back for more.

HOW TO GET IN TOUCH

John C. Campbell Folk School, 1 Folk School Rd., Brasstown, NC 28902, 800-365-5724, www.folkschool.org.

Clay County Chamber of Commerce, 828-389-3704, www.ncmtnchamber.com.

MORE CRAFTS SCHOOLS

- **Appalachian Center for Craft, Smithville, Tennessee.** Intensive courses in summer months ranging from three days to three weeks in textiles, metals, clay, blacksmithing, glass, and wood. Costs vary by course but start at $300; lodging and meals not included. *931-372-3051, www.tntech.edu/craftcenter/home/.*
- **Haystack Mountain School of Crafts, Deer Isle, Maine.** One- and two-week classes offered each summer including glass, basketry, printmaking, quilting, clay, wood turning, and metal. Tuition is $450 for a one-week class; $760 for two weeks; on-campus lodging starts at $175 per week. *207-348-2306, www.haystack-mtn.org.*
- **Mendocino Art Center, Mendocino, California.** Courses in fiber arts, ceramics, visual arts, jewelry, and sculpture. Costs range from $200–$300 plus materials for a weekend course; lodging and meals not included. *707-937-5818, www.mendocinoartcenter.org.*
- **North House Folk School, Grand Marais, Minnesota.** Boatbuilding, basketry, outdoor skills, painting, sailing, and fiber arts are among the half-day and weeks-long courses taught here. Course costs vary; lodging and meals not included. *218-387-9762, www.northhouse.org.*
- **Penland School of Crafts, Penland, North Carolina.** One-, two-, and eight-week workshops in textiles, drawing, clay, photography, metals, and other crafts. One-week classes start around $470; room and board varies, but starts at $407 per week in a dorm room. *828-765-2359, www.penland.org.*

step up your steps

NEW HAMPSHIRE & WEST VIRGINIA

There is a bit of insanity in dancing that does everybody a great deal of good.

—EDWIN DENBY, POET AND DANCE CRITIC (1903–1983)

72 There's a reason we still watch Fred Astaire and Ginger Rogers even now. When they glided across a dance floor, it was literally art in motion. No one can promise you'll be able to dip and swing with the same style and grace, but there's definitely no reason to be a wallflower. Weekend dance programs provide a no-pressure way to learn the basics of ballroom. Pretty soon, you'll feel like you're dancing on the stars, if not with them. These two dance weekend programs offer a friendly, supportive environment for beginners, but enough new moves to keep the fleet-footed on their toes too.

Pipestem Resort State Park. You'll find a similar dance getaway at Pipestem Resort State Park in West Virginia, where a weekend of dancing, including two nights lodging, dance instruction, and evening dances, runs just under $300 a couple.

"We can take care of the person who has never danced," says Sandi Elam, who serves as the disc jockey while her daughter and another couple work as instructors. "The scariest time is the first lesson, but that's with anything you do: a yoga class, a golf class, you're intimidated to no end. But to watch these people grow through a weekend, it's very rewarding."

Elam says she'll continue playing music as long as dancers want, sometimes well after midnight. "I play until they can't dance anymore."

While television shows like *Dancing with the Stars* have raised new awareness about ballroom dancing, it has been a mixed blessing, Elam says, "The stars complain how hard it is, and it scares some people away."

The resort, located about two hours southeast of Charleston, has a golf course and also offers fishing, hiking, and horseback riding. But Elam says most the options go unexplored. "None of them are going to go out hiking and run the risk of spraining an ankle and not being able to dance."

Pipestem Resort State Park, P.O. Box 150, Pipestem, WV 25979, 304-466-1800, www.pipestemresort.com.

Purity Spring Resort. For decades now, this resort in East Madison, New Hampshire, has hosted four dance weekends a year. For about $200 per person, including two night's accommodations and meals, guests get several group lessons and evening galas where they can try out their new moves. It's a bargain: Dance weekends at other locations can cost many times more.

"They make it fun," says Art Deleault, who took up dancing with his wife about four years ago and recently attended his first Purity Springs dance program. "It's very comfortable even for the novice. Even if you don't know much, you can pick it up."

$PLURGE

DANCING AT SEA

USA Dance, a national association promoting ballroom dancing, sponsors an annual weeklong Caribbean cruise that's open to nonmembers. The event includes 16 free class choices per day while at sea, and eight choices while in port. There are evening dance events and even dance-themed shore excursions. Instructors are nationally recognized. Prices begin at $599 per person, double occupancy. *USA Dance, 888-391-2680, www.dancecruise usadance.com.*

Each weekend focuses on two dance styles, like mambo and hustle, or waltz and fox-trot. The action kicks off Friday evening with an informal social dance. If you don't know what you're doing, the instructors will provide some basic tips to get you started. Saturday brings two-hour lessons in the morning and afternoon, which are followed by a black-tie optional dance that night. On Sunday morning, there's a chance to review the steps.

In between, the kitchen provides filling dishes, like prime rib, salmon, and vegetable lasagna. On Saturday night, it's served on a buffet so you can fuel up for hours of cha-cha. "When you're not dancing, you're eating," Deleault says. "It's a very relaxing weekend." Many visitors return year after year, but every weekend includes first-timers too. Although the music might seem old-fashioned, the dancing has wide appeal. Couples range in age from their 30s to 70s.

"I teach people to have fun with it," says Paul Demers, who runs the weekend with his wife, Doris. His approach is to teach basic steps that are easy for beginners, but that more skilled dancers can adapt into flashier moves.

The family-owned resort is an old-fashioned retreat at the southern end of the White Mountains. Although you probably won't have time away from the dance floor, there are hiking trails and canoeing and kayaking available, too. Tip: If you sign up for a dance weekend over Memorial Day, you can stay a third night for just the price of the meals, $27 per person.

Purity Spring Resort, 1251 Eaton Rd., Rte. 153, East Madison, NH 03849, 800-373-3754, www.purityspring.com.

bring in the laughs

CHICAGO, ILLINOIS

More of me comes out when I improvise.

—ARTIST EDWARD HOPPER (1882–1967)

73 It's hard work to be funny. A well-delivered line. An off-the-cuff comment. A crazy observation. All are usually products of study, practice, and amazing self-confidence.

What's almost as amazing is that you can begin to acquire these skills in weekend and weeklong workshops at Chicago's Second City. The theater company is North America's epicenter of comedy. A who's who of comics have passed through its halls and honed their craft on its stages: John and Jim Belushi, Bill Murray, John Candy, Steve Carell, Martin Short, Gilda Radner, Dan Aykroyd, Mike Myers, Bonnie Hunt, Eugene Levy, Stephen Colbert, and Tina Fey, to name a few.

While some students have dreams of guest starring on *Saturday Night Live,* many come because they've always wanted to see what it's like to improvise, or have friends who have laughed at their jokes for years and urged them to try. Classes range from introductory improvisation to comedy writing to physical comedy. Advanced and specialty classes are available for experienced students, many of whom stay for two weeks to complete an entire sequence of training.

Most classes are scheduled during the summer, but there are some offerings at other times. Three-day "intensives" and weeklong "immersions" both run $285. Since immersions last a half day, some students enroll in two courses at a time. Lodging's not included, but Second City, located in Chicago's Old Town neighborhood, has discount arrangements with nearby hotels. You can get a bed for $35 a night at a youth hostel, or pay $300 for a week in a college dormitory. Hotels begin at $89 a night. After classes, students often gravitate to nearby **Corcoran's Grill & Pub** (1615 N. Wells St., 312-440-0885) for reasonably priced appetizers, burgers, and salads. After performances, you'll likely find the cast at a favorite dive bar, **Old Town Alehouse** (219 W. North Ave., 312-944-7020). Bottom line: There won't be a big number on the bottom line after a week at Second City.

While many in the classes are college theater students or recent graduates, others are new to performing. You might find yourself making up lines in a skit about professional wrestling with lawyers, educators, and retirees. It's possible for families to attend, as children can enroll in Second City's youth day camps ($725 for two weeks) while parents take the adult classes.

Whatever you take, you can be sure a class will yield moments of hilarity that you'll treasure for years—a priceless souvenir. And you'll also leave with new faith in yourself and a tight set of friends.

"It's amazing how close you can get to a group in five days," says Kelsey Wagner, who had performed one night of improv near her home in San Jose, California, before she took her first Second City class. Now she's a regular with the ComedySportz troupe, which performs in the San Francisco Bay Area.

One reason students bond so quickly is the nature of improvisation. Since you're literally making up material on the spot, you'll only succeed if everyone works together. Students quickly learn they need to rely on one another.

It all starts out simply. In Wagner's first class, the students stood in a circle and their teacher started by throwing an imaginary red ball to someone across the room. That person then threw it to someone else and so forth. A moment later, the instructor tossed out an imaginary paper airplane, then a baby, then a wet cat, and then a chain saw. Soon the circle was alive with flying imaginary objects. The ice was broken, and the students began to see that they had the power to create something from nothing.

CHICAGO'S FAMOUS COMEDY CLUBS

The Windy City is the center of the comedy universe. Even if you can't attend a comedy class, you'll still find inspiration (and low-priced tickets) at some of the city's top clubs. Many offer free or discount performances featuring new students of comedy. It's a great bargain, but plan to order a drink to support the fledgling comics. Schedules and discounts change, so call ahead and ask about the latest deals.

- **The Annoyance Theatre & Bar.** A rotating schedule of popular shows. Look for $5 performances on Wednesdays, and discounted tickets Tuesdays and Sundays. *The Annoyance Theatre & Bar, 4830 N. Broadway, 773-561-4665, www.annoyanceproductions.com.*
- **ComedySportz Theatre.** Wednesday nights at ComedySportz are free, with Battle Prov taking place at nine, when a group of ComedySportz comedians takes on a team of college comedy students, and an hour of open mike at ten. *ComedySportz Theatre, 929 W. Belmont Ave., 773-549-8080, www.comedysportzchicago.com.*
- **The Playground Theater.** Described as the nation's first and only not-for-profit co-op theater devoted to improvisational comedy. Depending on the night, admission can be free or $5, and you'll rarely pay more than $10. *The Playground Theater, 3209 N. Halsted St., 773-871-3793, www.the-playground.com.*
- **Second City.** Two resident troupes and performances most evenings. Tickets usually run about $12. For a super bargain, catch student and workshop performances. Sketch-a-Sketch, a triple-bill, features new material on Thursday nights at 10:30 and is free. On Monday nights, the e.t.c. theater features Level 5 Conservatory students; tickets are just $5. *Second City, 1608 N. Wells St., 312-664-3959, www.secondcity.com.*

"It opens your brain up to how many possibilities there are," Wagner says.

After a day of literally putting yourself out there, you'll have homework, but no one will be complaining. The staff urges students to catch improv shows at Second City and all over Chicago. Students not only get a free ticket to a Second City performance, but they also receive a card good for free or discounted admission at comedy clubs around the city. Students relish the chance to study professionals using the same techniques they just learned—and then they get a chance to try it out in class the next day

Student Melissa Saunders became such a fan of the classes that she went three times in one year. The mother and educator said she yearned to get back in touch with her theatrical side, and found she couldn't get enough. "It just felt really free to be around so many creative people, to have an excuse to be silly and ridiculous and laugh and laugh and laugh."

Months later she could see the difference the class made when she was the announcer at a high school reunion and felt the confidence to speak all night in front of the crowd without notes or a chance for preparation.

Yes, it can be intense and intimidating, but the staff's goal is to build you up, not down. "The more successes students have in class, and the happier they are when they leave Second City, that's how we measure our success," says Matt Hovde, artistic director of the training center.

HOW TO GET IN TOUCH

Second City, 1608 N. Wells St., Chicago, IL 60614, 312-664-3959, www.secondcity.com.

sharpen your spanish

OAXACA, MEXICO

A different language is a different vision of life.

—FEDERICO FELLINI, ITALIAN FILM DIRECTOR (1920–1993)

74 A second—or third—language is more than just a communications tool. It's a way of exploring cultural intricacies and lets you soak up arts, food, politics, and humor in a way that's nearly impossible when the punch lines don't translate.

For North Americans who have so many Latin countries to the south, no second tongue is handier than Spanish. The best way to learn any language is to study and live in a place where your mother tongue is rarely spoken, so sign up for an immersion Spanish language course in Oaxaca, Mexico. For as little as a week—or months on end—you can spend a few hours each day studying with a teacher, with the rest of the time spent learning to make a mask, whisking up the perfect enchilada, and practicing your newfound skills daily with your host family or other locals.

The cozy colonial city of Oaxaca is home to the popular Instituto Cultural Oaxaca. On arrival, students are tested and grouped by ability; each morning they spend three hours in class before settling in for an hour of *intercambio*—chat—with a local resident. In the afternoons, many students opt for cultural courses, such as Mexican cinema, weaving, ceramics (the region is famous for its crafts, especially its black clay pottery), salsa dancing, and cooking.

Alternatively, students can choose to spend their afternoons wandering this mountain-rimmed town—a UNESCO World Heritage site filled with cafés spilling onto the main square, domed colonial churches (don't miss the Santo Domingo church's Altar of Gold), and graceful stucco buildings in brilliant cobalt or vermilion hues. Galleries and museums dot the center, carrying on the tradition of contemporary artists such as Rufino Tamayo, Rodolfo Morales, and Francisco Toledo. Indigenous locals dressed in bright traditional garb sell weavings and baskets of vanilla beans in the market; at night, a brass band often plays in the *zócalo,* or town square. Festivals are colorful and frequent, and the November 1 Day of the Dead celebration is celebrated with fanfare. Thanks to its setting, Oaxaca enjoys clear, dry, and comfortably cool (around 65°F) weather year-round.

Language-instruction programs plus the daily intercambio start at $120 per week, plus an initial $55 registration fee; adding on the afternoon cultural workshops raises the cost to $160 per week. Private classes and inexpensive excursions to outlying villages are also offered.

Many students stay with a host family arranged by the school, with fees starting at $13 per night including breakfast—an experience that often wins raves, especially among solo travelers.

BEYOND OAXACA

Lisa Yanke of North Carolina got hooked on learning Spanish for work and is now on a quest to perfect her skills. In the last few years, she has visited five programs—three in Costa Rica, one in Spain, one in Puerto Rico.

Her tips: (1) Pay attention to whether the school is affiliated with any U.S. colleges—a good marker for reliability. (2) Check out reviews from students who have been to the school at its current location. She once attended a school in San Juan, Puerto Rico, that had moved recently to an area that didn't feel safe; she left after a day.

At most programs, the longer you stay, the lower the price. All offer homestays and private accommodation at an additional price. Recommended programs include the following:

- **Antigua, Guatemala.** The epicenter of Central America's Spanish language programs, Antigua is home to 80 Spanish-language schools catering to foreigners, tucked into the glory of a cobbled colonial town. Among the many recommended schools are **Escuela de Español San Jose El Viejo** (www.sanjoseelviejo.com), **Centro Linguistico International Spanish School** (www.spanishcontact.com), and **Academia de Español Guatemala** (www.learnspanishinguatemala.com). Prices vary according to the program but generally start at $85 per week for a half day of classes; lodging extra.
- **Costa Rica. CPI Spanish Immersion School** (www.cpi-edu.com) holds classes in tourist-friendly places—in the cloud forest at Monteverde, on the coast in Guanacaste Province, and the town of Heredia. One-week classes cost $330 per week and include some activities; lodging extra.
- **Guanajuato, Mexico.** Travel writer Tim Leffel brought his wife and two young children to study here at **Escuela Mexicana** (www.escuelamexicana.com) and gave the experience a big thumbs up. Group classes start at $60 per week; lodging extra.

For eight weeks, Wisconsin college student Kathleen Neelson stayed in a private room with a family whose 18- and 20-year-old daughters took her to the local shops to buy bread and included her in activities. With no TV in her room and no Internet access at her host family's house, Neelson says she got used to entertaining herself with books—another learning experience.

Homestays are not required, however; students can stay wherever they choose. Oaxaca offers a range of lodging in apartments (starting around $450 per month) and local hotels and inns.

HOW TO GET IN TOUCH

Instituto Cultural Oaxaca, 52-951-515-3404, www.icomexico.com.

Mexico Office of Tourism, 800-446-3942, www.visitmexico.com.

Oaxaca Tourist Office, Palacio Municipal on Independencia, 52-951-514-6633, http://oaxaca-travel.com/.

soak up the suds

PORTLAND, OREGON

Without question, the greatest invention in the history of mankind is beer.
Oh, I grant you that the wheel was also a fine invention,
but the wheel does not go nearly as well with pizza.

— HUMORIST AND AUTHOR DAVE BARRY, *DAVE BARRY TURNS 40* (1990)

75 Any foodie knows that wine is a complex alchemy of soil and elements, grapes and the vintner's careful hand. Wine lovers have long crafted whole vacations built around wine, touring vineyards, and tasting the grape. But beer is just beer, right?

If you live in a bottled-beer city, you might think so. But the craft of beermaking has a long and rich history that equals that of winemaking, and for those more interested in hops than grapes, there are some celebrated beery places to visit—the beer-brewing monasteries of Belgium and the raucous beerhouses of Germany, to name but a couple. In America, the Pacific Northwest reigns supreme for the quantity and quality of its microbreweries, small specialty brewers making limited batches. And no place is more devoted to the craft than Portland, Oregon.

In the past 30 years, craft beers have blossomed here, fed by pristine waters of the Bull Run watershed out of the Cascade Range and the area's optimum growing conditions for hops, the bitter flower clusters used to counter the sweetness of malted barley. Today, Portland boasts more than 30 craft breweries, making it the largest craft brewing market in the U.S., according to the Oregon Brewers Guild—and one of the country's best places to appreciate the fresh, complex tastes that can vary widely from one specialty ale to the next.

To learn how craft beers are made, catch a tour like those led by Todd Fleming of **BridgePort BrewPub** (1313 N.W. Marshall St., 503-241-3612, www.bridgeportbrew.com, Sat.), the city's oldest continuously operating craft brewery. First, the barley is malted (that would be roasted, so it tastes a bit like grape nuts), cracked, and hauled off to the brewery in giant sacks. It's then mixed with heated pure Cascade water and mashed (steeped like tea), which releases the sugars from the barley to create a sticky liquid called wort. The water is drained, the wort is boiled for an hour, the hops get tossed in. The whole mess is drained and cooled; the yeast goes in and you've got beer.

Another brewery offering free scheduled tours is **Widmer Brothers** (929 N. Russell St., 503-281-2437, www.widmer.com).

Or catch the Oregon Brewers Guild's annual **Zwickelmania-Oregon Brewery Tour** that takes place during President's Day weekend (Feb.); details can be found online at http://oregonbeer.org/zwickelmania/.

To really appreciate the intricacies of flavors that can result, you need to do some tasting. You can do that by ordering a sampler of beers—six or eight short glasses—at either BridgePort, **Deschutes Brewery Portland Public House** (2010 N.W. 11th Ave., 503-296-4906, www.deschutesbrewery.com), or at any of the city's other craft beer houses serving fresh brews usually unavailable outside the city. You'll find that the darkest beers aren't necessarily the heaviest and the lightest aren't necessarily the sweetest. (Color and bitterness have to do with the roast of the barley, the type of hops, and the specific recipe.) And it's not just India pale ales and stouts: BridgePort ages its Stumptown Tart in Pinot Noir barrels to craft a raspberry flavor; Deschutes brews a gluten-free beer; **Laurelwood Public House & Brewery** (5115 N.E. Sandy Blvd., 503-282-0622, www.laurelwoodbrewpub.com) makes an organic beer. **Cascade Brewing** (7424 S.W. Beaverton-Hillsdale Hwy., 503-296-0110, www.cascadebrewing.com) has spearheaded a national movement with its award-winning sour beers.

IN PORTLAND, BEER MEANS MCMENAMINS

More than 25 years ago, Oregon passed a law allowing breweries to serve their suds on the same premises where they are crafted. Brothers Mike and Brian McMenamin swiftly opened the state's first brewpub. Today their company, **McMenamins** (www.mcmenamins.com), boasts more than 50 breweries in sometimes unexpected historic settings, including movie theaters, a former chapel, and a handful of brewpub hotels. You don't have to check in to belly up to the bar, but if you do, you won't have to worry about driving; your room is just down the hall.

McMenamins hotels in or near Portland include:

- **Crystal Hotel.** This downtown Portland hotel is opening winter 2011 in a 1911 pioneer residence turned tire shop. *Crystal Hotel, 303 S.W. 12th Ave., Portland.*
- **Grand Lodge.** This former 1922 Masonic lodge features a rolling green lawn, spa, and 10-hole disc golf course. From $115 with private bath, from $45 with shared bath. In Forest Grove, between Portland and the Oregon Coast. *Grand Lodge, 3505 Pacific Ave., Forest Grove, 877-992-9533.*
- **Kennedy School.** At this 1915 schoolhouse turned pub, guests drink in the Detention Bar, catch a movie in the auditorium, and sleep in a classroom turned guest room; from $109. *Kennedy School, 5736 N.E. 33rd Ave., Portland, 888-249-3983.*
- **White Eagle Saloon & Rock 'n' Roll Hotel.** Opened in 1905, Portland's oldest continuously operating bar is a hit with those who want to rock until the wee hours; from $45. *White Eagle Saloon & Rock 'n' Roll Hotel, 836 N. Russell St., Portland, 866-271-3377.*

If you want to go a step further and learn to brew yourself, check out classes at local home-brewing supply stores. **F. H. Steinbart** (234 S.E. 12th Ave., 503-232-8793, www.fhsteinbart.com, free classes) and the **Homebrew Exchange** (1907 N. Kilpatrick St., 503-286-0343, www.homebrewexchange.net, classes $10) periodically offer courses lasting a few hours. If those don't suit your schedule, check out the one-night courses occasionally offered by **Portland Community College** (503-244-6111, www.pcc.edu, $29).

And there's more to beer than pizza and dogs, you'll learn. The brew is an essential ingredient in many brewpub menu items, including venison stew (made with Deschutes' Obsidian Stout), mac and cheese (made with BridgePort's Ropewalk amber ale), and turkey pot pie (made with Black Bear Stout at **Alameda Brewing Company,** 4765 N.E. Fremont St., 503-460-9025, www.alamedabrewhouse.com). Some breweries also host occasional gourmet dinners with beer pairings; you can find out about those and other beer events (like barrel-aged beer tastings) online at www.portlandbeer.org.

EAT ON THE CHEAP

Portland deserves its reputation for inventive (though sometimes expensive) cuisine. Numerous food carts offer a price-sensitive—and yummy—alternative. At most, less than $7 will buy you a heaping plate of pad Thai, pork barbecue, Indian curry, a Korean taco, or the famous Czech schnitzelwich (an enormous sandwich made from a freshly cooked pork or chicken schnitzel).

The carts are scattered around downtown and nearly always open at lunch during weekdays; in summer you may also find them open evenings and Saturdays. Popular locations include the parking lot at S.W. Fifth Avenue and Oak Street; S.W. Third Avenue and Washington Street; and the area around Pioneer Courthouse Square. You can't go far wrong; just walk up to any of them and plunk down your cash. *www.foodcartsportland.com.*

If all that isn't enough to keep you brewed up, time your visit for one of the city's many beer festivals, including the **North American Organic Brewers Festival** (www.naobf.org) in late June; the **Oregon Brewers Festival** (www.oregonbrewfest.com) in July; the **Portland International Beer Festival** (www.seattlebeerfest.com), also in July; and the December **Holiday Ale Fest** (www.holidayale.com), held outdoors.

No wonder the city is called Beervana.

HOW TO GET IN TOUCH

Travel Portland, 800-962-3700 or 503-275-9750, www.travelportland.com.

learn to tie and cast that fly

CUMMING, GEORGIA

In our family, there was no clear line between religion and fly fishing.

—AUTHOR NORMAN FITZROY MACLEAN, *A RIVER RUNS THROUGH IT* (1976)

76 For someone who has never fly-fished, the pastime can seem an elite, closed society, a world with its own language, equipment, and rituals. Even watching it is different from traditional rod-and-reel fishing. Like a symphony conductor, a fly fisherman directs graceful loops of line that seem to float in the air. The bait isn't a worm or an engineered lure, but a nearly weightless mass of feathers. Somehow this is enough to land a trout—and fuel a lifelong obsession.

Since 1999 Scott Swartz and his Georgia-based school have worked to take the mystery out of the sport, at bargain prices. A weekend at **Atlanta Fly Fishing School,** located in Cumming, Georgia, is all it takes to teach the basics of fly-fishing and casting, and give you a chance to try out your skills on Georgia's 4,000 miles of trout-rich rivers and streams. The school's about an hour north of Atlanta, making it easy to fly in for a weekend.

Swartz said he purposely keeps class rates low. "We are, without a doubt, the most affordable fly-fishing school in the country because we wanted to make it that way." A five-hour Saturday class runs $125, as does the more advanced Fly Casting School, which lasts four hours. Several times a year, the school offers a "Double Header," teaching both classes in one day. Another popular option is the discounted two-day Learn-N-Go package, which combines one class with

L.L. BEAN WALK-ON ADVENTURES

Always wanted to try kayaking, clay shooting, or snowshoeing? L.L. Bean, the clothier and sports-supply retailer famous for its catalog and rubber-toed boots, will teach you the basics through its $15 Walk-On Adventures program. It's offered at L.L. Bean retail stores, which are located along the East Coast from Maine to Virginia and in Illinois. (The flagship store in Freeport, Maine, is open 24/7 and is a travel destination itself.)

Classes can include lessons on fly-casting, cross-country skiing, archery, geocaching, and more. The price covers all equipment and shuttle transportation to an off-site location. The classes last up to 2.5 hours and are open to anyone 8 and up; for shooting, the minimum age is 12. *L.L. Bean Inc., Freeport, ME 04033, 888-552-3261, www.llbean.com/outdoorsOnline/odp/walkon.*

a four-hour guided fishing excursion the following day. Prices, which include flies and equipment, are $260 for a floating trip on the Chattahoochee River and $270 for a wading trip. Swartz and his instructors are Master Certified Casting Instructors, accredited by the Federation of Fly Fishers, and the school even offers classes to those who want to become certified instructors themselves.

Out-of-town guests often stay in nearby Alpharetta, Georgia, which has a variety of chain hotels and motels. Rates vary depending on time of year, but expect to pay from $90 and up per night. The school provides a list of recommended accommodations.

In Georgia, Swartz's introductory class gives an overview of the sport before delving into techniques. Fly-fishing, he notes, was developed to mimic the look and action of an insect skittering along the surface of the water. (Rod and reel fishing uses bait that's presented below the water's surface.) Fly fishermen and -women must cast more often because the fly needs to be moving to attract a fish. "Many people find casting so enjoyable, that's why they fly-fish," says Swartz.

For novices, learning to cast is the hardest and the most intimidating aspect of fly-fishing. The trick is to stop in the middle of a cast and let the momentum carry the line out to the river. "It's kind of like a spring. You stop your arm and the rod does the work for you," Swartz says. "It's not hard to learn, it just seems counterintuitive."

Instructors use PowerPoint presentations and DVDs to present the information, and some advanced classes even use digital video and sophisticated monitors to carefully analyze casts. Classes include detailed manuals, so there's no need to scribble notes during presentations. The last hour of the introductory class is spent around a pond behind the school. Working with hookless flies (no one wants to be walking around with beginners tossing sharp objects in the air), the instructor works with each student on casting techniques.

Twenty-seven-year-old Thomas Simmons of Macon, Georgia, who took the class after his fiancée gave him a gift certificate, said the class was enough for him to fall for the sport. When he took out his fly rod three weeks later, he could tell how much he learned. "I was always trying to rush it, and pop it like a whip, but you realize it will come naturally. It's a rhythm that shouldn't be forced . . . It's an artisan craft."

$PLURGE

ORVIS

Orvis, a company long known for fly-fishing classes, also provides lessons at resorts around the country. Although many of the offerings are more expensive, the one-day class at Equinox Resort & Spa in Manchester, Vermont, runs a comparable $235 a day, not including lodging. *Orvis Fly-Fishing School, 802-362-4604, www.orvis.com.*

HOW TO GET IN TOUCH

Atlanta Fly Fishing School, 5060 Pittman Rd., Cumming, GA 30040, 404-550-6890, www.atlantaflyfishingschool.com.

follow the lighthouse trail

NOVA SCOTIA, CANADA

Lighthouses are more helpful than churches.

—BENJAMIN FRANKLIN, AMERICAN STATESMAN, PUBLISHER, AND INVENTOR (1706–1790)

77 Nova Scotia literally disappears when the fog rolls in from the Atlantic. The treacherous weather, an annoyance on land, can be deadly at sea, which is why you'll find more lighthouses here than any other U.S. state or Canadian province. More than 160 dot the coast at nearly every twist and turn along the serpentine shore. For the visitor, it's lighthouse heaven. The maritime province makes it easy to see and learn about these beacons with a dedicated Lighthouse Route.

One of the prettiest drives in North America, the route passes through fishing villages and by craggy coves, and endless oceanfront vistas. The route links the port of Yarmouth with the capital city of Halifax, and you can start at either end.

For Lighthouse Route drivers beginning in the northwest, the **Cape Forchu Lightstation** (end of Rte. 304, 902-742-4522, www.capeforchulight.com) makes a distinctive start to the trail. The beacon, built in 1964 to replace an earlier one, is one of the country's newest and looks like an apple core. The design is meant to minimize air resistance in this often windy spot. Visitors to the lighthouse can tour a small museum in the former keeper's house and have a cup of tea. The light, visible up to 30 miles away, was once projected by a Fresnel lens. These elaborate mirrored French-made prisms resemble a giant jewel, and you can see Cape Forchu's original one from 1839 at the **Yarmouth County Museum** (22 Collins St., 902-742-5539, http://yarmouthcountymuseum.ednet.ns.ca).

Heading south from Yarmouth, don't be surprised if you run into mysterious patches of fog. Perhaps that's why the area near Shag Harbor was said to be the site of a UFO crash landing in 1967. Residents reported seeing four mysterious lights floating in the sky. The area celebrates a **UFO festival** (www.shagharbourufo.com) every August.

Just a few miles more and you'll find another mysterious object, a red-and-white striped lighthouse in the hills well away from the seashore. **Seal Island Lighthouse** (Rte. 3, Barrington, 902-637-2185, www.capesablehistoricalsociety.com, $3 Canadian) wasn't originally located here, but when the Canadian government decommissioned the light in 1979, locals rose in protest.

They raised funds and built a new half-size base at its current location. The cast iron top was relocated by helicopter. Now you can climb a winding staircase and see the original lens that was lit by thousand-watt bulbs the size of ostrich eggs.

The beauty of the Lighthouse Route is that it allows plenty of time for exploring. Wander through **Shelburne,** which was settled by Loyalists escaping the American Revolution, and grab a bite to eat from **Mr. Fish** (104 King St., 902-875-3474), an unassuming shack that offers some of the best seafood in this seafood-savvy part of the world. Choose from fresh haddock, shrimp, and scallops. As you wind through small villages and past more lighthouses, set your bearings on **White Point** (White Point Beach, 800-565-5068, www.whitepoint.com), an old-fashioned waterfront resort. You can wander the grounds and see the bunnies that literally hop all over the property. Nightly rates start at $109 Canadian.

The next day wander over to the historic town of **Liverpool** for the **Fort Point Lighthouse** (21 Fort Ln., end of Main St., 902-354-5471). If you're lucky, an employee in period dress will be present to tell you about Liverpool's heyday, when the keeper was paid $36 a year to operate the light. Like nearly all lighthouses, the harbor beacon burned whale and seal oil. That changed when a Nova Scotian invented kerosene.

You'll want to allow plenty of time to explore **Lunenburg,** a fascinating town that dates from 1753 and is now a UNESCO World Heritage site. Visit the surprising **Fisheries Museum of the Atlantic** (68 Bluenose Dr., 902-634-4794, $10), devoted to the trade that kept the province fed for centuries. Check in to the restored **Lunenburg Arms Hotel** (94 Pelham St., 902-640-4040, www.eden.travel), with rooms from about $109 Canadian in

TITANIC SITES

Halifax has always been a city tied to the sea, so perhaps it's fitting that it looked after the victims of the *Titanic.* The liner sank 700 nautical miles away and ships from Halifax were dispatched to search for survivors and recover the dead.

Learn more about the disaster at the excellent **Maritime Museum of the Atlantic** (1675 Lower Water St., 902-424-7490, http://museum.gov.ns.ca/mmanew), located on the waterfront. You can see artifacts from the ship, including a deck chair, china, and the heart-breaking shoes from an unknown child. Only 705 of the ship's more than 2,200 people aboard survived.

One hundred fifty victims are buried at three city cemeteries, but most are at **Fairview Lawn** (3720 Windsor St., 902-490-4883). The area's well marked, and the graves all bear the same date: April 15, 1912.

the low season. At the **Homeport Motel** (167 Victoria Rd., 902-634-8234, www.homeportmotel.com), rooms begin at $79 Canadian, low season.

Now, it's time to visit the most photographed lighthouse in the world: **Peggy's Cove** (178 Peggy's Point Rd., 902-823-2564), perched above a tiny fishing village scattered with boats painted in primary colors. It sits on a rocky outcrop surrounded by surf and, at certain times of day, tourists. Never mind, you'll still love it.

Next up is the other endpoint of the route, the lively provincial capital, **Halifax,** population 287,000. You can take in galleries, clubs, and museums here, but first look out to the channel to see **George's Island,** home to the city's lighthouse. Although not open to the public, the light is visible around the city and has guarded the entrance to Halifax Harbor for centuries.

HOW TO GET IN TOUCH

Nova Scotia Department of Tourism, Culture, & Heritage, P.O. Box 456, Halifax, NS B3J 2R5, Canada, 800-565-0000 or 902-425-5781, www.novascotia.com.

Nova Scotia Lighthouse Preservation Society, www.nslps.com.

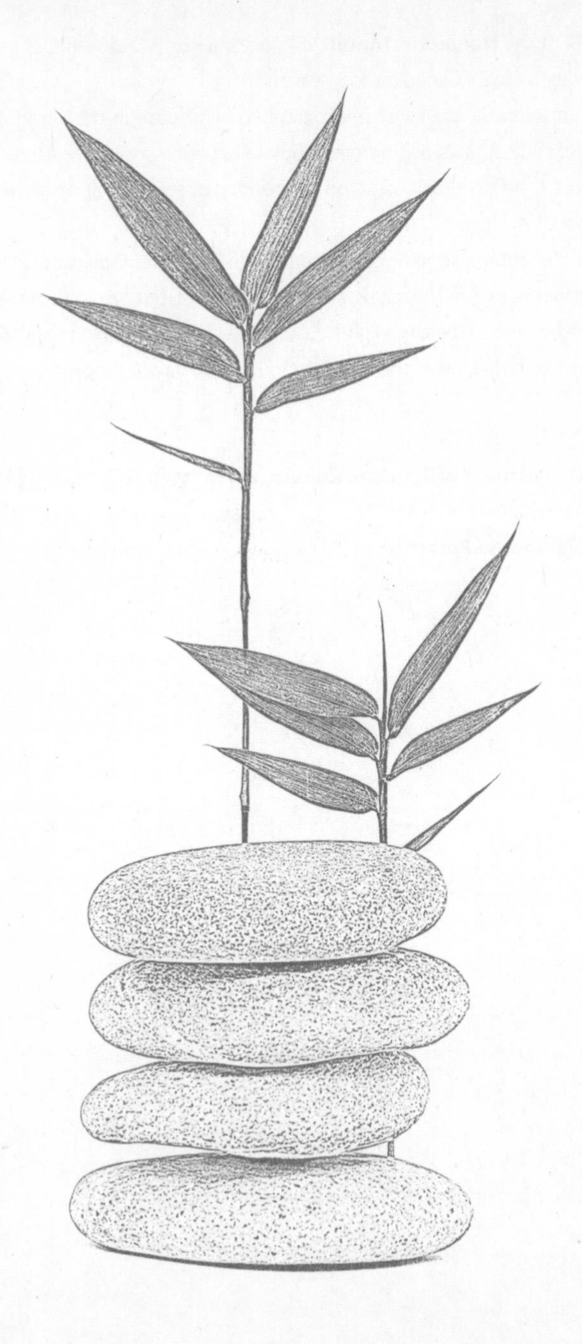

CHAPTER

4

body & soul

Why do we take vacations? The simple answer is to escape the routine of everyday life. But the underlying reason is renewal. When work and school and doctor visits are far away, we have the mental space to honor what's really important to us—whatever that may be.

A vacation can be a chance to indulge in cultural pursuits that are artsy, musical, and literary. You can spend days studying opera or abstract art or exploring the Bohemian experiment called Burning Man or the unfathomable world of fringe theater. If you're a romantic in disguise, you might immerse yourself in the plays of Shakespeare or stroll through the landscapes that inspired artist Andrew Wyeth.

A vacation is also an opportunity to look after yourself. Use it to develop healthy habits—or simply ease the stress away. Run through incredible scenery, dip into natural hot springs in the wilds of Montana, or breathe deeply and regain your serenity at a wellness retreat. Your body and mind will be thanking you for years to come.

A vacation can also be a chance to help other people and institutions. Underfunded parks and abandoned animals need your time. Scientists struggling to preserve the past seek willing hands to help out. From here in the United States, you can help poor people around the world by teaching at a training center or helping with administrative work.

How much of a difference can you make? Plenty. Even if you only have a week, the programs here can help you touch others. At the end of your vacation you may feel tired, but you'll also feel strengthened by a sense of mission and the knowledge that regardless of your place in it, this truly is one world.

slip into hot water

SOUTHWEST MONTANA

I can't think of any sorrow in the world that a hot bath wouldn't help, just a little bit.

—PULITZER PRIZE—WINNING PLAYWRIGHT AND AUTHOR SUSAN GLASPELL, *THE VISIONING* (1911)

78 Spas have boomed in the past decades, offering pleasure palaces in which to retreat and rejuvenate. But a spa doesn't have to be a climate-controlled room with piped-in Andean flute music located deep in a hotel. You can find peace and relaxation on the fringes of Yellowstone National Park, where you can soak in an open-air pool or a river eddy fed by natural hot springs. The greater Yellowstone area sits over a geothermal hot spot, which over eons has fueled volcanoes and geysers—and in the last century or so, spawned resorts, small inns, and naturally heated pools.

Start your supersoaking tour in **Chico Hot Springs,** located in Pray, Montana, just north of Yellowstone. This historic spring comforted Native Americans for centuries, and then became a favorite stop for miners. Now guests find two hot springs pools, with average temperatures from 96°F to 103°F (translation: just about perfect). Pools are free to hotel guests; room rates begin at $79 for a cabin for two. Chico has a day spa with a 30-minute spot massage running $50. [SPLURGE: **For a splurge try the hundred-minute geotherapy with spring-heated hot basalt stones for $170.**] And then have dinner in the hotel's celebrated restaurant. Try the barbecue bison short rib ravioli appetizer ($11) and, if you're truly indulgent, the beef Wellington for two ($55), which is carved tableside. Many of the vegetables are grown in the inn's geothermal-heated greenhouse.

Your next stop is within Yellowstone itself. At the **Boiling River** (307-344-7381, www.nps.gov/yell), bathers lounge in natural pools along the edge of the Gardner River, where chilly snowmelt mixes with natural heated water. Instead of turning a tap, you control the temperature by rearranging rocks to regulate the flow of water. The area is just 2 miles south of the park's North Entrance and then a half-mile hike from a parking lot. You'll find bathrooms for changing, but keep in mind the area's closed from spring to midsummer due to high water. While in Yellowstone, take a hike or two. Beaver Ponds Loop Trail, a 5-mile path located near the park's nearby Mammoth Hot Springs area, offers the chance to see wildlife, including moose and even bear.

To get to your next stop, leave the park via West Yellowstone, where you should grab a bite to eat at **Kiwi Takeaway** (237 Firehole Ave., 406-640-0187), which has huge burgers, meat pies, and fish-and-chips. Now head north on U.S. 191 to **Bozeman Hot Springs** ($8.50, towel and suit rentals

$1), a watery wonderland with nine pools ranging in temperature from 56°F to 106°F. Moving from hot to cold and back to hot pools is invigorating to say the least. Or visit the sauna and steam room. At bedtime, check into the nearby **Canyon Cabins Lodging** (101 Ruby Mountain Way, 406-763-4248, www.canyoncabinsmontana.com) in Gallatin Gateway, with bunkhouse cabins available from $95 from May to October.

Before soaking in water again, try riding on it. **Geyser Whitewater Expeditions** (800-914-9031, www.raftmontana.com) and **Montana Whitewater Raft Company** (800-799-4465, www.montanawhitewater.com) offer half-day excursions on the Gallatin River for around $50.

Look for a geodesic dome and you'll find your final stop, **Norris Hot Springs** ($5, suit and towel rentals $1), which calls itself the "water of the gods"; it's located in Norris on Highway 84, a quarter mile east of Route 287. This laid-back wooden pool uses sprayers and jets to cool the 120°F water. It also sports a café specializing in food sourced within 50 miles and is home to the No Loose Dogs bar, which serves Montana microbrews. There's live music Friday, Saturday, and Sunday after 7 p.m., when admission is $7.

While in the area, take a two-hour, 2-mile walking tour of **Lewis & Clark Caverns State Park** (Whitehall, 406-287-3541, http://fwp.mt.gov/parks/visit, closed Oct.–April, tours $10), home to a colony of western big-eared bats. Then for dinner, make the half-hour trip to **Willow Creek Cafe & Saloon** (21 Main St., Willow Creek, 406-285-3698), which serves some of the best barbecue ribs west of the Mississippi, with a half rack under $15.

HOW TO GET IN TOUCH

Bozeman Hot Springs, 81123 E. Gallatin Rd., U.S. 191, Bozeman, MT 59718, 406-586-6492, www.bozemanhotsprings.biz.

Chico Hot Springs, 1 Old Chico Rd., Pray, MT 59065, 800-468-9232 or 406-333-4933, www.chicohotsprings.com.

Norris Hot Springs, P. O. Box 2933, Norris, MT 59745, 406-685-3303, www.norrishotsprings.com.

MONTANA'S DINO COUNTRY

Dinosaur fossils have been unearthed across Montana and new wonders continue to be discovered. Some of the most spectacular finds are exhibited in the Siebel Dinosaur Complex at Bozeman's **Museum of the Rockies.** Displays include the world's largest *Tyrannosaurus rex* skull, a tail with fossilized skin impressions, and rare fossilized dinosaur embryos and nests.

But another star of the museum is curator and paleontologist Jack Horner. He discovered and named the duck-billed *Maiasaura,* or "good mother lizard," and proved that dinosaurs cared for their young. He also served as a technical adviser for the *Jurassic Park* films and is said to be the inspiration for one of its lead characters. Many of the exhibits showcase his finds and research. *Museum of the Rockies, 600 W. Kagy Blvd., Bozeman, MT 59717, 406-994-3466, www.museumoftherockies.org, $13.*

step into a wyeth painting

BRANDYWINE VALLEY, PENNSYLVANIA

I don't really have studios. I wander around, around people's attics, out in fields, in cellars, anyplace I find that invites me.

—PAINTER ANDREW WYETH (1917–2009)

79 Critics often derided the late Andrew Wyeth's paintings as illustrations. But for his many fans, the superrealistic depictions—of barren landscapes, the trappings of rural life, and his hardworking country neighbors—offer a hauntingly honest glimpse of America of the 1950s and beyond.

On a visit to Pennsylvania's Brandywine Valley region near the town of Chadds Ford, you can judge for yourself. Though the area has grown since Wyeth grew up here, in places this countryside 45 minutes southwest of Philadelphia looks much as it appears in Wyeth's paintings. In the red barn of the snug Kuerner Farm sits the stone tub once used to cool milk—a scene captured in Wyeth's "Spring Fed"—and the kitchen window of the wooden white farmhouse in "Groundhog Day." Nearby is the rolling hill of "Winter 1946" and "Snow Hill"—not far from the railroad crossing where his father and nephew were killed decades ago in what some suspect was an act of suicide.

Tours of the Kuerner Farm are offered Thursday through Sunday by the **Brandywine River Museum** (1 Hoffman's Mill Rd., Chadds Ford, 610-388-2700, www.brandywinemuseum.org, $10), a must-stop for anyone with an interest in the Wyeth family. Here you'll find a gallery of remarkable color illustrations that his father, acclaimed artist N. C. Wyeth, painted for James Fenimore Cooper's *Last of the Mohicans* and Robert Louis Stevenson's *Kidnapped* and *Treasure Island,* plus works by other regional artists, including family members Jamie Wyeth, Henriette Wyeth, Carolyn Wyeth, Peter Hurd, and John W. McCoy. And, of course, temperas and watercolors by Andrew Wyeth.

The museum also owns the 1911 house where Andrew Wyeth grew up, and if you've got the time, you'll want to visit it. N. C. Wyeth's studio lies behind the house and looks much as it did the day he died in 1945. The museum offers tours of the house and studio Thursday through Sunday for a fee of $5 per person in addition to the regular museum entry of $10 for adults. Both tours should be booked at least a day in advance at 610-388-8326.

For the ultimate Wyeth experience, time your visit to catch a guided gallery tour of the Brandywine River Museum led by Victoria Browning Wyeth (Andrew's granddaughter and Jamie's niece); she peppers her talk with family anecdotes. (Her aunt Carolyn, she may tell you, was such a character that the family disposed of her ashes in a firecracker.) Her tours are held most Thursdays and

THE WYETHS IN MAINE

The Wyeth family has long spent summers in the mid-coast region of Maine. **Rockland's Farnsworth Art Museum** (16 Museum St., 207-596-6457, www.farnsworthmuseum.org, $12) features an extensive collection of works by various Wyeth family members.

To fully experience Maine as portrayed in Andrew Wyeth's paintings, drive to Port Clyde (about 30 mins. S of Rockland) and take the hour-plus boat ride to **Monhegan Island** (207-372-8848, www.monheganboat.com, $32 round-trip, several times daily in summer but limited in winter). You probably won't run into any Wyeth family members—but you never know.

Fridays (July–Aug. excluded) on a first-come basis (free with regular museum entry).

The full Wyeth immersion requires a minimum of a day and a half. Diehard Wyeth fans can stay minutes from the Brandywine River Museum at the **Brandywine River Hotel** (1609 Baltimore Pike, Chadds Ford, 877-320-0664, www.brandywineriverhotel.com, rates for a double room from $139). Other accommodations can be found nearby in chain lodgings.

For cheap authentic eats, check out **Hank's Place** (corner of Rte. 1 & Rte. 100, 610-388-7061), an Andrew Wyeth favorite for meat loaf and other hearty fare where the entrees start under $10, and another Wyeth family favorite, **Jimmy John's Sandwich Shop** (1507 Wilmington Pike, West Chester, 610-459-3083), which is due to reopen in 2011 after a fire, for sandwiches and hot dogs. For an affordable splurge, hit the **Gables at Chadds Ford** (423 Baltimore Pike, 610-388-7700, www.thegablesatchaddsford.com) in a converted 1800s barn, where the contemporary menu (American with French and Asian twists) features dinner entrees around $30. Many are available in half portions.

When you're ready for a break from Wyeth family lore, stop in at the **Chaddsford Winery** (632 Baltimore Pike, 610-388-6221, www.chaddsford.com), open daily from 12 p.m. to 6 p.m. for free tours and tastings from $8. About 30 minutes away, in Nottingham, the **Herr's Snack Factory** (20 Herr Dr., 800-637-6225, www.herrs.com) offers free tours mornings Monday through Friday, and afternoons Monday through Thursday; reserve in advance. The 300-acre **Linvilla Orchards** (137 W. Knowlton Rd., Media, 610-876-7116, www.linvilla.com) features a farm market, hayrides, and seasonal activities.

HOW TO GET IN TOUCH

Brandywine Conference & Visitors Bureau, 800-343-3983, www.brandywinecountry.org.

nurture the big cats

ZOLFO SPRINGS, FLORIDA

Those who wish to pet and baby wild animals "love" them. But those who respect their natures and wish to let them live normal lives, love them more.

—EDWIN WAY TEALE, *CIRCLE OF THE SEASONS* (1953)

80 For a few months, a tiger kitten is cuddly, a baby bear irresistible. But something inevitably happens. It gets bigger, its teeth grow sharper, and its behavior becomes more destructive and dangerous. That's when many folks who have acquired wild animals as pets put them in cages, and sometimes begin to abuse them.

If the animals are lucky, the owner will come to their senses, or animal-welfare advocates will be alerted, and the creatures will end up at a place like Peace River Refuge & Ranch, founded in 1998 in Zolfo Springs, Florida, about 70 miles southeast of Tampa. The shelter takes in a host of wild animals, from cougars and leopards to wolves and fruit bats. Some come from pet owners, while others are seized by authorities from zoos or carnivals. What they all have in common is the need for care, and Peace River relies on the help of volunteers to help do the job. Visitors can come for as little as a weekend to help build cages or paint rooms. But the longer you stay, the more you can do.

Volunteers learn about the animals they're helping. Nearly all were raised in captivity and had never seen their own species until they came to Peace River. "They didn't even know what they were," says Lisa Stoner, the refuge's vice president. But over time, the animals revert to their natural state. "To sit and watch them roughhouse, to climb trees and destroy things. To watch wild behavior out of a captive-born animal is really rewarding."

Although it can be exciting to spend time near the wild animals, there's nothing glamorous about it. "It's hard," Stoner says. "It's Florida, it's hot, it's buggy."

Nearly all volunteers help prepare food for the sanctuary's hundred-plus animals. Preparing meals can require hours of chopping fruit or raw meat and then measuring out portions. Volunteers staying for several weeks may get a chance to feed the animals. The food is usually proffered on 18-inch tongs, pushed through cages. Feeding a feline can be particularly exciting because some crouch, sneak up, and then pounce on their food—as they'd do in the wild.

Janine Ellis of Reading, England, spent a month at Peace River on break from her job as an accountant. The refuge

HELP ABANDONED PETS

The country's biggest no-kill animal sanctuary, Best Friends of Kanab, Utah, welcomes volunteers to work with its dogs, cats, horses, waterfowl, pigs, parrots, and rabbits, to name its most common residents. On an average day, the shelter is home to 2,000 animals, rescued from all across the country.

You can spend your days grooming, playing with, and walking the residents. There's no cost, but you're responsible for accommodations and food. The shelter's Angel Canyon Guest Cottages offers Best Friends members ($25 for basic membership) cabins that sleep two for $55 a night off-season, $70 high season. You can even borrow a pet to keep overnight. *Best Friends Animal Society, 5001 Angel Canyon Rd., Kanab, UT 84741, 435-644-2001, www.bestfriends.org.*

offered her a chance to help monkeys, panthers, and other critters she never imagined she'd encounter. She particularly enjoyed watching spider monkeys. "They're very expressive. I enjoyed the whole thing, getting to know the animals and their quirky personalities." One of her jobs was to prepare enrichment activities, like placing peanut butter or other treats inside a paper towel tube, so animals are forced to find a way to reach the food.

For those able to volunteer for a month, the shelter charges $1,960 for housing and food, although volunteers need to prepare their meals. They must also have proof of a current negative TB test, and if they're going to work with bats, a rabies vaccination. Hepatitis B and tetanus vaccinations are also recommended. Accommodations are basic. Women stay in a house a few miles from the refuge. The few men who volunteer stay in an on-site trailer, which means they can hear the sanctuary's wolves howling at night.

If you can't stay a month, you must provide your own housing and food. Chain lodging is available in nearby Bowling Green, with rates starting about $80 per night.

No volunteers are allowed to physically interact with the animals, but they are invited to watch veterinary procedures and other special interactions. Part of Peace River's mission is education. "People come here loving the animals," Stoner says. "But they leave here knowing so much more than they ever did."

HOW TO GET IN TOUCH

Peace River Refuge & Ranch, P.O. Box 1127, 2545 Stoner Ln., Zolfo Springs, FL 33890, 863-735-0804, www.peaceriverrefuge.org.

hobnob with authors

MIAMI, FLORIDA

Always read something that will make you look good if you die in the middle of it.

—P. J. O'ROURKE, POLITICAL SATIRIST

81 Whether your idea of contemporary literature is Ann Patchett's heady novels or Stephen King's scare thrillers, dozens of literary festivals scattered across the United States offer a chance to shake hands with authors, ask about their writing, and trade words with fellow book lovers.

And nowhere is it more special perhaps than at the Miami Book Fair International. When independent bookseller Mitchell Kaplan of Miami-based Books & Books helped found the then Miami Book Fair in the early 1980s, the United States boasted only a few large book festivals. The Miami Book Fair International is now the oldest and largest consumer book festival in the country.

Book fairs serve as a community tent where people share ideas and passion for words, says Kaplan, a former president of the American Booksellers Association. And like good books themselves, the most intriguing fairs are a prism into time and place. "Most book fairs try to reflect the nature of where they are . . . by the authors who come, exhibitors, and by the book lovers who are drawn to that fair," Kaplan says.

The **Miami Book Fair International** (www.miamibookfair.com), held each November on the campus of Miami-Dade College, draws authors who write in Spanish and Creole as well as English. Local pen masters—including mystery writers Carl Hiaasen and Edna Buchanan, humorist Dave Barry, and Haitian-American novelist Edwidge Danticat—have taken the podium, along with such luminaries as Patchett, Barbara Kingsolver, Jacquelyn Mitchard, Mario Vargas Llosa, Al Gore, Margaret Atwood, Garrison Keillor, Iggy Pop, the late Carl Sagan, the late Julia Child, and Barack Obama before he was elected President.

Events spanning eight days include "Evenings with . . ." major authors that feature readings and Q&As and seminars on writing and book publishing. The apex is the weekend street fair featuring hundreds of vendors, music, food booths, a children's alley, and dozens of simultaneous and back-to-back author appearances. Prices vary, but most evening author events cost $10. The street fair costs $8 for adults; it's free for everyone else. If you're lucky, you'll catch a year when the Rock Bottom Remainders—a literary garage band made up of mega-authors Dave Barry, Amy Tan, Stephen King, Ridley Pearson, Greg Iles, Mitch Albom, Roy Blount, Jr., Kathi Kamen Goldmark, Matt Groening, James McBride, and Scott Turow—decide to play.

OTHER BOOK FESTIVALS THAT WELL-KNOWN AUTHORS FREQUENT

- **Baltimore Book Festival, Maryland.** Held over a weekend in late September, the festival attracts more than 50,000 attendees each year. Past authors have included Dr. Cornel West, Buzz Aldrin, Jane Goodall, Walter Mosley, Candace Bushnell, and Andrea Mitchell. Free. *410-752-8632, www.baltimorebookfestival.com.*
- **Los Angeles Times–UCLA Book Festival, California.** Held over a weekend in late April on the UCLA campus. Author events are ticketed at $1 per event. T. C. Boyle, Mary Higgins Clark, Brett Easton Ellis, Sebastian Junger, and Herman Wouk have all attended this festival. *213-237-2665, http://events.latimes.com/festivalofbooks/general-information.*
- **National Book Festival, Washington, D.C.** At this one-day festival held on a Saturday each September, dozens of tents on the National Mall feature presentations by authors of children's books, contemporary fiction, history, and poetry. Past authors have included Ken Follett, Isabel Allende, and Jules Feiffer. Free. *888-714-4696, www.loc.gov/bookfest.*
- **Wordstock, Portland, Oregon.** More than 200 international authors attend this event held over a weekend each October. The festival has featured James Ellroy, John Irving, Joyce Carol Oates, Norman Mailer, Alice Sebold, and Russell Banks. Entry costs $5. *503-546-1012, www.wordstockfestival.com.*

The college is within an easy people mover/Metrorail (www.miamidade.gov/transit) ride of the **Adrienne Arsht Center for the Performing Arts** (1300 Biscayne Blvd., 305-949-6722, www.arshtcenter.org), which offers a variety of performances year-round, and the bubbling café scene at the Mary Brickell Village. The Design District, Wynwood Arts District, and South Beach are less than 15 minutes away by taxi.

Convenient and wallet-friendly lodgings include **Villa Paradiso** (1415 Collins Ave., 305-532-0616, www.villaparadisohotel.com, rooms from $119), a historic South Beach apartment complex turned guesthouse two blocks from the sea, and Key Biscayne's **Silver Sands Resort** (301 Ocean Dr., 305-361-5441, www.silversandsbeachresort.net, rooms from $129), directly on the beach in tranquil-yet-urban Key Biscayne. [$PLURGE: For a splurge, go for the urban scene overlooking the city and river at the **Epic Hotel** (270 Biscayne Blvd. Way, 305-424-5226, www.epichotel.com, rooms from $300) in downtown or the first-rate **Mandarin Oriental** (500 Brickell Key Dr., 305-913-8288, www.mandarinoriental.com/miami, rooms from $350) on an urban island linked to downtown.]

Miami is a car town, which means that unless you're going to locations on the limited people mover/Metrorail link, you'll need to travel by taxi or car.

Miami is also a food town with endless options to choose from. Two establishments worth the price are **Michael's Genuine Food & Drink** (130 N.E. 40th St., 305-573-5550) in the Design

District, by award-winning chef Michael Schwartz, where the food is fresh and inventive but not fussy; and **Michy's** (6927 Biscayne Blvd., 305-759-2001), with American fare from award-winner Michelle Bernstein, on the burgeoning stretch of north Biscayne Boulevard between 50th and 79th Streets. For fun and cheap food, hit **Versailles** (3555 S.W. 8th St., 305-444-0240), a Cuban icon in Little Havana.

HOW TO GET IN TOUCH

Greater Miami Convention & Visitors Center, 305-539-3000, www.miamiandbeaches.com.

CITY SLEEPS ON THE CHEAP

Lodgings in big cities are notoriously expensive. These tips will help you find the best deals:

- Check with business hotels that, midweek, are expensive. On weekends they may have empty rooms—especially when there's no convention in town.
- Consider traveling just before or after a major holiday, when prices often plummet.
- Consider all costs—valet parking, taxes, resort fees, service fees, and more—to determine the true cost of your stay. In a big city, free breakfast can add up to a big bonus.
- If you're considering an upscale brand, compare the cost of staying on the Club floor, and find out what is included if you do. If the Club floor comes with cocktails, heavy hors d'oeuvres, and breakfast and costs only a little more than a regular room, it may be worth the rate.
- Consider short-term apartments for rent (see sidebar p. 61).
- In some big cities, an increasing number of hotels are offering bargain rooms with shared bath.
- If you collect hotel points, see how far they can take you. Points collected at value-oriented hotels in relatively inexpensive destinations can land you a free, well-located room in a major city in the United States or Europe.
- Discount hotel websites: It's always worth checking "blind" websites like Hotwire and Priceline, as well as regular online sites like Hotels.com, Quikbook, Expedia, Orbitz, and Travelocity. Check cancellation policies and fees before you book.

Here's how to ask for a better rate without feeling like a chump:

- Look first online to see the best available rate for the time you want to visit. Many hotels offer Web-only rates.
- If you're an AAA or AARP member, check those rates online. Don't assume you'll find them if you click "Best Available Rate."
- Call the hotel directly, not the 800-number. Ask if there are any specials or discounts available.

take a walk, go for a run

NATIONWIDE

Running has thrown me into adventures that I would otherwise have missed.

—AUTHOR BENJAMIN CHEEVER, *STRIDES* (2007)

82 Experienced travelers know the best way to see a city is on foot. And since it's always nice to have company, why not combine the two? Make your vacation an active getaway by building a trip around an organized run or walk. Nearly every community has one signature event, and in many cities, you can find them almost every weekend. Some competitors take the competition seriously, training for months and vying for large cash prices. If you're one of those, congratulations—and the rest of us will step quickly out of your way. But many participants plan to take the course at a walk or slow jog. They're there for the scenery, the company, and yes, an excuse for a party. But you'll have to plan ahead. The most popular runs sell out, so register and make room reservations early. Here are a few favorites to consider:

Gasparilla Distance Classic Race Weekend. Indulge your inner Blackbeard with this Tampa, Florida, event held in February. The pirate-themed weekend includes a 5K stroller run and 5K, 15K, half-marathon, and marathon runs. The routes skirt the Tampa Bay waterfront as they traverse the city's prettiest neighborhoods. Afterward, celebrate your success with a beer or a massage at the post-race party. Registration begins at $25, but if you're planning on getting new running gear anyway, check the race website for deals offering free registration with the purchase of certain running goods. A runner's unlikely to smoke cigars, granted, but it doesn't mean you won't like Ybor City,

CITY RUNS

Just because you're on vacation does not mean you need to give up your running routine. The website Run.com lists thousands of routes across the country that are contributed by runners. Just log on to find, for example, a 3-mile beach run in San Diego or a 5-mile loop around the monuments in Washington, D.C. Another option is to ask your hotel concierge or the front desk. Many accommodations have maps with running routes highlighted.

[$PLURGE: **For a splurge, consider City Running Tours (www.cityrunningtours.com), which offers guided runs in Boston; Charleston, South Carolina; Chicago; New York; Philadelphia; San Francisco; and Washington, D.C. Personalized runs begin at $60 for 6 miles, but if you're in town during a group run, the cost is just $20.**]

which was once the center of the cigarmaking industry. A $4 walking tour reveals the city's connection to the Spanish-American War—and stogies; the tour is offered Saturdays at 10:30 a.m. through the **Ybor City Museum State Park** (1818 9th Ave., 813-247-6323, www.floridastateparks.org/yborcity). Stay in the historic district at the **Don Vicente de Ybor Historic Inn** (1915 Republic de Cuba, 866-206-4545 or 813-241-4545, http://donvicenteinn.com), with rooms from $99 off-season and up.

Gasparilla Distance Classic Race Weekend, P.O. Box 1881, Tampa, FL 33601, 813-254-7866, www.tampabayrun.com.

Mackinac Bridge Walk. For soaring scenery, you can't beat the annual Labor Day walk across Michigan's Mackinac Bridge; the third longest suspension bridge in the world, it carries I-75 over the Straits of Mackinac. The 5-mile walk connects Michigan's Lower and Upper Peninsulas. At its height, the bridge soars 200 feet above the water, so to be safe running, racing, animals, and even playing tag aren't allowed. As you stroll, you will take in stunning views of Lake Michigan to the west and of Lake Huron to the east. The event starts at 7 a.m. in St. Ignace, at the bridge's north end, and finishes in Mackinaw City in the south. School buses will ferry participants ($5 per person) to St. Ignace, either to start the event, or to return to their car. Those completing the walk get a numbered certificate. Afterward, wander Mackinaw City or St. Ignace to see if your number is posted in a shop window, qualifying you for a prize. Since the walk starts so early, you'll want to stay nearby—and make reservations early. For simple but well-maintained accommodations, try the **Cedars Motel** (2040 I-75 Business Loop, St. Ignace, 906-643-9578, www.thecedarsmotel.net). It's worth crossing the bridge just for a hamburger from frozen-in-time **Clyde's Drive-In** (W. Hwy. 2, St. Ignace, 906-643-8303).

Mackinac Bridge Authority, 906-643-7600, www.mackinacbridge.org.

$PLURGE

STAY AT THE GRAND

It would be a shame to make it all the way to northern Michigan and not see Mackinac Island. The scenic vacation spot has been welcoming visitors for more than a century, and since cars aren't allowed there, it does feel like a step back in time. The Grand Hotel lives up to its name and it is a must-see. Rooms from $470 per couple (including breakfast and dinner). *Grand Hotel, 286 Grand Ave., P.O. Box 286, Mackinac Island, MI 49757, 906-847-3331, www.grandhotel.com.*

Not Since Moses. If running over the water doesn't sound good to you, why not take a stroll on the bottom of the ocean? The Not Since Moses Run offers a Charlton Heston–Red Sea experience off the coast of Nova Scotia, Canada, in mid-August. Staged at the Five Islands Provincial Park, an hour north of Halifax, the 10K and 5K walk/run is timed to take advantage of the Bay of Fundy's extreme tide changes, which can vary as much as 48 feet. The route takes participants along the seafloor, so this is not the course for your best Nikes—expect plenty of puddles and mud. But if your pace is slow, don't worry, you can step up to the coast and be picked up by a boat looking for stragglers. Cost is $45 Canadian, which includes a shirt and post-run party. You can find motels and inns along the shore, including in Parrsboro, 20 minutes away from the start. Consider the basic but cheerful **Sunshine Inn** (4487 Hwy. 2N, Parrsboro, 877-706-6835 or 902-254-3135, www.thesunshineinn.net, rates from $89 Canadian). There's also camping at **Five Islands Provincial Park** (902-254-2980, www.novascotiaparks.ca/parks/fiveislands.asp).

Not Since Moses, 951 Hwy. 2, Lower Five Islands, NS B0M 1K0, Canada, www.notsincemoses .com.

Surf City Marathon. You'll undoubtedly yell "Surf's Up" sometime during the Surf City Marathon in Huntington Beach, California, every February. More than 17,000 participants line up behind a brigade of classic woody sedans in this marathon, half-marathon, and 5K oceanfront event. The post-race party includes surf music, barbecue, and beer. Plus you'll treasure the surfboard-shaped medal awarded to all who complete the course. Registration begins at $25. **Huntington Dog Beach** (west side of Pacific Coast Highway bet. Seapoint St. & 21st St., www.dogbeach.org) is celebrated for its pet-friendly sands. Even if you're petless, it's worth a visit to see all the canines having fun in the sun. Another beachy must-see is the **International Surfing Museum** (411 Olive Ave., 714-960-3483, www.surfingmuseum.org), with vintage boards, classic surf music, and surf movies. Lodging can be pricey here, but the **Huntington Suites** (727 Yorktown Ave., 714-969-0450, http://thehuntingtonsuites.com) is a good budget choice with rooms from $88.

Kinane Events, 800 Grand Ave., Ste. C-10, Carlsbad, CA 92008, 888-422-0786, www.runsurf city.com.

get out on the fringe

EDMONTON, CANADA

I just want people to enjoy themselves for an hour, to make them laugh. The fringe is really a way for that to happen.

—CHRIS GIBBS, TORONTO-BASED FRINGE PERFORMER

83 The very name "fringe festival" hints at something wild and frenetic, and for those who give in to the temptation of seeing multiple performances per day—20 plays in five days isn't uncommon—a fringe can become a mad dash. But the real point behind fringe festivals isn't the quantity of shows you catch—or even, perhaps, the quality of them. It's the idea of self-produced, uncensored, unjuried dramatic freedom.

Anyone can apply for a spot at the fringe—whether they have acting or performing credentials or not. Musicals, comedies, one-man acts, children's shows—sometimes even naked dances—can be seen on stage. "Fringe takes art back into the hands of the people," says David Ortolano, producer of the Boulder International Fringe Festival. Because slots typically are assigned by lottery or a first-come, first-served basis, the creativity is fresh, unfettered—and often funky.

"There's no quality control. It could be the worst thing you've ever seen; conversely it could be the best thing you've ever seen," says T. J. Dawe, a Vancouver, Canada–based fringe playwright and performer. Which seems to be exactly what the audiences—teens to grandparents—seem to want. "Fringe audiences come to see something new. If you did Brecht, or Shakespeare, no one would want to see it."

At typical North American fringe festivals, $500–$700 buys a performer (or group) a half dozen time slots in an assigned venue (church hall, bar, nightclub, actual theater), technical support for the show, and a built-in audience primed for the experimental. Most shows last 60 to 90 minutes.

There are no advance reviews. Artists have to market their shows themselves, and it's not unusual to find them or their friends handing out fliers. Shows—and repeat artists—catch positive buzz, which can lead to sell-out audiences. At many festivals, the infrastructure is supported through private support and grants, so that the proceeds go back to the artists—which means the more tickets a show sells, the more that artist makes.

Festivals run multiple days to two weeks and may feature 200 different performances. Some include outdoor stages and street performers; nearly all have a beer tent. The price is right, with tickets to individual shows starting under $10, depending on the festival, and multishow passes that average out to several dollars less per performance. Food booths around the grounds serve up cheap eats.

"The fringe" takes its name from postwar Scotland, when counterculture artists clamored outside the then conventional Edinburgh Festival to get audiences for their experimental shows. Fringe came to the New World in 1982 in the form of the Edmonton Fringe Festival; today dozens of festivals are held throughout the United States and Canada.

The **Edmonton International Fringe Festival** (780-448-9000, www.fringetheatreadventures.ca) that spans ten days in mid-August is still North America's largest fringe fest, drawing more than 550,000 visitors for 1,200 shows, including many designed just for children. The festival takes place in the city's early 1900s historic district, **Old Strathcona** (www.oldstrathcona.ca), where crowds gather around two outdoor stages, food and crafts booths, and street performers who juggle in streets closed to traffic. (Need a snack? Don't miss the green onion cakes.)

But for theater buffs and the fanatics fondly dubbed "fringe fries," the indoor shows are the big attraction. *Miami Herald* journalist Madeleine Marr, who described herself as dashing from tent to tent to catch 25 plays in five days,

MORE FAVORITE FRINGE FESTS IN THE UNITED STATES & CANADA

- **Boulder International Fringe Festival, Boulder, Colorado.** Twelve days in mid-late August; tickets from $10. *303-803-5643, www.boulderfringe.com.*
- **Minnesota Fringe Festival, Minneapolis/St. Paul, Minnesota.** Ten days in early August; tickets from $12. *612-872-1212, www.fringefestival.org.*
- **New York International Fringe Festival, New York, New York.** Some 1,200 multiarts performances offered over 16 days in mid to late August; tickets from $15. Unlike other festivals, selection is competitive and based on quality. *212-279-4488, www.fringenyc.org.*
- **Orlando Fringe, Orlando, Florida.** The oldest fringe fest in the United States, held over 12 days in late May; tickets from $6. *407-648-0077, www.orlandofringe.org.*
- **Philadelphia Fringe Festival, Philadelphia, Pennsylvania.** Runs over two weeks in early September; tickets from $25 with discounts for multiple shows. *215-413-9006, www.livearts-fringe.org.*
- **San Francisco Fringe Festival, San Francisco, California.** Two and a half weeks in early to mid-September; tickets from $10. *415-931-1094, www.sffringe.org.*
- **Winnipeg Theatre Fringe Festival, Winnipeg, Manitoba, Canada.** The festival literally takes over the town of 680,000, and artists become instantly recognized celebrities—at least for the run of the show. About 80,000 typically attend over the 12-day show in mid-July; tickets cost about $9 Canadian. *877-446-4500, www.winnipegfringe.com.*

ENJOY THE SHOWS

Fringe regulars offer these tips:

- Book hotels in advance. Because the festivals span a number of days, you can usually find rooms . . . but the later you wait, the higher the rate may be.
- Keep an open mind. See something you aren't inclined to see; you may be surprised.
- Ask around. Once you hear a show is good, snag a ticket quickly.
- Consider a pass that includes a number of shows; it usually saves time and money.

rated the performances as 50 percent worthy, 50 percent dogs. "I enjoyed one play so much I bought the soundtrack," reads her review of the fringe festival for the *Miami Herald.* "On the other hand, I witnessed plays so pitiful that the actual cast walked off the stage in disgust." Good thing the max ticket price is only $15.

Convenient lodging can book up quickly and, with the exception of the International Hostel, isn't cheap. One choice is the **Campus Tower Suite Hotel** (11145 87th Ave., 780-439-6060), where advance-purchase rooms during the festival cost around $100. **Edmonton's Hostel** (10647 81st St., 866-762-4122, www.hihostels.ca/westerncanada/1404/HI-Edmonton.hostel) is convenient to the festival grounds; rates for a private room with shared bath start around $65; en suite rooms and dorm rooms are also available. At the **Varscona** (8208 106th St., 780-434-6111, www.varscona.com), festival-season rooms start at around $125. [$PLURGE: **For a splurge, consider the stylish Metterra Hotel (10454 82nd Ave. NW, 780-465-8150, www.metterra.com), where a room during festival season costs about $150.**]

HOW TO GET IN TOUCH

Edmonton Economic Development Corporation, 800-463-4667, www.edmonton.com.

help out at a national park

NATIONWIDE

The service we render to others is really the rent we pay for our room on this earth.

—SIR WILFRED GRENFELL, BRITISH MEDICAL MISSIONARY (1865–1940)

84 Several years ago visitors to Montana's Little Bighorn Battlefield got a surprise when they signed up for a free guided tour. As the guide opened his mouth, it was clear he wasn't a local. He had a Brooklyn accent you could cut with a knife.

Some travelers might have felt they were grabbing a cab at LaGuardia, not exploring the Great Plains. But if the guide ever saw disappointment, he never let on. Every day he led his group to the grassy battlefield and quickly put them in the minds of the soldiers on that fateful day in 1876. Soon the arrogance of the U.S. forces became clear, and everyone could see the inevitability of the army's defeat. Battlefields can be hard to visit. It's difficult to understand the bloodshed that shook what is now a peaceful meadow. But the New Yorker took his visitors back in time and made this crucial moment in history come alive. In short, he made their visit.

But the surprising thing is that this hard worker wasn't on the payroll. He was a volunteer.

You, too, can be a VIP—Volunteers-in-Parks, as the program is called. In 2009, nearly 200,000 people participated, contributing work valued at nearly $120 million.

The Little Bighorn guide was working a several-months-long stint. And if you have the time to give, there are literally scores of opportunities for you. If you have a particular interest or skill, contact a park where you'd like to serve or browse the VIP website, where you'll find listings of opportunities and an application form. You can do everything from operating a gristmill at San Antonio Missions National Historical Park in Texas to transcribing oral histories for the Flight 93 National Memorial in Somerset County, Pennsylvania.

Another long-term commitment is to work as campground host. Volunteers who can stay through a season collecting fees, cleaning common areas, and performing light maintenance can often stay free of charge at the campground. But even if you just have a week or only a few days, there are often ways you can assist. For example, parks often need help when they hold special events.

Joy Pietschmann, the National Park Service's volunteer program coordinator, urges visitors to call a park a few weeks before they arrive and ask about opportunities even if there are none listed on its website. "If the park knows they're coming, it can often find a project for them. They might paint tables and then get a tour." Pietschmann says the Park Service works to make volunteer opportunities mutually beneficial. "We don't want people to just come in and clean toilets if

NATIONAL PUBLIC LANDS DAY

Most of us want to volunteer but have trouble finding time. Well, here's a chance to change that. National Public Lands Day, now the nation's largest outdoor volunteer event, began in 1994 as a way to serve our national forests, parks, and other properties. In recent years, 150,000 people have come out on a Saturday in late September to pick up trash, fix trails, and remove invasive species. Other tasks are as varied as collecting native plant seeds in the tallgrass prairie near Homestead National Monument in Nebraska to improving the grounds surrounding the Lincoln Memorial in Washington, D.C. And to show their appreciation, both the National Park Service and Forest Service offer free admission to their units on the day. *National Environmental Education Foundation, National Public Lands Day, 4301 Connecticut Ave. NW, Ste. 160, Washington, DC 20008, 202-833-2933, www.publiclandsday.org.*

they're not getting anything out of it. We want people no matter what they're doing to be happy what they're doing."

That's not to say the work won't be hard.

At Florida's Everglades National Park, volunteers are constantly needed to trim growth from trails and help eradicate invasive plant species. One of the biggest restoration projects is called the Hole-in-the-Donut, a 6,600-acre area that had been covered with Brazilian pepper trees, which absorb water and crowd out native plants. Although the park bulldozed the area, the plant keeps returning and volunteers help by pulling up new plant shoots and using loppers, clippers, and saws to cut the resilient evergreen back.

Other volunteers work with biologists tracking down invasive fish, or even searching for snakes that are tagged with GPS transmitters. Although those jobs are usually reserved for long-term volunteers or groups, the park tries to place short-term guests with these ongoing projects. And then there are the day-to-day park needs like photocopying, painting, and trimming overgrown vegetation. Even if it's not as sexy, the work is just as crucial.

In gratitude, the park gives even one-day volunteers a weeklong pass good for free admission. Cerisa Swanberg, an Everglades ranger who works with volunteers, says people leave with an even more valuable gift. After working at a park, a visitor always feels connected to the site. "It does make it a more satisfying and more memorable visit," she says.

HOW TO GET IN TOUCH

Volunteers-in-Parks, National Park Service, Volunteer Coordinator, 1201 I St. NW, Ste. 2450, Washington, DC 20005, e-mail: volunteer@nps.gov, www.nps.gov/getinvolved/volunteer.htm.

just say "om"

COLORADO

Yoga teaches us to cure what need not be endured and endure what cannot be cured.

—B.K.S. IYENGAR, RENOWNED YOGA TEACHER AND FOUNDER OF IYENGAR YOGA (B. 1918)

85 Yoga and meditation have become so popular in America that classes are taught in offices, high schools, and even the smallest heartland towns. While doctors laud yoga's physical benefits—flexibility, strength, and posture—for most people with hectic lives, it's the serenity that comes with an hour of measured breathing and thoughtful poses that makes the practice endurable.

Travel and fitness writer Debra Bokur was introduced to yoga by a physical therapist following a horseback-riding accident more than 20 years ago. "My horse and I fell at a jump, and both of my legs were injured. At the time, I didn't know a thing about yoga, but found that it not only helped with my recovery, it also had personal benefits I hadn't anticipated: My stress level lowered, I slept better, and my overall flexibility increased dramatically," she says. "In the years since that first session in a medical center, I've also found that yoga practice helps me to connect with a community of people who usually share many of my own values, including a mindful approach to moving through life."

If a once-a-week class isn't enough to chill you out, a retreat may be what you need. These days, you don't need to go all the way to Bali to find one you can afford. Many yoga and meditation centers in the United States offer programs that allow you to camp out or bunk in a shared space. Most also offer private accommodations for those who want more amenities and space.

Bokur, who now works with *Healing Lifestyles & Spas* magazine, recommends two Colorado retreats set in landscapes that offer their own healing magic:

Shambhala Mountain Center. This northern Colorado retreat near the town of Red Feather Lakes sprawls across 600 acres in a mountain valley. Founded in the 1970s as a Buddhist retreat—the grounds feature a Buddhist stupa completed in 2001—Shambhala offers an unusual array of programs centered on mindfulness, yoga, and Tibetan Buddhism. Programs centered around drumming, writing, ikebana (the Japanese art of flower arrangement),

GET STARTED ON YOUR DOWNWARD DOG

Travel and fitness writer Debra Bokur offers these tips:

- Get qualified, certified instruction before practicing on your own.
- Try different styles and traditions to find the one that best serves your needs.
- Take your time, and don't compare yourself to anyone else.
- Don't practice on a full stomach.
- Wear comfortable, appropriate clothing during practice.
- Pay attention to your breathing during your practice.
- Invest in your own mat—it's healthier than sharing.

gardening, and photography are designed to stir the creative soul; meditation to soothe the tired and tortured. Physical activities as a form of meditation become the centerpiece of programs focused on distance running and walking, Chinese qigong, and tai chi. Yoga weekends may be focused on helping you establish your practice at home or helping you manage depression; yoga styles vary. Weekend yoga programs start at $310 and include lodging in a dormitory, meals, and seminars; private rooms are offered.

Shambhala Mountain Center, 921 County Rd. 68C, Red Feather Lakes, CO 80545, 970-881-2184, www.shambhalamountain.org.

Shoshoni Yoga Retreat. Meditation, walks, breathing exercises, and hatha yoga practice are designed to help visitors allay stress during their stay at this retreat near Boulder. Guests can design retreats that start and end when they want for as many days as they want, space allowing. Each overnight of your stay includes morning and evening meditation programs, two yoga classes, and three vegetarian meals. Prices start at $95 per person for space in a single-gender dorm room, $70 if you camp out and bring your own tent. Several private-room options are offered for around $180 per night. Occasional family weekends are also offered—which might be just the antidote if you've got a soul-searching teen in tow. If you're up for a splurge, sign up for an ayurvedic treatment including a facial or scrub.

Shoshoni Yoga Retreat, P.O. Box 400, Rollinsville, CO 80474, 303-642-0116, www.shoshoni.org.

Colorado not convenient? Here are a few other affordable options:

- **Esalen Institute, Big Sur, California.** Weekend yoga workshops, including meals, movement classes, lodging, and use of grounds, start at $385 per person in a shared sleeping-bag room. *Esalen Institute, 831-667-3000, www.esalen.org.*
- **Kripalu Center for Yoga and Health, Stockbridge, Massachusetts.** This well-known center in the Berkshire Hills offers retreat-and-renewal packages that include three meals

daily, yoga classes, and outdoor activities from $160 per night in a dorm space with shared bath. *Kripalu Center for Yoga and Health, 866-200-5203, www.kripalu.org.*

- **Omega Institute, Rhinebeck, New York.** All-inclusive packages at the Omega include three vegetarian meals; daily open classes in yoga, tai chi, and meditation start at $160 for a two-night package for campers with their own gear, $244 for a dorm single for a two-night package. Longer packages and private accommodations available. *Omega Institute, 877-944-2002, www.eomega.org.*
- **Sivananda Ashram Yoga Retreat, Nassau, Bahamas.** Yoga vacation programs start at $15 per day in summer, $29 per day in winter, plus an accommodations fee starting in summer at $59 if you bring your own tent, or $69 for a dorm space or tent hut. Prices are slightly higher in winter. Rates include two meals daily. Class attendance is mandatory—a factor behind some unfavorable reviews on the Internet review site TripAdvisor. *Sivananda Ashram Yoga Retreat, 866-446-5934, www.sivanandabahamas.org.*

see opera outdoors

SANTA FE, NEW MEXICO

Opera is credible drama now, and it costs less than going to a football match.
What have you got to lose?

—LESLEY GARRETT (B. 1955), BRITISH SOPRANO

86 Summer sunsets bring two kinds of drama to the foothills of the Jemez Mountains. As the day ends, New Mexico's sky fills with pinks and vermilions—and on most nights in July and August, the soaring notes of opera.

"You really get a feeling that's electric," says Oliver Prezant, a longtime lecturer and educator with the Santa Fe Opera, which has performed here for more than a half century.

If you want to be immersed in opera, Santa Fe is one of the best places to go. As generations of patrons have discovered, the art form translates beautifully to the outdoors. Although the amphitheater is covered, the wall behind the stage is left open before performances, and the side walls often are too. With the evening breeze comes a relaxed atmosphere. Some people do wear black-tie, but dressy casual clothes are fine, too.

Every summer, the celebrated company runs five operas in rotation, which might include classic works from the 1700s and world premieres. Each performance is preceded by a free lecture providing context and background for the show.

Although a trip devoted to opera doesn't sound like an affordable vacation, it's possible to take in performances without breaking the bank. Seated tickets begin at a reasonable $27, and each seat includes a private screen placed on the back of the seat in front of you, which provides translation of the opera in English or Spanish. Even cheaper is standing-room admission ($10), which gets you an assigned spot with a rail to lean on, and a libretto screen as well. There's no shame in going this route, but since performances might last several hours, be sure to wear comfortable shoes.

Guests with children can take advantage of special performances designed for families. On four evenings each summer, Youth Nights provide budget tickets for the second-to-final dress rehearsal before a production begins. One adult and two youths (ages 6–22) costs $32, and two adults and three youths runs $56. Additional youth tickets are $8. Don't try to sneak in without a kid, though. Since the tickets are underwritten by grants, the opera makes sure youths are actually attending.

But anyone can take a 9 a.m. backstage tour ($5), available daily but Sunday, from May 31 to August 28. If you go early in the season, you'll see more activity as the company busily prepares for upcoming productions. "There's a whole cadre of docents who get wonderful training," Prezant says. "They can tell you which side of the yak the hair for the wig comes from." Answer: The belly, which is more supple since it isn't exposed to the weather.

Visitors in mid- to late August can take in performances by the opera's apprentices on two consecutive Sunday nights, with tickets running from $5–$15. These talented singers undergo an extensive audition process to get the prestigious posts. They serve in chorus and in minor roles during the operas, and also as understudies for the stars. Several apprentices, such as Joyce DiDonato, Dimitri Pittas, and Samuel Ramey, have gone on to stardom.

You can also hear the apprentices during Opera Week at **Vanessie** (434 W. San Francisco St., 505-982-9966), a restaurant and lounge. The multinight fund-raiser, usually held in late July, features the singers in two sets at the piano bar. Cover is $10. The restaurant's a favorite with performers, and throughout the season, you might find opera singers kicking back and singing at the restaurant's piano bar on nights the amphitheater's dark.

But on performance nights, the drama starts well before the first note is sung. Like football fans, opera lovers tailgate in Santa Fe, often setting up elaborate meals in the amphitheater parking lot. Some may have chandeliers and champagne set up on folding tables. "It's a strange and wonderful and absolutely delightful thing," Prezant says.

ARIAS UNDER THE STARS IN NEW YORK

Just north of the Baseball Hall of Fame in Cooperstown, New York, Glimmerglass Opera company has been performing in the innovative Alice Busch Opera Theater since 1987. The 900-seat venue can slide open its walls, allowing patrons to enjoy an evening breeze between arias.

The company runs four productions every summer, and guests in August can sometimes see all of them in one packed weekend. There's also a free backstage tour on Saturday mornings and free pre-opera lectures an hour before each performance. These include audio clips and are held in a preview pavilion. Changeover Talks are held Saturday afternoons between the matinee and evening performances. Audience members can watch as walls are moved and the stage is transformed from, say, ancient Rome to medieval Spain. A production staffer explains what's happening on stage. "We have two hours. It's synchronized and choreographed," says Brittany Lesavoy of the opera company. "Some companies have automatic stages, but all our changes are done by hand." Patrons are welcome to picnic before performances on the grounds. **Danny's Main Street Market** (92 Main St., 607-547-4053) offers inexpensive sandwiches and bottles of wine.

Tickets start at $26, with discounts available for children, students, and educators. *Glimmerglass Opera, 7300 Hwy. 80, Cooperstown, NY 13326, 607-547-2255, www.glimmerglass.org.*

If you're not on a caviar budget, you can pick up gourmet takeout and a bottle of wine at a bargain price from the grocery store **Trader Joe's** (530 W. Cordova Rd., 505-995-8145). Even cheaper, but authentic and still acceptable, is a green-chile cheeseburger from nearby **Blake's Lotaburger** (3200 Cerrillos Rd., 505-471-2433).

[$PLURGE: **For a splurge, sign up for the opera's Preview Buffet ($52 per person), which includes dinner, wine, and dessert in an open-air venue. The meal finishes with a guest speaker, who discusses the night's performance while dessert is served.**]

Santa Fe lodging isn't generally cheap. For budget accommodation, look along Cerrillos Road. For example, **King's Rest Court Inn** (1452 Cerrillos Rd., 505-983-8879) often has rooms in the $50 range.

HOW TO GET IN TOUCH

Santa Fe Opera, 7 Governor Miles Rd., Santa Fe, NM 87506, 505-986-5900, www.santafeopera.org.

spread your wings

OSHKOSH, WISCONSIN

There is no sport equal to that which aviators enjoy while being carried through the air on great white wings.

—PIONEER AVIATOR WILBUR WRIGHT (1905)

87 Before commercial airlines became flying cattle cars, aviation was a sport of passion, romance, and exploration. For the estimated 500,000 private pilots in America who claim small-plane flying as their hobby, that's still the case. "Up there you get a perspective you just don't get from the ground," says Dick Knapinski, who flies a 1967 Piper Cherokee. "You look at the countryside below and see how everything fits together." And there's a sense of accomplishment, he says, of just learning to fly the machine.

If you long to play Charles Lindbergh or Amelia Earhart but find flying lessons pricey, head to Oshkosh, Wisconsin, in late July to check out the EAA AirVenture Oshkosh, a fly-in convention that has been a tradition since 1953. (EAA—Experimental Aircraft Association—sponsor of the convention, is a membership organization that encourages recreational aviation.) Some 2,500 small planes—vintage aircraft, experimentals, homebuilts, military planes, seaplanes, warbirds—fly in for a week of demonstrations, afternoon aerobatics displays, training sessions, seminars, workshops on planebuilding, and camaraderie at the country's largest air show. Evening entertainment includes bands—one year the Beach Boys, another Chicago—and "fly in" movies. Activities include a kid's hangar, play dates, and a teen dance. And whether you're looking for airplane models, historic patches, or the latest avionics gear, you'll find it here.

The show draws pilots and enthusiasts from corporate CEOs with the newest equipment to working people who have scrimped for years to build ultralights or kit planes, says Knapinski, who works with the show. "It's celebrating the fact that yes, we can fly."

Entry for an adult costs $37 per day. (If you're planning to attend for at least two days, pay $40 for an EAA membership, which brings the entry fee down to $25 per day and $21 for your spouse.) Included is that day's admission to the **AirVenture Museum** (920-426-4800, www.airventuremuseum.org, regular entry $12.50 adults).

EAA membership also allows you to camp at the show site, with tent sites starting at $22 per night with a three-night minimum. For a price-savvy alternative, book a room in a local college dorm room, often for less than $50 per night. Options include the **University of Wisconsin-Oshkosh** (920-424-3326, e-mail: uwoeaa@mio.uwosh.edu), **Lawrence University** (920-832-7024, e-mail:

NOTABLE HISTORIC AIRCRAFT AND WHERE TO FIND THEM

- **1903 Wright Brothers Flier.** National Air and Space Museum, Washington, DC, 202-633-1000, www.nasm.si.edu.
- **1916 Curtiss JN-4D "Jenny" Military Tractor.** College Park Aviation Museum, College Park, MD, 301-864-6029, www.collegeparkaviationmuseum.com.
- **1918 Fokker D-VIII.** Fantasy of Flight, Polk City, FL, 863-984-3500, www.fantasyofflight.com.
- **1944 Grumman Duck.** EEA Aviation Center, Oshkosh, WI, 920-426-4800, www.airventure museum.org.
- **Original Air Force One**. Museum of Flight, Seattle, WA, 206-764-5720, www.museumof flight.org.
- **Saturn V Rocket.** Kennedy Space Center, Cape Canaveral, FL, 866-737-5235, www.kennedy spacecenter.com.

outreach@lawrence.edu) in Appleton, and **Marian University** (800-262-7426, e-mail: eaa@marianuniversity.edu) in Fond du Lac. Many local homeowners rent out rooms during the show.

If you really want to try your wings, sign up for an airplane ride. While those in specialized vintage planes may run hundreds of dollars, other show flights may cost as little as $40—a bargain by flying standards.

For those in your group who haven't been fully struck with aero-obsession, Oshkosh offers other diversions. They include the **Barlow Planetarium** (1478 Midway Rd., Menasha, 920-832-2848, www.barlowplanetarium.com, shows from $7); the **Paine Art Center and Gardens** (1410 Algoma Blvd., 920-235-6903, www.thepaine.org, $9), a 1920s-era mansion turned museum; and the **Bergstrom-Mahler Museum** (165 N. Park Ave., Neenah, 920-751-4658, www.paperweight museum.com), home to one of the world's finest collections of glass paperweights.

And as for the burning question: Are Oshkosh B'gosh children's overalls made here? The answer is no longer, though the company keeps a corporate office here.

HOW TO GET IN TOUCH

EAA AirVenture Oshkosh, 3000 Poberezny Rd., Oshkosh, WI 54902, 920-426-4800, www.air venture.org.

Oshkosh Convention & Visitors Bureau, 920-303-9200, www.visitoshkosh.com.

join the art parade

HOUSTON, TEXAS

Every child is an artist. The problem is how to remain an artist once we grow up.

—ARTIST PABLO PICASSO (1881–1973)

88 Houston ranks as the nation's fifth largest arts scene, says a recent study by Americans for the Arts. But what sets it apart from New York, Los Angeles, Miami, and London, says Houston Arts Alliance CEO Jonathon Glus, is the wide range of visual arts, from the funky Art Car Parade and Beer Can House to major museums.

For sheer exuberant self-expression, few displays in the country beat Houston's annual rite of spring, the Art Car Parade, organized by the Orange Show Center for Visionary Art, an organization that promotes self-expression through art. Since 1988, Houstonians (and now, out-of-towners in for the fun) have transformed cars, bicycles, lawn mowers, go-karts, roller skates, motorcycles—just about any kind of personal conveyance—into rolling works of joy.

A giant sunflower affixed to a curvy auto painted spring green, a Beetle with another full-scale Beetle affixed on its roof upside down and painted to match, a psychedelic Flower Power mobile, a sedan topped with a hand swiped from a giant, a winged plaid-covered hot rod with its driver in plaid pajamas, a bicycle transformed into 1950s-style ice-cream cart. All have joined the caravan of 250-plus vehicles that parades down Allen Avenue on a Saturday afternoon in early May.

The spectacle is so popular that it's grown into a weekend of events. Thursday night kicks off with the Art Car Ball street party ($25–$30), featuring live entertainment. Friday morning, a phalanx of cars visits local schools, hospitals, and community centers as part of the Main Street Drag. Friday night, supporters gather at the downtown Discovery Green for a sneak peek at the parade participants.

On Saturday comes the parade itself. Many people arrive in the morning to watch the cars line up near the intersection of Allen Parkway and Taft Street. About 100,000 enthusiasts turn out for the free frolic, angling for views along Allen Parkway between Taft and Bagby Streets in downtown.

The festivities officially begin at 1 p.m., and the parade sometimes even features a celebrity grand marshal. (In 2010, Dan Aykroyd was the honoree.) If you'd like to see the event in comfort and style, $125 will buy you a bleacher seat and box lunch at the VIPit Party. The money goes to defray parade costs. Creating an art car isn't cheap. To honor both effort and creativity, a panel of judges awards $10,000 in prizes. These are handed out on Sunday at the Art Car Brunch and Awards Ceremony.

HOUSTON'S OTHER ARTY SIDE

Oil money and a wildcatting spirit of independence have made Houston an unexpected center for visual arts that's well worth a visit any time of year. Houston's **Museum District** (www.houstonmuseumdistrict.org) alone is home to 19 museums. Note: Museums don't open until midday on Sunday and are closed on Monday.

The private **Menil Collection** (1515 Sul Ross St., 713-525-9400, www.menil.org), created by the late Houston collectors John and Dominique de Menil, is Houston's must-see museum. Set in a tranquil residential neighborhood, its airy main space—designed by Renzo Piano—is home to ceremonial masks from Africa and Oceania plus modern paintings by Magritte, Picasso, and Tanguy. A second Piano-designed space houses sculptures, paintings, and works on paper by Cy Twombly. Two blocks away stand a pair of chapels; one built to house fragments of an ancient Byzantine fresco (4011 Yupon St.), the other for a series of monochromatic paintings by Mark Rothko (3900 Yupon St.). All are free.

Another important stop for art lovers is the **Museum of Fine Arts, Houston** (1001 Bissonnet St., 713-639-7300, www.mfah.org, $7). Founded in the 1920s, today's MFA features exhibition buildings designed by Mies van der Rohe and Rafael Moneo and a sculpture garden designed by Isamu Noguchi. Collections include Native American art, Renaissance and baroque masterpieces, Impressionist works, antiquities, modern and Old World masters, Asian and African art, and pre-Columbian gold. Don't miss the light tunnel by contemporary artist James Turrell and the thought-provoking "End Game" sculpture by Damien Hirst. Plan to spend the day here; you'll need that and more.

If you're into the gallery scene, a number of galleries, including a half dozen galleries on quiet Colquitt Street, lie a short taxi ride from the Museum of Fine Arts, including the following:

- **Goldesberry Gallery.** A gallery dedicated to contemporary crafts. *2625 Colquitt St., 713-528-0405, www.goldesberrygallery.com.*
- **McClain Gallery.** This blue-chip gallery has shown the works of Frank Stella, Julian Schnabel, Cy Twombly, and James Rosenquist. *2242 Richmond Ave., 713-520-9988, www.mcclaingallery.com.*
- **Meredith Long Gallery.** Opened in 1957 by Houston art-scene pioneer Meredith Long, this gallery with longtime New York connections lists Helen Frankenthaler, Robert Motherwell, and Jules Olitski among its artists. *2323 San Felipe St., 713-523-6671, www.meredithlonggallery.com.*
- **Texas Gallery.** Fredericka Hunter owns this River Oaks district space focusing on contemporary artists. *2012 Peden St., 713-524-1593, www.texgal.com.*
- **Sicardi Gallery.** Next door to the McClain Gallery, the Sicardi specializes in contemporary Latin American artists. *2246 Richmond Ave., 713-529-1313, www.sicardi.com.*

The Orange Show also acts as steward for two of the city's funkiest year-round attractions. The **Orange Show Monument** (2402 Munger St., $1) is a massive, 3,000-square-foot folk art installation including a pond, museum, and upper deck, single-handedly built over 22 years by a late postal worker. The **Beer Can House** (222 Malone St., $2) was started in 1968 by a retired upholsterer who reportedly got sick of mowing the grass; the yard and house are now a monument to recycling, featuring an estimated 50,000 cans. Both attractions are open Saturdays and Sundays (12 p.m.–5 p.m.).

Lodgingwise, your most convenient choices for the Art Car weekend are downtown, where there are chain hotels and motels. Some may offer discount rates for event attendees, but you'll need to book early.

HOW TO GET IN TOUCH

Orange Show Center for Visionary Art, 2402 Munger St., 713-926-6368, www.orangeshow.org.
Greater Houston Convention & Visitors Bureau, 800-446-8786, www.visithoustontexas.com.
Houston Art Dealers Association (713-520-7767, www.arthouston.com)
Houston Arts Alliance (713-527-9330, www.houstonartsalliance.com)
***PaperCity* magazine** (www.papercitymag.com).

foster self-sufficiency for those in need

PERRYVILLE, ARKANSAS

These children don't need a cup, they need a cow.

—DAN WEST (1893–1971), FOUNDER OF HEIFER INTERNATIONAL, WHO LADLED RATIONS OF MILK TO CHILDREN DURING THE SPANISH CIVIL WAR

89 Imagine living in a refugee camp. You have no food and water. Your home is a makeshift shelter offering minimal protection from heat or rain. No one speaks your language. It's an abstraction that's hard to appreciate until you live that way yourself.

The innovative charity Heifer International helps visitors understand the reality of poverty with its immersive Global Gateway program, at the group's 1,200-acre farm in Perryville, Arkansas, about 50 miles northwest of Little Rock. In one of its most popular programs, guests are randomly assigned to spend the night in a mock-up of a poor community modeled on homes in Guatemala, Thailand, Zambia, Tibet, Appalachia, an urban slum, or a refugee camp. There's enough food for everyone, but resources are unevenly distributed. The slum might have rice, Appalachia could have wood for cooking fires, and Guatemala might be blessed with water. True to life, the refugees have nothing. It's only by cooperating through barter or trade—or not—that participants can eat and sleep in relative comfort.

It's one of the most unique learning opportunities offered by the charity, best known for its original approach to philanthropy. Instead of trying to fight global poverty by giving away money, it donates animals—sheep, goats, water buffalo, camels, rabbits, guinea pigs, llamas, and, yes, heifers—to villagers around the world. The livestock can provide a livelihood for the poor, giving them a chance to feed their family and eventually provide animals to others.

The one-night Global Gateway experience is usually only open to school groups, but on select dates it is open to individual guests for $43. Heifer International's philosophy is that the world has enough food—grain, vegetables, fruit, and meat—to supply everyone with a full diet, which the village experience tries to make clear to participants. The charity doesn't preach redistribution as a solution. The goal is self-sufficiency, so everyone can feed themselves.

$PLURGE

SEEING PHILANTHROPY AT WORK OVERSEAS

Heifer International's overseas study tours immerse visitors in the culture and lives of project beneficiaries. Tour participants, for example, might see how a generator powered by manure helps farmers in China or join with families harvesting honey in Poland.

For travelers, it can be an emotional experience watching Peruvian villagers accept a donation of alpacas that will help sustain their family, or to see how the charity helps Kenyan children orphaned by AIDS. Travelers will stay in hotels most evenings, although there may be an overnight in a village. While the focus is on Heifer programs, there often is a chance for some sightseeing. Fees run from $1,000 to $4,000, but do not include airfare. *Heifer International, www.heifer.org/studytours.*

But as guests see, that's much easier said than done.

As participants learn, their fate is really a matter of luck. And once they're assigned to a "village" they simply have to make the most of it. Some participants are shocked when others won't cooperate with them. Sometimes those with water will demand others wash their dishes before they'll share their supply. It might sound like *Lord of the Flies,* but the experience delivers a profound and lasting lesson.

"We try to put people a little bit out of their comfort zone," says Michelle Dusek Izaguirre, the charity's senior director of Learning Centers. "But if everyone works together and shares, there's plenty of food, and normally a good meal out of the deal." The shelters are based on actual villages where Heifer International works. Thus the Zambian home resembles the roundhouses found in that African country. The Guatemalan shelter, though, does make a few concessions for visitors—it and the accompanying pit toilet are handicapped accessible.

Participants make breakfast the next morning, which requires more bartering and cooperation between the village inhabitants. Later that day, after they've done their dishes and cleaned their village, the program participants gather for a debriefing. "We talk a lot about being global citizens," says Izaguirre. "How everyone's not the same and we all have different realities."

Heifer offers two other programs that individuals can sign up for:

- **Farm Program.** This service and education program costs $335 for a five-night visit, including food and accommodations, and focuses on either beekeeping or animal health care. Program participants arrive on Sunday night and check into an air-conditioned lodge. On Monday, they begin their farm chores, such as feeding animals, changing hay, and harvesting produce from a garden. The program's experiences build on each other throughout the week. Participants may milk goats one day, learn to make cheese another, and then use the cheese to make a pizza. These aren't just make-work activities. Heifer

International maintains the farms to train workers and to demonstrate how its international programs work.

- **Women's Lambing Program.** This spring program open to women only is scheduled around the lambing season. It runs $275 for a weekend and $600 for a week. The women work farm chores and learn how the charity uses sheep to help families. Participants get an in-depth education about the animal's life cycle and gestation process, and often get to witness the inspiring moment when a lamb takes its first wobbly steps.

HOW TO GET IN TOUCH

Heifer International, 1 World Ave., Little Rock, AR 72202, 800-422-0474, www.heifer.org. Minimum age and other requirements vary by program.

relax at a spa

IXTAPAN DE LA SAL, MEXICO

Healing is a matter of time, but it is sometimes also a matter of opportunity.

—PRECEPTS, PART OF THE HIPPOCRATIC CORPUS,
ATTRIBUTED TO HIPPOCRATES (CA 460 B.C.–375 B.C.)

90 Spa visits aren't usually on the affordable vacations list. But women from Oregon to New Jersey have discovered the secret of **Hotel Spa Ixtapan,** set near the town of Ixtapan de la Sal in the Mexican mountains, where a four-night package, including exercise and yoga classes, lodging, all meals, and many spa treatments, costs less than a single day at an upscale urban spa. If you share a room with a friend or spouse, the package costs $770; if you go solo, the cost rises to $870. Longer stays and sports packages are also offered.

Some visitors come for the health benefits, some simply to relax. Most of the 33,000 American women who come here each year are 50-plus, says owner Roberto San Roman, whose grandfather first developed the resort in the 1940s. (Men are welcome, too.)

Many guests are repeaters, like Rosemary Owens of Dallas, who has been visiting since the mid-1990s with a crowd of fellow airline employees. "It's lovely. It's affordable. They have beautiful service and food," she says. "You get a whole lot of bang for the buck. And the treatments are really good; each year they've improved."

Treatments run the gamut of what you'd expect to find at a destination spa, including firming facials, reflexology, deep massage, loofah, mani- and pedicures, scalp massage, Thai massage, and aromatherapy. Some treatments are included in packages; others may require an extra fee. Some massages take place in the main hotel building; others are offered in the newer Holistic Spa, a serene space of high light ceilings and trickling pools.

Hotel Spa Ixtapan isn't a luxury resort, but the open-air lobby, twin swimming pools, and spacious, cheery rooms (sans AC, but in the mountains, cool enough even in summer) are more than comfortable. A constant refrain of tweets sounds from the treetops sheltering the 13-acre park of fountains and lawns. The tennis club, golf course, and a children's play area make the resort popular with Mexican families during holidays, though the campus is large enough that you're not likely to be distracted.

The resort has two restaurants; one features healthy fare, the other offers international and Mexican dishes. If you take all your meals at the health-conscious restaurant, you'll consume less than 1,000 calories a day. Breakfast illustrates the differences: In the healthy restaurant, you dine on fresh fruit, cereals, and fresh juices—including an unappealing looking cactus diuretic that actually tastes pretty good—and eggs cooked to order. Looking for croissants or butter? Head for the other restaurant—but say goodbye to your weight-watching intentions.

For visitors coming from the United States, the only drawback is distance from the airport at Mexico City, a two-hour drive away. The hotel will provide transportation in its own vehicles for $360 round-trip for up to four people—a hefty fee if you're on your own, but reasonable if you are traveling with friends. Alternatively, you can fly into the nearby airport at Toluca.

MORE BLISS FOR THE BUCK

At $250 or more for a half day of spa treatments at most U.S. resorts, you have to wonder whether a visit is worth the money. But some places do offer great value. You just have to know how to find them.

Look for spa deal weeks and months, usually held in the low season at resorts where business tends to be seasonal. For instance, during Miami's Spa Month each July (www.miamispamonth.com), dozens of spas offer treatments and packages for $99. Hundreds of spas in other cities—including New York, Chicago, and Seattle—participate in a national spa week (www.spaweek.com), held in April and sometimes again in the fall, when some treatments are priced at $50.

Check out the "Spa Tapas" or "Spa Sampler" menus of mini treatments being offered at spas nationwide. It's a top trend in this slow economic recovery, says the International Spa Association.

Look for day spas when you travel that may charge 40 or 50 percent less for that massage or facial than you'd pay at your hotel. You can find them by doing a simple Google search online.

If you're opting for a high-priced spa treatment, do it at a resort with expanded facilities that includes use of them for the day with your spa treatment. At some, you can get a spa treatment then spend the rest of the day in the fitness facilities, steam room, relaxation room, or by the pool.

Diane Bair and Pamela Wright, who cover spas for AirTran's *GO* magazine, recommend the following spas for value:

- **Birdwing Spa.** Set in a 300-acre woodland, this 15-room destination spa 70 miles east of Minneapolis has won a slew of awards, thanks to killer packages like this one: Two nights (Fri.–Sun.) with five meals, fitness classes, wellness presentations, massage, and choice of a facial or herbal body wrap for $515. *Birdwing Spa, 21398 575th Ave., Litchfield, MN 55355, 320-693-6064, www.birdwingspa.com.*
- **The Oaks at Ojai.** Charmingly low-key, the Oaks is widely regarded as the best affordable destination spa in the country. Owner Sheila Cluff, who ice-skates competitively at age 71, is her own best advertisement. Look for fabulous specials online, like the popular mother-daughter 50 percent–off deal, offered twice a year. Weekend rates start at $195 per person per night, including fitness classes and meals. *The Oaks at Ojai, 122 E. Ojai Ave., Ojai, CA 93023, 800-753-6257, www.oaksspa.com.*

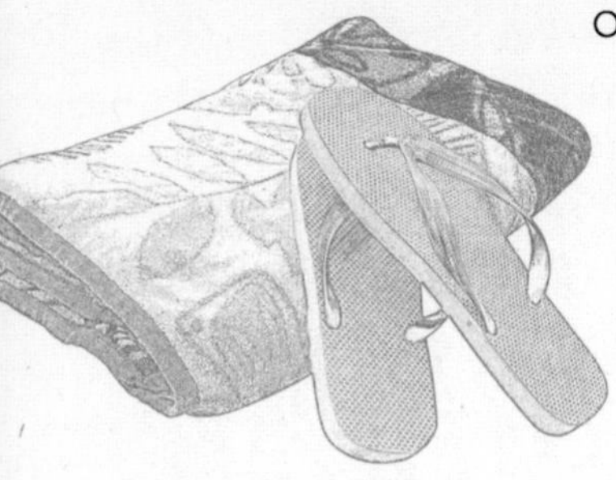

Once you are in the mountains, you can easily visit the colonial towns of **Taxco**—famed for its silver—and **Cuernavaca**—known for its gardens—on day trips, which can be arranged by the hotel upon request. Taxco is an hour away, Cuernavaca an hour and a half.

Or you can just wander into the sweet town of Ixtapan de la Sal, scooping up silver jewelry and locally made face creams and clay piggy banks, then stroll back to lounge by the hotel pool, margarita in hand. That won't help you lose weight, but it just might be what you need.

HOW TO GET IN TOUCH

Hotel Spa Ixtapan, Ixtapan de la Sal, Mexico, 800-638-7950, www.spamexico.com.

go it alone

NATIONWIDE

One travels more usefully when alone, because he reflects more.

—THOMAS JEFFERSON, LETTER TO J. BANNISTER, JR., DURING JEFFERSON'S PRIVATE TRAVELS IN FRANCE (1787)

91 Traveling solo isn't everyone's first choice, but for many of us, it's the only practical option. If friends and family don't share your travel interests, you either go alone—or don't go at all.

That's been the lesson for co-author Jane Wooldridge. As a college student, she headed off on a European backpacking trip with a male friend. Their budgets and interests were so different that by the end of the first week, the two parted ways.

He took their only guidebook. In those pre-Internet days, she was left to jot down youth hostel addresses from borrowed copies of *Let's Go Europe.* "I was terrified," she says. It was her first trip outside the United States.

Lonely and scary though it was, that first solo trip literally changed her life. "It proved to me that I could manage on my own, just about anywhere—even in a foreign country." That trip gave her the confidence to move to unfamiliar cities, take new jobs, visit Asia and Africa, and drive alone across the United States (28 days, 5,000 miles). Now married, she's visited more than a hundred countries—some on vacation, and some as part of what became a travel-writing career.

Her advice: "Be safe, be smart, be money-wise. But don't bypass the places you want to see just because no one in your circle has the time, money, or inclination to go with you."

Here are her suggestions for three trips to take on your own:

San Francisco, California. Great restaurants, terrific sites—what's not to like about San Francisco? What makes it a great choice for traveling alone is that it is a bustling city with good public transportation (making it relatively cheap and safe to get around), busy walking districts that bustle at all hours (meaning you'll have plenty of company on the streets), and lots of business and single people (meaning you can pull up a chair at a communal table in a great restaurant, or dine alone and not look out of place). And if you go out of season (Dec.–May) or on a slow weekend, you'll have a better chance of snagging a value rate at one of the city's downtown hotels.

Top choices for things to do in the City by the Bay: Ride the **F-Market & Wharves streetcar line** (www.streetcar.org, $2) that

SOLO SAFETY

Here are some of Jane's tips for traveling safely on your own:

Traveling by car

- Check all working parts (tires, belts, etc.) before you start out on a long trip.
- Fill up on fuel; never let your tank go below one-third.
- Use a GPS or have good maps handy.
- Avoid the roads less taken—a romantic idea, but potentially dangerous.

Lodging

- Stay only in hotels/motels with enclosed hallways; be sure the hallways are well lit.
- In cities, stay in hotels in bustling (but not too loud) business districts where you're likely to find lots of people on the street, day and night; be sure the front door has night security.

In cities

- Stick with public transportation when possible.
- Ride only in official taxis—not gypsy cabs. Be sure the driver turns on the meter when you get in, or negotiate the flat rate before he takes off. (And if he tries to overcharge you, get out of the car and hand him the cash you think is fair, then walk off.)

Keeping in touch

- Give your itinerary to someone you trust. If plans are loose, have general check-in times with friends so they know all is well.
- Don't post your movements on a blog or via Twitter unless (a) you feel confident your home is secure and won't be bothered by Internet-savvy crooks and (b) you've already left the place you're posting about.
- Keep your cell phone charged.

Going out

- Stick with casual restaurants, upscale restaurants familiar with business travelers, and trendy restaurants with communal tables.
- Take a book to dinner—a sure sign that you're not looking for company.
- Dress appropriately—whatever that means. Being overdressed, underdressed, or too bare will draw attention you may not want.
- Do not let anyone except the bartender touch your drink; stories about date-rape drugs aren't urban myth.

runs between the Castro District and Fisherman's Wharf, visit **Alcatraz** (www.nps.gov/alcatraz, www.alcatrazcruises.com, day tours including ferry start at $26), join a free **walking tour** (www.sfcityguides.org), and take in the view from the sky-high lounge **Top of the Mark** (Mark Hopkins Intercontinental Hotel, 999 California St., 415-616-6916, www.intercontinentalmarkhopkins.com).

Other great cities for a solo visit: Chicago; New York; Quebec; Philadelphia; Seattle; Portland, Oregon; and Washington, D.C.

Only in San Francisco, 415-391-2000, www.onlyinsanfrancisco.com.

"Spoleto USA," Charleston, South Carolina. For solo travelers, arts performances create a shared experience that doesn't require knowing the people around you. In a darkened theater, you're all characters in a play, witnesses to the despair and exuberance and the complexities of emotion that are often best portrayed through music and theater.

The U.S. and Canadian arts calendars are blessed with festivals centered on music, theater, and dance. Spoleto USA offers the best of interdisciplinary worlds. For nearly three weeks each year, in late May and early June, the stages of Charleston, South Carolina, are filled with performances of jazz, modern dance, ballet, opera, chamber music, and musical and dramatic theater. Ticket prices vary by event, but some cost as little as $10. Lodging can be pricey during the festival, but if you stay just outside the city, you'll have access to the arts at a value price; for instance, in the cozy town of **Summerville** (www.visitsummerville.com), bed-and-breakfast rooms start at around $75.

Other great festivals for solo travelers to attend: Jacob's Pillow Dance Festival, western Massachusetts (June–Aug.); Williamstown Theatre Festival, western Massachusetts (June–Aug.); Aspen Music Festival, Colorado (July–Aug.; classical music); Tanglewood Music Festival, western Massachusetts (summer; classical music and jazz; see pp. 274–275); Toronto Fringe Festival (early July; fringe theater); Oregon Shakespeare Festival, Ashland, Oregon (Feb.–Oct.; see p. 261); Summerfest, Milwaukee (late June–early July; rock); South by Southwest, Austin (March; new media, music, and film).

Spoleto USA, 843-579-3100, www.spoletousa.org.

ALONE, NOT LONELY

Traveling solo doesn't mean you have to be lonely. Here are a few tips for connecting with others:

- Before you leave, get names and numbers of friends of friends and colleagues who live where you're going. Touch base in advance and make a date for coffee.
- Join a tour. Even a two-hour walking tour, ranger talk, or excursion will help you connect with others.
- Museums, colleges, women's tour companies, and adventure firms offer group trips—often with affordable single rates. Choose a trip based on a passionate interest or go to a place you've always wanted to visit; if you don't like your fellow travelers, you'll still have a worthy experience.

Yellowstone National Park, Wyoming. National parks are great (and generally safe) places to get out and enjoy nature, yet still be within shouting distance of help. You'll find plenty of other people on the trail, too,

$PLURGE

YELLOWSTONE LODGES

Yellowstone has nine lodges scattered around its interior; many of them offer the choice of accommodations in the lodge or cabins. The most requested lodging in the park is Old Faithful Inn, a national historic landmark that, as its name suggests, stands next to the park's iconic geyser. The Victorian-era eponymous Lake Yellowstone Hotel was the first lodge built in the park. Rooms at Yellowstone's lodges offer few frills and can run $145 and up, but the experience is worth the expense. *Yellowstone National Park Lodges, www.yellowstonenationalparklodges.com.*

although most will be polite enough not to intrude. Ranger-led tours offer chances to connect with others if you'd like, and learn about the ecology as well.

At more than two million acres, Wyoming's Yellowstone National Park offers you plenty of space and a wide diversity of attractions and activities. You can drive from one fluorescent boiling mudpot to the next, learn why Old Faithful's timing isn't what it used to be, marvel at Mammoth Hot Springs terraces, hike into the woods, go fly-fishing, catch a tour in a historic open-topped car, and sign up for a horse-riding trip.

Unless you are camping, which can be a little daunting on your own, and unless you're traveling in the off-season, staying within the park can be expensive. Fortunately, the towns of **Cody** (Wyoming; www.codychamber.org) and **West Yellowstone** (Montana; www.destinationyellowstone.com), both located near a park entrance, have plenty of clean, cheap accommodations. In addition, the towns present an interesting mix of charm and honky-tonk.

Other great national parks for a solo visit are California's Yosemite National Park and Arizona's Grand Canyon National Park (especially the South Rim).

Yellowstone National Park, 307-344-7381, www.nps.gov/yell.

restore the trails

NATIONWIDE

Me thinks that the moment my legs begin to move, my thoughts begin to flow.

—HENRY DAVID THOREAU, JOURNAL (AUGUST 19, 1851)

92 Ever wonder about that park footpath that takes you up to a mountain peak? It didn't just appear there. Someone had to move the rocks, build the footbridges, and map the route all so that years later, you could have a memorable hike.

That someone can be you. For more than 30 years, the American Hiking Society has run volunteer vacations to build and maintain trails on public lands across the nation. The trips mix the best of an outdoor adventure with public service. You travel to some of the prettiest places on the planet—places like the San Juan Islands of Washington, the Colorado Rockies, and the Virgin Islands—and get to know them literally from the ground up. You have to pay for your transportation to the volunteer site, but once you arrive, the price for a weeklong adventure is an incredible bargain, $265. That includes all food, local transportation, and lodging, plus membership in the American Hiking Society, which includes subscriptions to *American Hiker* and *Backpacker* magazines. And if you do more than one trip in a calendar year, additional trips run just $175.

Now there are a few caveats. That lodging? It may be a tent pitched on a mountainside miles from civilization. But not necessarily. Other trips are based in developed campgrounds with flush toilets and hot showers, and some even use lodges or cabins. You can check out all the details before you sign up.

And that volunteer work? It really is work. "It's not just a hiking vacation, there is a purpose to it," says Libby Wile, the society's volunteer programs manager. Expect to be digging, moving rocks, and building structures. Shirley Banks, a longtime American Hiking Society volunteer, says most people are surprised how strong they are, and how much they and their small group can accomplish in a week. "You are *working,*" she says. "There will always be a couple people who are really burly and pound the rocks. And there are other people who want to use the loppers and trim back brush. But it's always OK to take breaks."

Sometimes it's quite an adventure just reaching your work site. When Banks volunteered in Olympic National Park in Washington State, llamas packed in her supplies. But she and others in her workgroup still had to backpack in their tent, sleeping bag, clothes, and personal gear. "It was 5 miles," she said. "Straight up." For the last several years she has been a team leader on a project in the Big South

NATIONAL TRAILS DAY

Even if you can't devote a week to the country's hiking trails, you can still make a day of it. Every June, usually on the first Saturday, the American Hiking Society sponsors National Trails Day, devoted to celebrating and maintaining the country's 200,000 miles of trails. (The Interstate Highway System, by contrast, covers less than 50,000 miles.) Trails Day includes up to 1,500 activities across the nation. For one day, volunteers will work on trails of all sorts, including paths for hiking, biking, and paddling. For information, visit the society's National Trails Day Web page. *American Hiking Society, www.americanhiking.org/NTD.aspx.*

Fork National River and Recreation Area in Kentucky. A truck brings in gear, and Banks is in charge of ordering food and other supplies.

Whatever the work, you won't go hungry, she says. Trips include three meals a day, plus snacks. You'll have to help prepare some of the food, but everyone takes turns, and groups grow close in just a week. Banks says that meals are never an afterthought. "If you feed people and feed them a lot and it's good food, anything else can go wrong and they'll still have a good time." After dinner, there's time for conversation around the campfire, but most people turn in early, pleasantly tired from the day's work.

Still, all work and no play doesn't make for much of a vacation, so each group gets one fun day to tour the area, whether it be a hike, museum, or field trip. Volunteers working in San Francisco's Golden Gate Park, for example, get a private tour of Alcatraz. And Banks remembers fondly her day trip to Mount Hood's lodge when she got a day off from working in Oregon's Columbia River Basin.

Banks says there's another benefit, too: the feeling of giving back. "Being a modern urban American, we use up a lot of resources, and I feel I owe the Earth a little bit. This is my tiny act of reparation. I can't tell you how much it has enriched my life."

The American Hiking Society runs about 60 trips throughout the year, although most are concentrated in the summer. Participants range in age from the early teens to the 80s, although there are some age restrictions on certain trips. Each group has about ten volunteers.

HOW TO GET IN TOUCH

American Hiking Society, 1422 Fenwick Ln., Silver Spring, MD 20910, 800-972-8608, www.americanhiking.org.

celebrate the bard

STAUNTON, VIRGINIA

All the world's a stage,
And all the men and women merely players.

—PLAYWRIGHT WILLIAM SHAKESPEARE, *AS YOU LIKE IT* (CA 1600)

93 The debate over playwright William Shakespeare's true identity may rage forever. But whether he was truly an English nobleman writing under a pen name or a humble scribe from Stratford upon Avon, the Bard remains one of the English-speaking world's most beloved storytellers.

It's a distinction far easier to appreciate on stage than in a high-school classroom—and thanks to the many performances in North America, there's no need to cross the pond to soak up Shakespeare.

To experience a Shakespeare performance as it might have been in the days of old, head to the Blue Ridge town of Staunton, Virginia, where a year-round program of Shakespeare is offered in a setting the Bard might recognize. In 2001, the town's **American Shakespeare Center** (10 S. Market St., 540-885-5588, www.americanshakespearecenter.com) opened a 300-seat re-creation of England's original Globe Theatre, which first staged many of Shakespeare's plays. However, the construction costs for Staunton's Blackfriars Playhouse ran far higher than in Shakespeare's time—$3.6 million—and included the modern conveniences of electricity, heat, and bathrooms that were not part of Shakespeare's world.

But aside from women cast members—an illegal practice in the 16th century that landed Gwyneth Paltrow's *Shakespeare in Love* film character in a hapless marriage—the performances are intended to be much the same as they might have been in the Shakespeare's own time. Seating is on bare wooden benches (it's worth paying a few dollars extra for a cushion or a Lords' Chair seat with back and padding). Music is provided by voice and guitar, costumes are simple, the audience is close at hand and often engaged. And yes, gender crossover still turns up on stage.

WHO WROTE THE PLAYS OF WILLIAM SHAKESPEARE?

Scholars debate whether a merchant's son who never attended university could have penned these complex plays—or whether they were in fact written by a nobleman seeking to hide his own identity. Candidates include the statesman Francis Bacon, playwright Christopher Marlowe, and Edward de Vere, the 17th Earl of Oxford. Or it might have been a poet from Stratford upon Avon named William Shakespeare.

WELL-KNOWN SHAKESPEARE FESTIVALS

- **Oregon Shakespeare Festival, Ashland, Oregon.** Founded in 1935, the Oregon Shakespeare Festival is the nation's oldest. Held February–October; tickets from $20. *Oregon Shakespeare Festival, 800-219-8161, www.orshakes.org.*
- **Stratford Festival of Canada, Stratford, Ontario.** Held late April–early November; tickets from $35 U.S.; family discounts, last-minute tickets, and other discounts available. *Stratford Festival of Canada, 800-567-1600, www.stratfordfestival.ca.*
- **Shakespeare in the Park, New York, New York.** Staged in Central Park's Delacorte Theater in June and July; tickets are free, but expect to get in line hours in advance on the day of performance or use the new online virtual ticketing, available after 12:01 a.m. on the day of the performance. *Shakespeare in the Park, 212-539-8750, www.shakespeareinthepark.org.*

Adult tickets cost $20–$22. Performance schedules are arranged so that theatergoers can catch two different plays on a Saturday, and three over a weekend. Tours are offered throughout the week at set times for $5; they include a chance for visitors to try out dialogue from their own Shakespeare favorites.

Despite its small size—population about 24,000—the historic town of Staunton offers plenty to fill a weekend, including a cheery Saturday farmers market, the **Woodrow Wilson Presidential Library and Museum** (888-496-6376, www.woodrowwilson.org, $12), and myriad antiques and crafts shops. If you want to balance your nighttime culture with a dose of nature, both **Shenandoah National Park** (540-999-3500, www.nps.gov/shen, $10–$15 per car, depending on the time of year) and **Luray Caverns** (540-743-6551, www.luraycaverns.com, $23) are located close enough to town for day visits.

Lodging is limited, and your best bet may be to ask about Shakespeare packages. At the **Frederick House B&B** (28 N. New St., 800-334-5575, www.frederickhouse.com), rates start at $95. At the renovated **Stonewall Jackson Hotel** (24 S. Market St., 540-885-4848, www.stonewalljacksonhotel.com), weekend rates start around $100. Just outside town are a few chain lodgings.

HOW TO GET IN TOUCH

Staunton Convention & Visitors Bureau, 800-342-7982, www.visitstaunton.com.

transform the desert, become a burning man

NEVADA

It's a community of really creative people, who are hard to find day-to-day.

—REPORTER MEREDITH MAY, WHO FIRST COVERED THE EVENT FOR THE *SAN FRANCISCO CHRONICLE* IN 1998 AND FOUND HERSELF RETURNING AGAIN AND AGAIN

94 The week before Labor Day, a desolate corner of Nevada transforms into Black Rock City, a place where imagination runs wild and the concept of controlled anarchy is put to the test.

This is a place where cars transform into giant armadillos, where someone dressed like Scarlett O'Hara might bike around offering manicures to strangers, and where you shouldn't be surprised to see a temporary roller disco somehow appear in the desert overnight.

It's hard to describe the Burning Man festival. It's an art project, a place that tries to unleash the wild creativity of the nearly 50,000 participants eager to escape the predictability of everyday life. It's also where you're likely to be battered by sandstorms, and you're certain to encounter nudity and intoxicants. But Burners, as repeat visitors are called, say the festival is much more than sex and drugs—although it must be said that you'll find those if you want.

In this C-shaped temporary settlement no commerce is allowed, except for the sale of coffee, ice, and soft drinks. Even people bringing in rental trucks are requested to cover the company logos. Most participants are in their 20s and 30s, but you'll also find plenty in their 40s, 50s, and 60s.

The spectacle that is Burning Man began in 1986 when two men constructed a wooden human-shaped figure and burned it in front of 20 strangers on a San Francisco beach. The annual ritual eventually moved east to the Nevada desert, and it is now the climax of an eight-day festival in late August/early September. Tickets run $300 per person, although a limited number of discounted tickets are

$PLURGE

LIVE LIKE A KING IN BLACK ROCK CITY

The most comfortable way to stay at Burning Man is to rent an RV. The vehicle will provide shelter from sandstorms and a place to take a shower. As the week goes on, you'll feel a little more human than the mass of dusty neighbors around you. A weeklong rental can run $3,000 and should be reserved months in advance. *www.cruiseamerica.com.*

available when Internet sales begin for that year's festival in January. Burning Man closes its gates to visitors on Friday before Labor Day to prevent day visitors from coming just to gawk, and then torches the 50-foot-tall neon ringed statue on Saturday night.

It sounds (and feels) a little pagan, but like much else at Burning Man, nothing's that simple. Black Rock City, located about 100 miles north of Reno, thrives on what it calls a gift economy. Everyone is encouraged to offer gifts to others. It may be alcohol, a foot massage, a poem, or anything else you dream up.

Although Burning Man has a children's camp, veterans advise against bringing kids due to the open sexuality. As for the nudity, you'll quickly grow immune to it. As May says, "It's always Murphy's law. The people who you don't want to see with their clothes off, take them off. And the people you might want to see, keep them on."

10 PRINCIPLES OF BURNING MAN

- Radical inclusion
- Gifting
- Decommodification
- Radical self-reliance
- Radical self-expression
- Communal effort
- Civic responsibility
- Leaving no trace
- Participation
- Immediacy

Like real cities, Black Rock has a violent side, although it tends to be restricted to a "sport." Crowds gather at the Thunderdome, a giant geodesic arena out of a Mad Max movie, where two fighters are suspended from bungee harnesses. A referee, who appears to be as much sorceress as human, gives the signal and the combatants pummel each other to the roar of the crowd. Blood and injuries are not uncommon.

But more typical are the incredible leaps of imagination. You'll find fields of solar-charged pods that change color when you jump on them, or giant mechanical dragons shooting lasers skyward from their eyes. There might be a tree made from cattle bones, or a bowling alley that uses flaming balls. Many of these attractions are found in theme camps, where participants create an experience for other guests.

Black Rock City has newspapers and more than a dozen pirate radio stations to help you keep track of all the spectacles. But even if you stay the whole week, you'll never see it all.

True to its independent roots, a visit to Burning Man requires preparation and resourcefulness, what festival organizers call "radical self-reliance." Given that Black Rock City covers 7 square miles, an important item to bring is a bicycle, preferably a single-speed ride and one you don't have too much invested in, monetarily or emotionally. "Inevitably people will borrow it," May says. Also

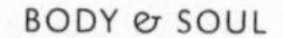

bring a strong stomach, and toilet paper. The portable toilets get increasingly grim toward the end of the day.

You will also need to bring water—at least 1.5 gallons per person per day. And shelter. A mere pup tent won't do much good in the middle of a sandstorm. Veteran Burners suggest picking up a sun cover, or better, a temporary garage made from PVC pipes and canvas walls, available from home improvement stores. If you put your tent inside the shelter, you may avoid some of the dust and the burning desert heat. Remember to pack food that doesn't require refrigeration and don't forget the earplugs. Self-expression isn't always quiet, and often it comes in the middle of the night.

HOW TO GET IN TOUCH

Burning Man, LLC, 415-863-5263, www.burningman.com.

rebuild together

NEW ORLEANS, LOUISIANA

Home is a name, a word, it is a strong one;
stronger than magician ever spoke,
or spirit ever answered to, in the strongest conjuration.

—AUTHOR CHARLES DICKENS,
THE LIFE AND ADVENTURES OF MARTIN CHUZZLEWIT (SERIALIZED 1943–1944)

95 From songs by Sugarland to Simon and Garfunkel, we're reminded of that basic truth we all know so well: Home is sacred. But for many American homeowners who are poor, elderly, or disabled, the costs of food and medicine overtake all but the most basic household maintenance. Increasingly this includes returning war veterans.

Thanks to the efforts of high-profile volunteers such as President Jimmy Carter, many of us are familiar with Habitat for Humanity, which works with recipients to build new houses. Perhaps less known is Rebuilding Together. Founded in 1976, this national organization is dedicated to helping people stay in their own familiar surroundings—homes that often are important assets, perhaps belonging to a family for generations. With donated goods, skilled labor, and the elbow grease of volunteers, the 200 Rebuilding Together affiliates across the United States work with low-income homeowners to address major maintenance issues and make homes both safe and physically accessible. There is no cost to the homeowners, who are nominated by local social service agencies.

Most Rebuilding Together projects draw on local residents who pitch in for a day at a time to rebuild 10,000 homes each year. But some needs are greater than a single community can handle.

Since Hurricane Katrina hit the Gulf Coast in 2005, the national organization has pulled together volunteers who go to the area for a week at a time to refurbish homes that suffered less than 60 percent damage and ensure the homes are safe, warm, and dry. Projects are scheduled several times throughout the year, starting Sunday afternoons with an orientation on why a particular homeowner has been chosen, so volunteers feel more connected to the mission. Volunteers pay $260–$285 each, depending on the project, and provide their own transportation to the Gulf Coast. Meals, basic lodging, and transportation to the work site are included with the fee.

GREAT CHEAP EATS IN NEW ORLEANS

- **Beignets.** These fried dough balls are made fresh, 24/7, but may be best at the end of a long night of music and cocktails, and paired with café au lait. **Café du Monde** (800 Decatur St., 504-587-0833) makes beignets that are worth the trip.
- **Debris biscuits.** These homemade biscuits sopped in the gravy and bits of roast beef are a specialty at **Mother's** (401 Poydras St., 504-523-2956). Hint: Go for breakfast to be sure they've still got 'em.
- **Muffuletta sandwiches.** The originals come from **Central Grocery Co.** (923 Decatur St., 504-523-1620). A loaf of focaccia-like bread is stuffed with capicola, salami, and mortadella meats, Emmentaler and provolone cheeses, and marinated olive salad. Plan to share; these things are huge.

These organized workweeks—currently scheduled through the end of 2011—end Saturday mornings, so volunteers may still have time to go out on the town.

"People come to New Orleans because they know they're going to have a good time. But they also want to be involved with something worthwhile and long lasting, and feel like they've made a difference," says Alyssa Provencio, volunteer coordinator.

Got a group of your own? Or heading to New Orleans when a workweek isn't scheduled? If you want to help out, Rebuilding Together's New Orleans office can put you to use for a few days, a week, or months on end—even if you don't have handyman experience, says Provencio.

"It's a different experience for everyone," she says. "The most popular comment I get is that people thought they were just rebuilding a house, and they end up creating this connection to the homeowner. It becomes more of an all-encompassing experience. Most of them want to come back and do it again."

HOW TO GET IN TOUCH

Rebuilding Together New Orleans, 923 Tchoupitoulas St., New Orleans, LA 70130, 504-581-7032, www.rtno.org.

find inspiration at an art colony

MARFA, TEXAS

As the sun colors flowers, so does art color life.

—JOHN LUBBOCK, ENGLISH BIOLOGIST AND ARCHAEOLOGIST, *THE PLEASURES OF LIFE* (1889)

96 One normally associates the West Texas plains with cowboys, oil wells, and wide-open spaces. How about artists, performance venues, and independent film? The town of Marfa, population 2,400, some 185 miles southwest of Odessa, is full of surprises. Some have called it the new Taos, citing the tiny New Mexico city that has long attracted creative types.

Since the early 1990s, the area has attracted international acclaim as an unlikely art colony. And as inevitably happens, where artists go, culture follows. This flyspeck of a town on the northern edge of the Chihuahuan Desert now has an innovative dining and shopping scene.

But don't worry—Marfa hasn't given up its Texas roots and gone all Manhattan on us. Consider the newest lodging choices. **Elcosmico** (802 S. Highland Ave., 432-729-1950, www.elcosmico.com) rents out parked vintage trailers, yurts, and tepees from $65 per night, and when gallery hopping begins to wear you out, you can always come back to your trailer and sack out in the hammock grove, a stand of elms offering shade and a perfect place to nap. Or stay downtown at the historic **Hotel Paisano** (207 N. Highland Ave., 866-729-3669 or 432-729-3669, www.hotelpaisano.com). Tiny historic rooms start at $99—ask for the one where James Dean stayed while filming *Giant*.

Modern Marfa owes its existence to one man. Minimalist artist Donald Judd first came to the area in 1971 and eventually bought a 340-acre abandoned military base, which is now home to the **Chinati Foundation** (1 Cavalry Row, 432-729-4362, www.chinati.org). Judd, who died in 1994, founded the organization to present permanent large-scale installations by a limited number of artists. It's open by guided tours only, offered Wednesday through Sunday. The collection is so spread out that the tour's split into two parts: the first half at 10 a.m. and the second at 2 p.m. Admission $10; reservations suggested. A shorter tour is also offered Thursday through Sunday at 3:45 p.m. for $5.

The separate **Judd Foundation** (104 S. Highland Ave., 432-729-4406, www.juddfoundation.org) offers tours of Donald Judd's home and his main studios Wednesday through Sunday at

4:30 p.m. Visitors see his early works and his 12,000-volume personal library. Tours of his other studios are offered Friday and Saturday at 2 p.m., and are limited to six people at a time. Tours of the house, informally called "The Block," run $20; studio tours cost $30.

But while both foundations charge a fee, it's always free to tour Marfa's art galleries. (Just don't come on Monday or Tuesday, when most everything in town is closed.)

To meet a Judd contemporary, stop by **Arber & Son Editions** (128 E. El Paso St., 432-729-3981, www.30x30cmproject.com). Robert Arber once made prints for Judd and now runs a gallery featuring printed woodcuts and lithographs in an old movie theater—he and his wife live in the former projection booth. "Judd came here for the landscape," Arber says, and eventually other artists followed. "Marfa's definitely changed, but it has changed for the better."

And the shopping's as varied as the art. Browse through **JM Drygoods** (107 S. Dean St., 917-548-7606, www.jmdrygoodsmarfa.com), which is full of vintage and ranch eclectic clothes and housewares. **Fancy Pony Land** (203 E. San Antonio St., 206-890-7658 or 432-729-1850, www.fancyponyland.com) has handmade Western wear and train-squashed penny jewelry, while **Wool and Hoop** (203 E. San Antonio St., 432-729-1850, www.woolandhoop.com) specializes in wool embroidery on linen, called crewel. The **Marfa Book Co.** (105 S. Highland Ave.,

MORE ARTY SPOTS

- **Grand Marais Art Colony, Grand Marais, Minnesota.** A nonprofit group based in a renovated church has been hosting and training artists for more than 60 years in areas as varied as painting, ceramics, printmaking, and mixed media. *800-385-9585, www.grandmaraisartcolony.org.*
- **Monhegan Island, Maine.** For more than a century, this car-free island has attracted artists drawn by its nautical beauty. Accessible by ferry from Port Clyde, Boothbay Harbor, and New Harbor. *www.monheganwelcome.com.*
- **Salt Spring Island, British Columbia, Canada.** The island's 30-plus galleries and studios welcome visitors throughout the summer (and some by appointment year-round). Pick up a studio guide on the ferry ride over. *www.saltspringstudiotour.com.*
- **Todos Santos, Baja California Sur, Mexico.** The desert setting, the colonial architecture, and the nearby Pacific have enticed both artists and visitors to this town, an hour north of Cabo San Lucas. *www.todossantos.cc.*
- **Towles Court, Sarasota, Florida.** This once blighted area has been reborn in the past decade thanks to a city plan to attract artists. Try to catch the monthly Gallery Walk on the third Friday. *www.towlescourt.com.*

432-729-3906, www.marfabookco.com) sponsors free events and readings. For more events on offer, check the schedule at **Ballroom Marfa** (108 E. San Antonio St., 432-729-3600, www.ballroommarfa.org), a foundation that sponsors musical and theatrical performances around town, sometimes at no cost.

To tool around in style, rent a bike at the **Thunderbird Hotel** (601 W. San Antonio St., 432-729-1984, www.thunderbirdmarfa.com). The town sits on a plateau, so everything's flat, but doing the gallery trek on foot can be brutal in the desert sun, where temperatures sometimes hit the 100s. Still, the town's busier in the summer than in winter.

As expected, good food has followed good art—but with a funky Texas twist. Grab a Marfalafel and humus from **Food Shark** (432-386-6540), a catering truck usually parked under the pavilion between the railroad tracks and the Marfa Book Co. **Pizza Foundation** (100 E. San Antonio St., 432-729-3377) offers Brooklyn style pies, served from an old gas station. And if you want to dine somewhere truly unique, be sure to stop by **Pardes** (209 W. El Paso St., 432-729-4425), a bar that serves gumbo and bratwursts in a former funeral home.

HOW TO GET IN TOUCH

Marfa Chamber of Commerce, 207 N. Highland Ave., P.O. Box 635, Marfa, TX 79843, 800-650-9696 or 432-729-4942, www.marfacc.com.

teach english to newcomers

AUSTIN, MINNESOTA

Give me your tired, your poor,
Your huddled masses yearning to breathe free,
The wretched refuse of your teeming shore.

—POET EMMA LAZARUS, "THE NEW COLOSSUS" (1883)

97 Imagine the life of an immigrant child living in a strange land where he doesn't know the language or local customs. Whatever your feeling about immigration, there's no denying that it's particularly hard on children.

"They didn't come here because they chose to, they're here because their parents chose to," says Bud Philbrook, co-founder of Global Volunteers, an organization founded in 1984 that helps altruistic travelers find opportunities to help other people. Although the St. Paul, Minnesota–based group works around the world, it decided it couldn't turn its back on the needs of children in its own backyard, which led it to develop a volunteer program in Austin, Minnesota. The program adheres to the same tenets of other Global Volunteers projects from West Virginia to Ghana. The idea is not to give people a hand out, but to help them help themselves.

For years now, a dedicated cadre of volunteers has spent a summer week in Austin, about two hours south of Minneapolis, working with some of its youngest and newest residents. The children are mainly from Mexico, although there are some from Vietnam, Laos, Bosnia, and Somalia. In all, about 30 languages are spoken in Austin, a small town best known for being the home of Hormel Foods.

The volunteers stay in dormitory-type rooms at a community college and eat basic cafeteria food. Their job is to help run an education program to teach children English. "During the summer months, they go home and play with kids of the same culture and their language skills regress," Philbrook explains. "This is to give those kids an opportunity to jump-start themselves for the academic year."

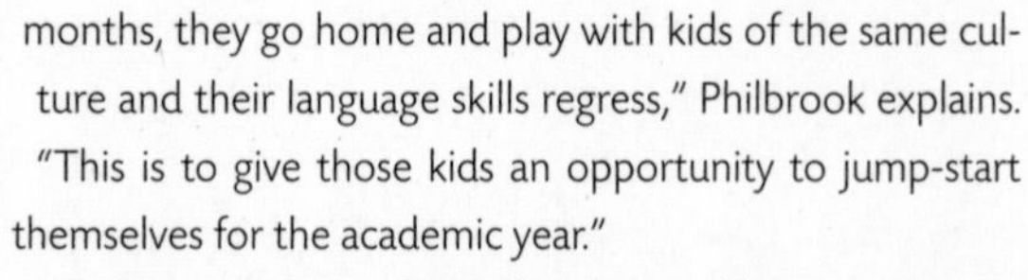

Participants pay $995 for the weeklong experience (transportation not included). Each additional family member participating, up to four, receives a $100 discount,

$PLURGE

LA DOLCE VITA VOLUNTEERING

Although all Global Volunteers programs require hard work, some benefit from geography. Consider the teaching-English program in the Puglia region of Italy (on the heel of the boot). This is one of the country's poorest areas, and many families can't afford after-school English classes for their children, which are quite common in Italy. Volunteers come for two weeks and work on conversational skills with kids. In between, they get to enjoy Italy. "We stay in very nice hotels," Global Volunteers co-founder Philbrook says. "We eat wonderful Italian food, and we drink wonderful Italian red wine. I don't know how else to say it." The cost? $3,195, not including transportation.

while students and repeaters get a $50 price break. The organization strives to attract a diverse group of volunteers. Philbrook says he's learned that groups function best when there are members representing all ages, from teens to seniors. Each brings a different perspective, and makes for a stronger team.

For volunteers, days start with planning and teambuilding sessions. Along with the practical discussions of the day's assignments and a review of the previous day's activities, each group member takes a turn to share a message of the day, be it poetry, a song, or a quote. Albert Schweitzer's message, "Only those who serve will be truly happy," is shared often, but so are the words of Martin Luther King, Jr., and Mahatma Gandhi.

Then the volunteers head to work. Sometimes, they'll read to a group of first graders, or team-teach a conversational English class to ten-year-olds. In the afternoon, the kids may play games. But even if it's kickball, it's still an English lesson: They can't say *segundo,* it must be "second" base. There are also tours of the college campus and field trips. Toward the end of the week, the children stage a variety show. It's hard to tell who is more proud, the parents or the volunteers.

Participants usually take a field trip during the week and have dinner with an immigrant family.

Linda Parkinson of Kansas City says she has used two Global Volunteers programs for family vacations. It was hard work, but it provided incredible insights into the lives of immigrant children, she says. And the week in Austin did offer the positive benefits of a vacation. "Because it's so different and you're being forced to live differently, it's rejuvenating," she says. "It's gotten you out of your patterns."

Global Volunteers also offers two other experiences in North America:

- **Blackfeet Indian Reservation, Montana.** As in Austin, some volunteers work with children, but others visit the elderly, or work on construction and renovation projects alongside troubled teens and young adults. Accommodations are on a community college campus, although the group has a cook to prepare meals.

- **Southern Appalachian Labor School, West Virginia.** The program teaches skills to high school dropouts. Even if volunteers can't hammer a nail straight, they can still make a difference. "For the kids, the most valuable thing is that some doctor or professor or cop or truck driver will come all the way from California or Texas to the hollows of West Virginia to speak with them," Philbrook says.

HOW TO GET IN TOUCH

Global Volunteers, 375 E. Little Canada Rd., St. Paul, MN 55117, 800-487-1074, www.globalvolunteers.org.

go with the girls

NATIONWIDE

It is the friends you can call up at 4 a.m. that matter.

—ACTRESS MARLENE DIETRICH (1901–1992)

98 For women, traveling with other women is about more than place, food, activity—even shopping. "Women talk about personal things. They get to know each other on a much deeper level, using the trip as the prop," says Phyllis Stoller.

Stoller should know. She founded the Women's Travel Club in 1992, before the current girlfriend getaways craze really took off. She has since sold the club, but during the decade or so she ran it, Stoller arranged dozens of women's trips in the United States and abroad. And although her trips often included women who didn't know each other in advance, she says the appeal is the same whether you're lifelong friends or new acquaintances.

"Women like to take internal experiences and talk about them, and men typically don't. Women want to share immediate reactions to things," she says.

Other bonuses of traveling with women: If you don't look good or feel good, you don't have to cover it up. With other women, it's less embarrassing to call for a bathroom stop or find you've spilled food on your shirt.

Most important, though, is the opportunity to share. "It's a great catharsis. We're all somewhat isolated today," she says.

WOMEN-ONLY TRAVEL

The following organizations offer small-group trips on specific dates for women only:

- **AdventureWomen.** Adventure and nature trips; some center on physical activity such as hiking, rafting, and horseback riding, others focus on exotic destinations such as Africa and Mongolia. *800-804-8686, www.adventurewomen.com.*
- **Gutsy Women Travel.** Offerings include short city trips in North America and tours of a week or more in Asia, Europe, Latin America, and Africa; most are moderately priced. *866-464-8879, www.gutsywomentravel.com.*
- **Sports Travel Adventure Therapy.** Active and culture trips around the world, incorporating spiritual activities such as yoga. *203-618-0854, www.stattrip.com.*
- **The Women's Travel Club.** Reasonably priced trips to spas and destinations around the world including Europe, Asia, and Africa. *800-480-4448, www.womenstravelclub.com.*

Today a number of companies specialize in trips for women, and many general-interest tour operators and outfitters offer women-only trips. If you don't have a traveling companion in mind, these trips often offer the option of pairing you with a roommate; others try to keep single supplements to a minimum. Choices include culinary tours to Italy, rafting tours down the Colorado River, biking tours in Vermont, surf-and-yoga retreats to Costa Rica, sea kayaking in Nova Scotia, fly-fishing in Alaska, and cultural tours to Asia and South America.

For women who have friends at the ready, women's travel expert Marybeth Bond has two books that can help: *Best Girlfriends Getaways Worldwide* and *50 Best Girlfriends Getaways in North America* (both from National Geographic Books). She suggests the following budget-friendly trips because of the abundance of inexpensive lodging nearby:

Asheville, North Carolina. For a girlfriend gathering replete with shopping in locally owned craft stores, nature, and a superior selection of lovely accommodations and restaurants, look to this mountain town set in western North Carolina, edging the scenic Blue Ridge Parkway. Long a haven for craftspeople, Asheville has drawn contemporary artists as well in recent years, giving the town an upscale bohemian feel. Stroll the art deco–era downtown, wander through antiques shops, then drive or bike up to the Blue Ridge Parkway. Be sure to stop in at the moderately priced **Tupelo Honey Café** (12 College St., 828-255-4863) in downtown Asheville for a home-cooked Southern breakfast served any time of day.

Buncombe County Tourism Development Authority, 828-258-6101, www.exploreasheville .com.

Door County, Wisconsin. This 80-mile peninsula jutting into Green Bay on the west and Lake Michigan on the east offers 300 miles of coast with dunes and historic lighthouses, earning it the nickname "Cape Cod of the Midwest." Cozy towns showcase antiques and local crafts and artwork. The county is also home to 2,000 acres of cherry orchards, a handful of apple orchards, five wineries, and miles of dairy farms, making for excellent gourmet food shopping. May brings the cherry blossoms; for the best of local produce, visit between mid-July and October. If you're up for outdoor activities, rent a kayak or a bike. Don't miss the jams, jellies, and pies at **Seaquist Orchard Farm Market** (11482 Hwy. 42, 920-854-4199), 2 miles north of the town of Sister Bay.

Door County Visitor Bureau, 800-527-3589, www.doorcounty.com.

Tanglewood Music Festival, Lenox, Massachusetts. The Tanglewood Music Festival, held by the Boston Symphony Orchestra at the Tanglewood estate, set in the lovely Berkshire Hills, 120 miles west of Boston, is just the thing for ladies in need of the curative effects of music, nature, relaxation, and shopping. Pop stars like James Taylor and Bonnie Raitt and the Boston Symphony Orchestra appear at concerts throughout the summer in a variety of venues. Come on a weekend and get a bargain ticket for space on the lawn around the open-air Koussevitzky Music Shed; bring your own chairs and picnic, too. When the music ends, you can explore 7 miles of trails along Lenox Mountain in the **Pleasant Valley Wildlife Sanctuary** (472 W. Mountain Rd., Lenox, 413-637-0320, www.massaudubon.org) or visit **The Mount** (2 Plunkett St., Lenox, 413-551-5111, www.edithwharton.org), the estate and gardens of author Edith Wharton.

Tanglewood Music Festival, 617-266-1492, www.tanglewood.org; **Berkshire Visitors Bureau,** 800-237-5747 or 413-743-4500, www.berkshires.org.

TIPS FOR TRAVELING WITH A FRIEND

Whenever and however you travel with a non-romantic friend, consider the following:

Before you go

- Talk honestly about your travel styles—especially if you're not going in a group. If one of you is always late, or one has to be in charge all the time, you're in for trouble. And if one of you has strong preferences for food types, you'll want to know that in advance.
- Set a basic itinerary—especially if your trip doesn't have a set schedule. Manage expectations about how much time—and money—you expect to devote to activities like museum visits, concerts, hikes, spa services, etc.
- Map out a budget. If you're not going on a tour, be sure you agree on the rate you expect to spend per night on lodging and on meals. Talk about your philosophy regarding tips for meals and services.
- Decide how much time you expect to be together. Are both comfortable if one of you strikes out for the afternoon on your own or with a new friend?
- If you plan to share a room, discuss sleeping and grooming habits. Does one of you snore? Hog the shower? Smoke? Be prepared—or get separate rooms.
- Bring a book, Kindle, or some other reading device—perfect for when you need alone time but don't have separate space.

On the road

- Keep a list of expenses. Invariably one person ends up paying for one thing, the next person for something else. Keeping a log makes it all clear.
- Set up a kitty. Even if you intend to pay for everything separately, you're bound to have some joint expenses.
- Be mindful of space; you might find it useful to determine a boundary line as soon as you get into your room.
- Be flexible and take your sense of humor. Both are essential to keeping your friendship intact throughout the trip and beyond it.

help preserve the past

NATIONAL FORESTS & BUREAU OF LAND MANAGEMENT LANDS NATIONWIDE

Most people enjoy the process of fieldwork more than just about anything else. It's the perfect combination of physical activity and mental work . . . Field archaeology is just too much fun.

—AUTHOR ADRIAN PRAETZELLIS, *DUG TO DEATH* (2003)

99 Archaeology isn't quite like an Indiana Jones movie. A typical day on the job rarely involves dodging deathly booby traps or menacing villains. You're more likely to encounter mosquitoes and long hours of physical labor.

But that reality hasn't stopped thousands of volunteers from literally getting their hands dirty on archaeological and historic preservation projects through the U.S. Forest Service's Passport in Time program. The work, they say, is fascinating.

Anne Grove, a 55-year-old Colorado resident, spent a week surveying an aspen forest in Wyoming looking for carvings on tree trunks left a half century ago by lonely Basque sheepherders. She found everything from initials to stylized nudes, and took photos, made drawings, and recorded GPS coordinates so researchers could document the life of these former residents. Working with specialists on other projects, she also has rebuilt a Civil War–era log cabin in Missouri's Mark Twain National Forest and repaired an aging adobe church in Colorado's Comanche National Grassland.

"It's work, it's hard work, a lot of times it's dirty work," says Grove, who has been on more than a dozen PIT projects, as the Passport in Time program is known. "But it feels good to volunteer, and I learn a lot."

The program began in 1989 as a way to provide labor for an archaeological study on U.S. Forest Service land in Minnesota. Since then it has grown to include the U.S. Bureau of Land Management and some state parks. Potential volunteers find a world of choices from excavations deep in the wilderness to detailed lab work.

Volunteers have to provide transportation to the project. Often basic accommodations are provided, usually a bunkhouse or dormitory. But sometimes, it's tent camping. Food is only sometimes included. Some volunteers, like Grove, specifically seek out projects where she can bring her RV.

Most programs attract volunteers in their 50s, 60s, and 70s, although some projects include teenagers as long as they're accompanied by a parent. "It's fun," Grove says. "The people for the most part are of similar mind-set. The whining and complaining is virtually nonexistent."

Despite the Spartan conditions, organizers have no problem filling several dozen annual projects. There's often a waiting list, so volunteers are encouraged to apply for more than one opportunity at a time. Group leaders are requested to reserve some slots for new volunteers, so it's likely you'll be accepted for something.

"It's the popularity of the program that has kept it alive all these years," says national PIT director Jill Osborn. "The archaeologists love it because they get to be with these incredibly enthusiastic volunteers."

The project requirements vary from site to site. Some projects seek people who are comfortable camping in the backcountry, or willing to do long hours of physical labor, while others may require walking or surveying plants or wildlife.

The lab work has its own fans, too. Larry and Sandy Tradlener have rebuilt log flumes and searched the Wyoming plains for ancient antelope tracks. But they were both drawn to a project in California's Lassen National Forest that had them working indoors documenting artifacts collected long ago on western-immigrant wagon trails. "We've both been interested in archaeology almost all our lives," Larry says. "This gives us an opportunity that's very satisfying to research our heritage."

Some of the projects in the archaeology and historic preservation program resemble our vision of archaeology: digging pits, sifting through dirt, and cleaning artifacts with toothbrushes. But these activities represent just a few of the needs in PIT projects. Other projects are devoted to historic—or more modern—research, requiring different skill sets. One New Mexico project, for example, involved aviation

$PLURGE

EARTHWATCH EXPEDITIONS

Earthwatch Institute offers an opportunity to join research scientists around the globe, assisting with field studies and research. Most programs involve wildlife—for example, you can help track bottlenose dolphins off the Mediterranean coast of Greece (8 days, $2,350), or work with Kenya's Samburu people to preserve the endangered Grevy's zebra (13 days, $2,950)—but some are cultural: A program in Bordeaux, France, for instance, has volunteers working in vineyards helping to test and improve wine-growing practices (5 days, $3,395); accommodations are in a chalet and meals are prepared by a French chef.

Prices do not include airfare, but can be considered tax-deductible contributions. *Earthwatch Institute–U.S., 114 Western Ave., Boston, MA 02134, 800-776-0188 or 978-461-0081, www.earthwatch.org.*

archaeology: tracking down beacons that had been placed in the wilderness nearly a century ago to help guide some of the earliest transcontinental pilots.

For many volunteers, their favorite program is Sierran Footsteps. Volunteers spend four days with the Me-Wuk Indians in central California's Stanislaus National Forest harvesting reeds and then making baskets. They also learn Indian legends and cook traditional foods. The project is designed to help keep these Indian traditions alive.

It might sound like summer camp, but this program, and all the others, has a serious side.

"We don't stage projects for the public," says Osborn, the national director. "It's actually engaging the volunteers in our job, in what we do on a day-to-day basis as archaeologists and preservationists in the government."

HOW TO GET IN TOUCH

Passport in Time Clearinghouse, P.O. Box 15728, Rio Rancho, NM 87174, 800-281-9176, www.passportintime.com.

see the *other* niagara

NIAGARA-ON-THE-LAKE, ONTARIO, CANADA

I dislike feeling at home when I am abroad.

—PLAYWRIGHT GEORGE BERNARD SHAW, *WIDOWERS' HOUSES* (1892)

100 Niagara Falls arguably rates as one of North America's kitschiest icons, its spectacular cascade flanked by a casino, a Ripley's Believe It or Not! museum, and a phalanx of clubs. A short drive away from the falls' Canadian side lies its alter ego, the gracious town of Niagara-on-the-Lake. (All prices given below are in Canadian dollars.)

The lake in question is Lake Ontario, on the village edge near the continent's oldest golf course (Niagara-on-the-Lake Golf Club, 1895), and a few blocks from the cafés and 150-year-old storefronts along Queen Street. It's a decidedly pretty—and yes, *homey*—place, with flowers spilling from baskets along the street and horse carriages offering rides. But what sets it apart from other sweet towns is both wine—a host of vineyards dot the surrounding countryside—and the literary blooms presented annually at the Shaw Festival.

The sometimes sardonic Irish playwright, who died in 1950, never came here. (Given his statement above, perhaps that is just as well.) But enthusiasm for his work led to the festival bearing his name that features plays by Shaw and his contemporaries. Since its founding in 1962, the **Shaw Festival** (800-511-7429, www.shawfest.com) has outgrown its original space in the historic courthouse as well as its original season; today, plays are presented from April to November in specially built spaces. Tickets start at $30 midweek; buy tickets for two performances on Sundays and you'll usually find special deals. Packages including theater tickets, meals, and hotel are also available.

With your soul sated, it's time to take care of your psyche—or at least your thirst for the grape. More than 20 wineries (www.wineriesofniagaraonthelake.com) lie within a few minutes' drive of the town itself—which means you could even bike from place to place if you promised not to indulge *too* much. Some of the vineyards are small family-owned or craft operations, but some—like Jackson-Triggs, Inniskillin, Peller, and Reif—produce table wines and vintages sold internationally. Best known is the region's ice wine, a sweet after-dinner drink made from grapes that have been frozen and left on the vine to finish, celebrated at the end of each January with the **Niagara Icewine Festival.**

Most of the wineries accept visitors and offer tours for free or for a minimal charge on weekends and in summer; tastings generally are priced at $2–$3. At **Stonechurch Vineyards**

(1242 Irvine Rd., 866-935-3500, www.stonechurch.com), you can tour the vineyards by wagon for $5 per person, ten-person minimum. Some vineyards boast restaurants offering everything from gourmet cuisine, such as **Peller Estates** (290 John St. E., 888-673-5537 or 905-468-4678, www.peller.com), to handmade pizza, such as at the organic **Southbrook Vineyards** (581 Niagara Stone Rd., 888-581-1581 or 905-641-2548, www.southbrook.com). [$PLURGE: **Throughout most of the year you can take cooking classes at the Wine Country Cooking School (905-468-8304, www.winecountrycooking.com), located at the Strewn Winery (1339 Lakeshore Rd., 905-468-1229, www.strewnwinery.com)—though at $195 per person for a daylong class, it's a splurge.**]

Lodging prices vary by season, but expect to pay $95 and up for a double room in a bed-and-breakfast. In summer, you can find two-bedroom suites with kitchen at the **Niagara College Residence** (137 Taylor Rd., 877-225-8664, www.stayrcc.com), starting around $104. The closest campground is at **Shalamar Lake** (Line 8 at Niagara Pkwy., 888-968-6067 or 905-262-4895, www.shalamarlake.com), open May to mid-October, where a campsite without hookups costs $32. You'll find a wider variety of hotels, motels, and bed-and-breakfasts in Niagara Falls itself, though published rates even at motels start around $80 midweek; be sure to check for value packages on the Niagara Falls tourism website.

Regardless of where you stay, be sure to stop in at the clubby **Prince of Wales Hotel** (6 Picton St., 905-468-3246, www.vintage-hotels.com), the town's nexus since 1864, and the 1824 **Oban Inn** (160 Front St., 905-468-2165, www.obaninn.ca), restored after a 1992 fire to retain its original Old World ambience.

If all this sounds a bit too pricey, walk around the town or by the river, stop in at the farmers market, and just take in the fresh air. All are free.

And then, if it wasn't your first stop, head for the falls, once the world's honeymoon capital for nervous brides and grooms. Though the shores are lined with man-made distractions, the cascade itself is a thing of sheer glory, spewing more than 1.5 million gallons per second over a 170-foot drop. "I felt how near to my creator I was standing,

NOTABLE WATERFALLS WORLDWIDE

- **Angel Falls,** Venezuela. World's highest falls at 3,212 feet tall.
- **Iguazu Falls,** Brazil/Argentina/Paraguay. 270-plus falls measuring 8,850 feet wide, 210–250 feet tall.
- **Victoria Falls,** Zimbabwe/Zambia. 5,600 feet wide, 360 feet tall.
- **Niagara Falls,** Canada/U.S.A. 3,300–3,945 feet wide (depending on measurement standard), 170 feet tall.

the first effect, and the enduring one—instant and lasting—of the tremendous spectacle, was peace," author Charles Dickens wrote after his 1841 visit. The most stellar views come from the Canadian side, at Table Rock, and from the ***Maid of the Mist* boat tours** (716-284-8897, www.maidofthemist.com, $15.60) that run regularly. Close your eyes, feel the spray; the romance lives on.

HOW TO GET IN TOUCH

Niagara Falls Tourism (Canadian side), 800-563-2557, www.niagarafallstourism.com.
Niagara Tourism & Convention Corp. (U.S. side), 877-325-5787, www.niagara-usa.com.
Niagara-on-the-Lake Visitor & Convention Bureau, 905-468-1950, www.niagaraonthelake.com.
Niagara-on-the-Lake Bed-and-Breakfast Association, 866-855-0123, www.bba.notl.on.ca.

acknowledgments

It's impossible to do this kind of project without the help of friends, family, and the many contacts–long-standing and new–who answered weekend e-mails and calls to provide ideas, check facts, and keep us inspired. Thanking them all would be impossible. But for each of us, there are a few people without whom this could not have happened.

Although I questioned her sanity a few times, my dear friend Jane Wooldridge gave me an incredible opportunity to explore new horizons, both professional and literal, when she suggested I join her in this project. My son, Harrison, whose travel adventures are just beginning, provided more inspiration than he will ever realize. And of course my wife, Liz, who enriches my travels–and my life–gets the most thanks of all.

–Larry Bleiberg

For my part, I have to thank my longtime colleague, friend, adviser, and co-author, Larry Bleiberg, who rescued me when my day job threatened to eat this book, not to mention my life. And most especially, I have to thank my husband, Stetson, who soldiered on throughout endless weekends of spousal absenteeism as I poured over the computer instead of tidying the house or hosting friends for dinner. I'm a lousy excuse for a wife, but a helluva travel companion.

–Jane Wooldridge

The publishers also wish to thank Jane Sunderland for editing the book, Nick Rosenbach for researching it, Judith Klein for her keen eye, and Melissa Phillips, our design intern.

index

N